A YEAR ON THE TUMP

WRITTEN AND ILLUSTRATED BY
DANIEL P.T. THOMAS

Every attempt has been made to obtain the necessary permissions for copyright material. I apologize for any omissions in this respect and will be pleased to make the appropriate acknowledgments in any future edition.

Also by Daniel P. T. Thomas

The Come'ere: from Wales to Chincoteague Island

TABLE OF CONTENTS

SPRING

SUMMER

FALL

WINTER

COMING FULL CIRCLE

DEDICATION

I dedicate this book to Debbie Hennel.

Chincoteague is not merely a home for us. It is a way of life that embraces more than just existing day by day. Here, we are truly living, surrounded by wonderful people and the marvel of nature.

PREFACE

The first Irish settlers to visit Chincoteague Island off the coast of Virginia referred to it as the "Tump." A tump is an Irish word for an insignificant, uninhabitable chunk of land in the shape of a hill or mound sticking out of the water. The Merriam-Webster dictionary defines tump as "a mound or hummock," but locals, affectionately known as Teaguers, define it their way: "home."

Teaguers have since embraced the name bestowed on them by the Irish and refer to the island today as the "Tump." Teaguers also refer to those that move here as "Come'eres" whereas the Irish might say "Blow-ins."

The Tump is a wonderful place to live, but without its people, it would be little more than another hump of marsh sticking out of the bay. For many Teaguers, the marsh landscape settles into them, rather like one cultivates a taste for coffee or tea and couldn't imagine starting a day without it. Generations of Teaguers have spent their lives hunting in the marsh for clams and dredging for oysters, and as such, they have become at one with the land. Many depend on it to feed them and so regard it as part of their family.

Because the island is separated from the mainland by a four-and-a-half mile causeway, it magnifies Teaguers daily lives. They focus on what's going in their own worlds, attentive to what is going on in town. The island has forged a community with strong ties, built up because of the water, its proximity, and the work it has provided for generations. Time and schedules are necessary for other places—not on Chincoteague. The slower pace of life affects Teaguers. The smallest of pleasures receive their due attention, and the habit of slowing down becomes contagious after one has been here a while.

Debbie and I visited Chincoteague many times since 2004 to escape our stressful lives in New Jersey. Every time we drove the causeway from the mainland, it was as if we entered another world. Our bodies immediately settled into what Teaguers refer to as "island time" as we fell under its spell and began to relax and absorb the enchanting atmosphere on the Tump. We didn't know on those early sojourns that we would buy one of the older historical houses on the island and move here permanently.

This book is our story of how we summoned the courage to make this dramatic, life-changing move, what it is like to be a resident and not a tourist, and how we adjusted to a very unfamiliar culture. The slower pace of life that we love here can sometimes drive us crazy—for example, when we need work done on the house. However, the delights of life among the Teaguers far outweigh any occasional frustrations. We've made it a practice to keep our sense of humor, and this has made the transition much easier.

My book documents a year on the Tump in all its seasons, the pleasure of nature on the wildlife refuge, and amazing stories from some of the older Teaguers. Many have lived a life very different from today. Those whose stories I share here were very open about their lives on the island. I hope I have done justice to them. I am sure you will be as fascinated as I have been to learn what this island means to them.

I invite you to kick off your shoes and let me take you there. Imagine your toes nuzzled in the soft Assateague sand, the sun warming your face, and a gentle, salt-scented ocean breeze cooling the air. I hope you enjoy reading about our year on this beautiful island.

THE EASTERN SHORE

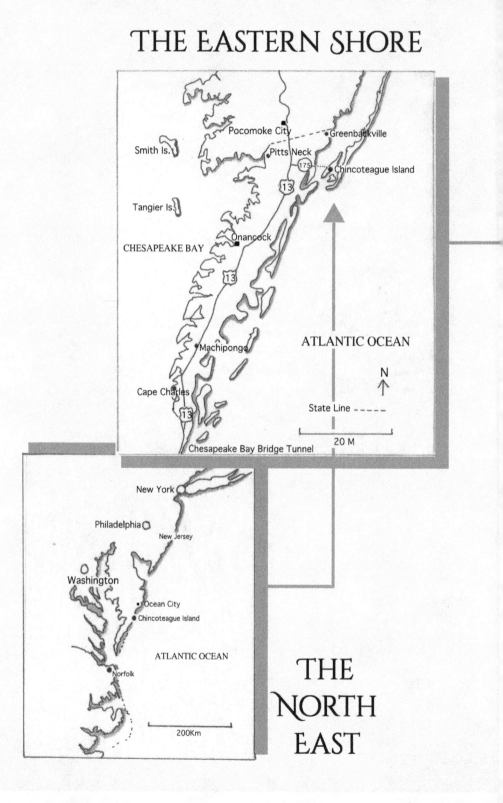

CHINCOTEAGUE ISLAND

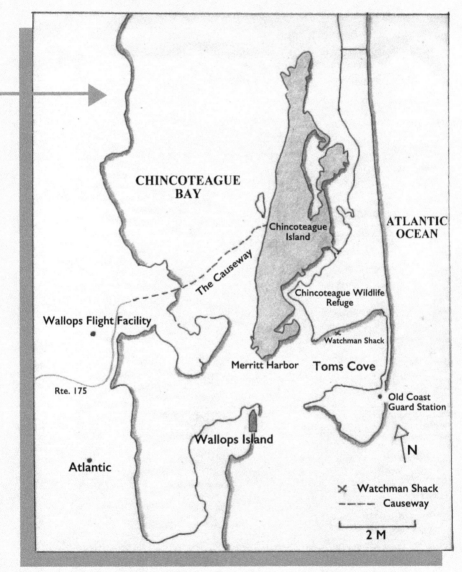

CHINCOTEAGUE
BAY

ATLANTIC
OCEAN

Chincoteague
Island

The Causeway

Chincoteague Wildlife
Refuge

Wallops Flight Facility

Watchman Shack

Merritt Harbor

Toms Cove

Rte. 175

Old Coast
Guard Station

Wallops Island

Atlantic

N

✕ Watchman Shack
----- Causeway

2 M

1

CHIRP

It was early evening, a typically beautiful one on Chincoteague Island. Debbie and I had made it happen. We had made a move—leaving hectic lives behind in New Jersey to what we anticipated to be the quintessential dream of living on an island off the coast of Virginia. We were enjoying the first of what surely would be a lifetime of lovely summer evenings sitting on our front porch watching the bay in front. Here we were, finally enjoying "island time" and beginning a new chapter in our lives.

"Would you like a glass of white wine?" I asked Debbie.

"Yes," she replied, "that would be lovely."

I went inside to retrieve the wine glasses from our small bar area and open a chilled bottle of Sauvignon Blanc. As I poured the wine, I heard a single chirping "cree" coming from our kitchen. The garden was alive with sounds, so I thought it was probably some insect outside or one stuck on one of the window screens.

When I returned to the front porch, I handed Debbie her wine glass and said, "Let's toast this wonderful evening in our lovely place. One of many nights I am sure we will enjoy on our front porch."

We savored the time discussing all the exciting plans for our new home. I offered to refill our glasses and so headed back in. I paused on the way to pick up the book I was reading when I heard two further "cree crees" even louder than the earlier one. I was curious and went into the kitchen to find out where the sound was coming from.

When I flicked the lights on, there were six of them staring back at me from the hardwood floor. Each was ominous, a nasty, shiny black color with twitching antennae that waved menacingly up at me. I panicked, immediately grabbing our long-handled fly swatter from the top of the fridge, and wacked as many of them as I could. Their armor-plated backs defied my blows, and I swore they laughed at me as they scurried behind the cabinets and appliances.

When I returned outside, I told Debbie.

"What do you expect?" she asked. "It's summer, and this is just what happens." She had no idea how big and horrible they looked.

The next evening I managed to capture some by stealthily approaching them from above and swiftly dropping a plastic cup over them. I then slid a strip of cardboard under the cup and took them outside where they could watch the Perseid Meteor shower instead. At first, I believed they just paid us a visit for some snacks, but soon their numbers increased. My initial approach of capture-and-release rapidly progressed into giving no mercy, or as we British might say, "no quarter." They appeared in greater numbers, extending their foray into our family room where they suddenly materialized from behind the couch. They freaked us out by perching quietly, their antennae wavering, on the arm of the sofa or creeping across the floor beneath our feet. If they weren't chirping, they were unnervingly silent as they appeared unexpectedly with a hopping dash across the carpet. It was as if we were living in our own real-life sci-fi movie—"The War of the Worlds," "The Swarm," or...eww... "Arachnophobia."

When Debbie went up to the third floor they were there as well, having scaled the joists that ran uninterrupted up the entire interior of the house from the crawlspace below. We didn't know how to get rid of them, so it became a horrific experience. After all, how many houses had this kind of invasion? I dreaded when evening came. As soon as it grew dark, such were the numbers entering our house that we needed to attack them head on using some drastic and effective treatment.

When we retired to bed, an incessant trilling from all areas of the house made it difficult to sleep. I paid a visit to our bathroom in the middle of the night where, when I turned the light on, one greeted me from the light cover above my head. Its large, dark shape scratched around inside the cover as the critter tried to escape.

The infestation was our worst nightmare, something we would never have anticipated to find in our wonderful new home. Where were they coming from? Why our place? And how would we rid ourselves of the damn pests?

2

CHINCOTEAGUE ISLAND

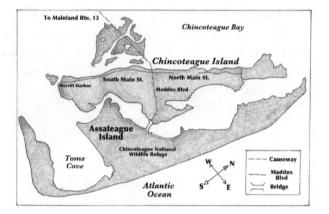

A gentle, wide turn took us off the mainland onto the nearly five-mile causeway to the island. I grew excited as the scenery opened up before us. The causeway is virtually at sea level, lending the illusion that we were driving on top of the water. The only way to navigate the complex system of channels that twisted, grooved, and furrowed their way through the marsh was by boat. The grand setting enveloped us, cleared our minds, and took away the stresses from the mainland.

Even from the car, I felt immersed in nature—so much so that it was palpable. As we sensed its calming effect, I allowed my shoulders to drop and relax. Giant clumps of Loblolly Pines stood out on the horizon, and from their dark green canopies, a blackness descended into the woods below. All around was a vast, beautiful, wide-open vista. An endless sky set above the marsh offered a view with no reprieve, iPad-flat and unadorned.

It was spring 2013 on Chincoteague Island off the coast of Virginia, a place we discovered in 2004 when Debbie and I brought our kids for a quick getaway. The island offered everything we enjoyed doing: the outdoors, birding, and the perfect place to pursue my art. We loved visiting for the tranquility and slower pace it offered compared to our busy lives in New Jersey—so much so that we thought about living there.

Before we left Princeton, Debbie set the odometer on her car to zero to record the mileage down to the island.

As she turned onto the causeway, Debbie turned to me and asked, "Guess what the mileage is on the odometer"?

"I have no idea, maybe 250 or thereabouts?"

"It's 222."

I knew that was a special number for Debbie—it was her dad's lucky number. Whenever the number 222 showed up in her life, she would make note of it to consider if it might be a message from him. After all, two twos might not be rare, but three twos surely were more than a coincidence.

"Maybe it's a sign from him that I am meant to be here," she said.

Indeed, I wondered.

The snapshot of the 222 on the odometer that day

The barrier island of Chincoteague on the Eastern Shore of Virginia is small—just seven and a half miles long by one and a half miles wide and barely six feet above sea level at its highest point. Of the island's thirty-seven square miles, only ten are dry. There are only three traffic lights on the island, and the speed limit everywhere is twenty-five miles per hour.

According to history, it was named for the indigenous inhabitants, the Gingo-Teague tribe. Colonel Daniel Jenifer was granted fifteen hundred acres when the British settled Chincoteague Island in 1671. He established a primitive settlement with thirty colonists, post-dating Captain John Smith's visit in 1608 by over sixty years.

Of the key industries in Chincoteague—tourism, seafood, and aerospace—the only one that has seen a marked decline is the traditional seafood industry. There used to be a substantial fishing fleet based in Chincoteague, but that has, sadly, declined over time due in part to government restrictions on sizes of catch over the years.

An island limits us to the experiences we have on them. It focuses our senses and protects them from the distractions pervasive on the mainland. Everything becomes much clearer and more immersed on Chincoteague. The sights, sounds, smells, tastes, and sensations on Chincoteague are not part of our previous mainland existence. These senses are strange experiences that Debbie and I have adapted to slowly. We try to encourage people who visit us to leave their laptops and smartphones at home and unplug to enjoy a simple way of life for a few days. Chincoteague makes it very easy to do this, as the pace is much slower. I am sure even the gas pumps at the island gas stations work slower than the mainland.

Chincoteague is a small, quaint seaside town with plenty of Americana architecture, such as the Roxy movie theatre, to remind people of days gone by. This is not your average beach town that one typically finds along the East Coast. There isn't a vast selection of restaurants, boutiques, spas, and high-rise hotels. In fact, the beach has no real estate development at all. The limit for building height on the island is thirty-six feet, which makes for a more pleasant skyline than many beach towns on the East Coast, and there isn't even a boardwalk filled with tacky souvenir shops and arcades.

Instead, this laid-back town makes one sense as if one had stepped back to a time when life was much more straightforward. A favorite place to meet people in town is Sundial Books, run by Jon and Jane Richstein. The community describes their store as the soul of the downtown area. When one enters, Jon and Jane always offer a warm welcome, and the charm of the place becomes immediately apparent. The bookstore is a bit like an intriguing rabbit warren, as the ground floor leads one through to back rooms piled high with books, and then upstairs to explore any genre further where one can lose oneself happily in compact nooks and crannies for hours. Jon and Jane do wonderful work in the Chincoteague community and help to organize many events on the island.

Watercolor of Main Street, Chincoteague

If one scans literature over the years, it is interesting to learn that the popularity of books written about islands far outweighs their share of the earth's surface area. Islands can conceal deep mysteries, making them ideal settings for many adventure stories, so they conjure up a romance entirely to themselves.

Many who come here fall in love with the marsh landscape. Its diversity and ability to survive great weather extremes provide everyone with great opportunities. The outdoor enthusiasts can walk, kayak, fish, or hunt at specific times of the year. Artists and photographers are keen to capture beauty in any season. And let us not forget the island's main draw, the wild Chincoteague ponies. As one drives around Chincoteague viewing the marsh, what plays out is a sense of peace and tranquility—in effect, nature on a grand, wide-screen TV. Nowhere are the vistas more open than from a boat in the marsh.

The island is an enchanting place, beautifully wrapped up in clapboard and watermen's cottages with great conch shells arranged in rows in gardens and along walls. The charm brings to mind nautical telescopes, hidden treasure, blooming hibiscus, and random footpaths that lead to secret romantic places.

Around the island are the old neighborhoods with peculiar names like Up the Neck to the North, Tick Town, Dodge City, Wildcat, Snotty Ridge, Deep Hole, Mad Calf, Down the Marsh, and Buzzard Swamp. Over the years, the Teaguer accent differentiated itself, depending on what part of the island one lived on. It seems the Eastside spoke a more pronounced Teaguer accent, whereas downtown it was more refined. Snotty Ridge supposedly got its name because the kids who lived there wiped their noses on their hands or arms. The older generation of Teaguers know these customs better. Some had their watermen's houses moved from Assateague Island many years ago and floated over to the island. Today on Pension Street and Willow Street, one can see examples of this particular home style.

At certain times of the year, the landscape transforms into a wilderness of wonder, especially after a heavy snowstorm, which we experienced in our first year. No matter the season, the island conveys a steady, gentle, constant rhythm. No day is the same, whether it is a particular light, amount of water in the pools, a changing wind, or the latest incoming species of birds. A Dutchman years ago described the marsh as "beautifully level."

Many well-known writers have connections to islands. Here are a few quotes I particularly enjoy.

An island always pleases my imagination...

Henry David Thoreau

If ever you've lived on an island
If ever you've lived by the sea
You'll never return to the mainland
Once your spirit has been set free

J. Earnhart

If once you have slept on an island, you'll never be quite the same.

Rachel Field

The general knowledge of time on an island depends, curiously enough, on the direction of the wind.

John Millington Synge

Island living means having a front-row seat of nature's performance

A. Merhing

Loss is nothing else but change, and change is Nature's delight.

Marcus Aurelius

As the American naturalist E. O. Wilson once stated,

Humanity is exalted not because we are so far above other liv-
ing creatures, but because knowing them well elevates the very
concept of life.

The concept of life here on the island is nearby. Knowing the seasons and what they bring, puts us directly in touch with life. The writer Mark Cocker stated,

At its fullest, studying the life of another creature is a way of engaging all of your faculties. It's a way of being intensely alive and recognizing that you are so. You appreciate that everything is connected to everything else. You are part of this big picture.

Rachel Carson said,

Those who contemplate the beauty of the earth find reserves of strength that will endure as long as life lasts. There is something infinitely healing in the repeated refrains of nature – the assurance that dawn comes after night, and spring after winter.

At the end of her life, Jane Austen's theme was constancy. She quoted the words, "Loving longest when hope was gone." Both she and Charles Darwin understood constant change as the way of the world, whether the microcosm under consideration was geological, biological, social, or literary. Both grasped the importance of scale in making observations.

Here in the land of marsh, scale is everywhere and so is constancy of change. Above us, the sky changes frequently. One evening when I stood out on the beach to view the stars, I thought about the universe, how constant it is from the days Columbus observed it.

In a world where we are so used to connecting to technology, some have forgotten, and many don't know what the world is like outside. Remember that phrase: "Go out and play"? My parents used to say that to me years ago. Often I came back well after dark, but these days our youth experience none of the freedom and adventure I enjoyed.

Richard Louv's book, *Last Child in the Woods: Saving Our Children From Nature-Deficit Disorder,* examines how our children have lost touch with the wondrous world around us.

Previously less common illnesses like depression and unhappiness have grown, products of the distance we have set with the world. Our children live connected to technology inside their homes.

Our physical experiences shape our brains. If people don't get outdoors and experience nature, they miss an enormous part of living and experiencing our planet—the smells, sounds, and tastes around us. I, for one, relish here on Chincoteague the fresh smell after the rain has fallen in the bay and across the marsh on a hot summer's day, the intoxicating scent of lilacs wafting in the spring air, or the tickling sensation of sand between my toes at the beach. Even the sight of pelicans effortlessly riding the waves to catch the updrafts I find a daily wonder.

The general population has a distrust of marshes. Movies like *Curse of the Swamp Creature* that depict the marsh as dangerous, inhospitable, and riddled with snakes are sure deterrents to days spent in delightful exploration.

Watercolor of Old Hunting Lodges at Gargatha

Those who rush through this landscape take marshes for granted and don't know how important they are. Too many of us drive past their dull swathes in winter and hardly notice them. The thousands of people who descend on the island in summer miss the diversity of life that exists within the four-and-a-half miles of marsh they passed through to get here. To them, it is simply a beautiful green carpet, and yet these slices of color host a teeming life that merits a closer look. In the marsh, everything has its place; the biome is interwoven and dependent on other creatures to survive, a place where the elements meet every day. The continually moving boundary line of solid ground shifting to soft watery mud separates aquatic and terrestrial. Both plants and animals must be hardy and adaptable to survive this environment of harsh changes, where salt is everywhere and on everything.

Creatures like fishes, mollusks, and crabs confront the elements twice a day. The incoming tide covers them; then they lie dry and prone to sun, wind, and rain in between. I cannot imagine being a creature that is subject to such abrasion for the entire day; it must be exhausting. While they tolerate this twice-daily weathering, they have the additional fear of becoming a meal for someone else.

These words from Rachel Carson in *Under the Sea-Wind* capture the essence of life in the marsh:

> *To stand at the edge of the sea, to sense the ebb and the flow of the tides, to feel the breath of a mist moving over a great salt marsh, to watch the flight of shore birds that have swept up and down the surf lines of the continents for untold thousands of years, to see the running of the old eels and the young shad to the sea, is to have knowledge of things that are as nearly eternal as any earthly life can be.*

It is just this constant rhythm, the ebb and flow of earthy life that attracts me and Debbie and so many others to this landscape.

3

THE OLD HOUSE

We arrived on Chincoteague and stayed at Miss Molly's Inn Bed and Breakfast. We had been looking online at Chincoteague real estate for years. The following day, Debbie suggested that we go out with a realtor, something we had hesitated to do on past visits. It was a whim, and we did not expect to find anything desirable, but we figured it would give us an idea of what our Jersey house money could get us on Chincoteague.

Lin and Sam at Miss Molly's recommended Tom Cardaci at Dockside Properties. Tom is a jovial gentleman, with big rosy cheeks and his hair swept back. He knows the real estate business inside out. Tom was accommodating and introduced the types of properties on the island and their locations.

Initially, Tom showed us a cheap fixer-upper house up the north end of the island, which was dark, dreary, and damp with tiny rooms. It was quite depressing and didn't bode well for the day. The subsequent home was at 3594 South Main Street. Tom explained that the owner, Loraine, had kept the house in excellent condition and had installed many upgrades. When we turned the corner, we saw it was a real gem. The moment we turned into the driveway, we fell in love with the house's historic character and charm. The clear wide-angle view of the marsh and bay in the front was spectacular.

Because the house at 3594 South Main Street was built during Queen Victoria's reign, it was considered a traditional Victorian home. It has endured many awful storms since then, so we knew it was solid; nonetheless, we did have some trepidation about moving into a place close to the water. The first child of the owners, William C. Bunting, Sr. and Hattie Mumford Bunting, was born in the house in 1889. It had only four owners in its century-plus history, mostly involving the Bunting family, which we would learn more about.

Despite the dark Victorian furniture, heavy drapes everywhere, and smaller rooms and closets, we loved the original features and atmosphere of the house. We overlooked the wallpaper in every room and the dated but immaculate kitchen and baths. It ticked all of our boxes—we wasted no time in imagining where our furniture fitted, the best spots for our garden plants, and where we would put Debbie's piano. We were so excited that we needed to bring ourselves back to earth and think seriously about how we could buy it. The hardest part was both of us still had houses to sell, and neither of us had jobs on the Eastern Shore. It would be a huge gamble, but we were confident we could make a go of it.

We needed a second opinion, so we asked our friends Lin and Sam from Miss Molly's to come and see the place. Their response was "You'd be stupid *not* to buy this place."

Tom Cardaci introduced us to one of his realtors, Lynne Ballerini, who he thought would be perfect to help us, as Lynne was from "De Bronx." When she came to Chincoteague in 1995, she fell in love with the place and moved down two weeks later. We immediately loved her fresh "tell-you-how-it-was" approach to life. "You's will love it here," she told us at our first meeting. We discovered that Lynne isn't always on island time, meaning she isn't laid back and slower about the way she does things. She has an acute sense of business and is one of the more astute realtors on the island—just what we needed to make our transition from hard-driving Jersey to a commitment to a more casual lifestyle. She was always honest and upfront about everything and made a huge difference in terms of making us comfortable about our move.

In one of her emails to us, she wrote "CI is waiting for you's" and boy, was she correct. Once we signed the contract, Lynne wrote, "I am really looking forward to adding you's guys to the Island so you's need to get down here for good."

We met the owner of the house during the summer of 2013. Loraine behaved in an unfriendly manner the first time we met her. She answered the door and seemed unwilling to let us in to view the property. After a discussion with Lynne, Lorraine permitted us to look around.

Loraine also owned the waterfront lot across the street and was willing to sell it, but we didn't have the money to buy that as well.

To make a long story short, with the help of some creative financing and some further awkward moments with the seller, we decided to purchase the house in October 2013, six months after we first looked at it. Who would have thought we'd make such a quick and vital life-changing decision at that time? It would require a complete uprooting of both our homes and our lives in New Jersey and the start of a new life in the South.

We were optimistic early on. I knew I could get a job teaching Business/Financial Literacy, which I taught in New Jersey, because it was required in Virginia schools, but Debbie would give up teaching German. We agreed that we would put my house on the market, while we would both keep working. I would continue substitute teaching in New Jersey until I found a job in one of the local Virginia schools and could move down.

We visited our new house on weekends and school breaks and worked to get rooms ready before we moved our furniture.

When we closed on the purchase of our new home, we learned more about the quirky nature of the seller. Loraine had given us some headaches during our contract negotiations. She had behaved in an unfriendly manner the first time we had met her and seemed to have a dual personality, so we never knew which Loraine we would meet. While walking through the house with our Realtor for the last time, Loraine told us it was haunted, and we should not sleep in the front bedroom. She explained she had never slept there because of Hattie, the original owner of the property. Rather, Loraine had placed a rocking chair in the bedroom by the window.

"That is where Hattie Bunting used to sit," Loraine told us. "Hattie was waiting for her husband to come home."

Apparently, he'd run off with one of their servants. She continued by telling us that she could have sworn that the lid on her trunk opened as it was lifted into her truck on moving day and that Hattie's spirit had climbed into it. I looked at her son who was helping her move, and he just shook his head as if to say, "Don't believe a word of it." This confirmed our suspicions that she was quite odd.

A stunning shock was yet to come, however. After we had wandered through our house and signed the paperwork, Loraine sprang a rather nasty surprise on us and informed us she had decided after all to build on the property directly across the street from us, thereby obscuring much of our beautiful view. She showed us the plans for her new house while we stared at each other with our mouths open.

Loraine's New House

The architectural plans for her house didn't appear to be that large or imposing, and with the required setbacks, we hoped we would see either side and hopefully under as well. We were naturally stunned and upset that she revealed her decision on the day of our closing, but were also determined that it wouldn't ruin our new life on the island.

Even though Lorraine was quirky, she had written a short history of the house, which she gave to us at closing. We celebrated our purchase with Lynne Ballerini and a glass of champagne. After taking a few photos on the porch, we retired to Miss Molly's Inn to drink a toast with Lin and Sam.

We came down for our first winter to get acquainted with the ambiance of the house and to do some initial decorating before we moved in. If Debbie and I could redecorate as much as possible before we moved our belongings down from New Jersey, so much the better. We enjoyed stripping the wallpaper and painting each room one at a time. We decorated the living room, and we started decorating the family room.

We also experienced our first significant winter storm, which reminded us of the awful wind that we had endured during Hurricane Sandy in 2012 back in New Jersey. Cold, high winds blew in off the bay, unobstructed due to the vast open space in front of us, and permeated the house. We were confident we could address the draft issues and make it a warm home to live in.

For a vintage house, the floorboards hardly made a sound, unlike the windows that creaked during the storm. When the heating system kicked on, however, the huge York heat pumps drove so much air through the vents that the house sounded like the howling wind from a hurricane. The new washing machine we inherited sounded like a jet plane passing overhead when it cycled down. It was a monstrous size with all kinds of fancy buttons, some of which I hoped might cook a roast dinner while the clothes were washed.

In certain places around our house, my six-foot five-inch height bumped into the low ceiling lights, so I had to watch my head. The kitchen cabinets were poorly organized, and there was a nasty cold draft behind the cutlery drawer, which we had to investigate. We suspected this was due to no insulation in the walls behind the cabinets where a chimney once had been. Also, it wasn't comfortable living without a dishwasher, which we planned to install.

During our winter stay, we met Anne, our neighbor. Anne Davis was the granddaughter of Hattie and William Bunting and the only living Bunting descendant that we knew of. According to Anne, her grandfather was quite a character—a sincere man and wonderful at business, but he liked women and his bottle.

"He had girlfriends on the side," Anne told us. When her mother was only two years old, he left home, and as Anne put it, "went with a lady named Ms. Mary who used to sew for my grandmother."

In Anne's words, found on the Chincoteague Library oral history archives, she stated, "Ms. Mary lived down the street here, and so at night when it would get dark in the winter rather quickly, my grandmother would tell my grandfather, "Will you walk Ms. Mary home? It's too dark for her to be out.

Well, he kind of liked Ms. Mary and so one time he simply didn't come back."

Anne continued to say, "My grandmother was, therefore, left alone down the marsh here."

Now we knew the context for the story Loraine told that Hattie used to sit in a rocking chair in the window upstairs, waiting for her husband to come home. Despite Loraine's warnings, we have not yet experienced any strange noises or encounters in the house. Maybe Hattie likes us better than she liked Loraine.

We began to understand more about our island home. A dichotomy exists on the island, whereby the northern part of the island has some costly homes, and not six miles away, in places like Inlet View, some homes are not in such great condition. There are those, however, that love Inlet View and cherish it as their piece of heaven with few rules. Numerous rundown trailers increase real estate diversity around the island. Everyone has an opinion of what they prefer.

We found out we could get a two-dollar discount to see the movies because we are residents. This was a welcome surprise given the cost of movies these days. When I signed up for my library card, I received a simple flyer with the library hours. On the top of the flyer was written: "Toes in Sand, Nose in Book, Life is Sweet." It rather summed up the place. When I begrudgingly visited the dentist, a sign at the main desk declared: "You are on island time now."

Over a year, we condensed our two four bedroom houses in New Jersey into one, along with our kids' stuff. Over time, we had to reduce everything we each had collected over the years.

Right away, we learned that by putting screens in every window, the house breathed wonderfully and we avoided much use of the air conditioning system. Our house is a typical Eastern Shore design, common in the days before air conditioning—tall with windows on all sides that invite a cross breeze. Ventilation flows through every room, even the attic.

Rising early is the way to live as the seagulls wake us anyhow, and the construction of Loraine's new house opposite started promptly each morning at 6:30 a.m.

When the workers arrived at her house, their vehicles sported characteristic Eastern Shore decals. One truck had two Dixie flags flying off the back of the cab with the words "Roll with me" on the tailgate, and the other with "Shore Girl" emblazoned across the rear window.

The Workers' Vehicles at Loraine's House

There was also the natural harmony of the island as each day we experienced distinctive smells and sounds, such as the omnipresent duck noises, willets with their distinctive calls settling on the clam beds out front, and the salty, sulfurous marsh smell in the air as it wafted over onto the front porch.

Because our house is located in a mixed-use area, I was able to get a business license to open an art gallery. Running my business out of the house meant we could assess the viability without investing in another location. Depending on our success, we could decide later if it warranted building a dedicated business space in the back of our property.

The license required that we have space to park four cars. I dug out an immense area of the yard to create a parking lot and then ordered three hundred cubic feet of crushed shells, which I spread to fill the space. The shells smelt awful, as many had the marine life still living in them, but people told us the smell would die down after a few months once the hot sun and repeated crushing by our cars had worked its magic.

So here we were, together, beginning a new chapter in each of our lives, living on an island four-and-a-half miles off the mainland, about to find out what it meant to be islanders and not tourists anymore. We had summoned the courage to make this dramatic move, but now Debbie and I had to embrace it and live it. What was it going to be like running a business and mixing with the community? What would this culture be like? Who were the main characters on the island? What happened when the tourists left in the fall?

4

THE CULTURE

Watercolor of Sundial Bookstore - The Heart of Downtown

Howard Thurman once wrote:

Community cannot for long feed on itself. It can only flourish with the coming of others from beyond, their unknown and undiscovered brothers.

It was certainly a culture shock coming to Chincoteague. Visiting as tourists on previous occasions, we hadn't experienced the day-to-day lifestyle or mingled socially with the locals.

We have a fair number of retired academics living on the island—former professors and presidents of colleges from the mainland. Several musicians add a creative flair and vibrancy to the island art scene. A person who is not born and raised on Chincoteague Island is called a Come'ere. Many of these Come'ere characters have their quirks, which makes for some interesting conversations. Early on, Debbie and I received advice to be careful about what we said and keep our opinions about our neighbors to ourselves. Since I was from Wales and possibly more exotic than what most people were used to, the locals showed more interest in us than usual. They asked us why we chose to move here, in this land between two waters.

There now exist many more activities celebrating the arts on the island than when we first visited back in 2004. The Chincoteague Cultural Alliance (CCA) regularly brings in some top outside talent to perform at their monthly coffeehouse events. I have heard that some islanders, however, see this as competition with their local businesses, so they tend to stick to themselves. The locals wholeheartedly support the month-long annual Volunteer Fireman's Carnival in July, which has been an established tradition for nearly a century.

Mostly Come'eres attend the CCA coffeehouse events, so an interesting dilemma exists—the sort of struggle that occurs in many places that have their strong history. The Come'eres don't know the roots of traditions that go back a while, whereas the locals do. Still, I quickly came to appreciate that both Come'eres and Teaguers are learning to work together to do what is appropriate for the island.

One thing they both seemed to agree upon is their dislike of the brash developers who seek to build yet another hotel complex on the island. Residents also become wary of those visitors who strive to make it more of a party place during the summer.

Some Islanders refer to some of the summer visitors as dumb damn tourists or (DDTs.) They are thrilled to make money off them, though, during the summer, but can't wait for them to go home come the fall. Those who bring their city "all-night-party" mentalities with them are not welcomed— they don't contribute to the island, and should have gone to

Ocean City further north instead, the locals might say. The town regularly issues ordinances to curb unwanted activity from among these partygoers, such as not permitting teenagers to ride in the open beds of trucks.

Friends told us that Islanders got up early for three reasons: hunting, their kids, and church. On Chincoteague, people with money live with many who don't, and yet they seem to get on well. We liked that people were not about impressing us. We had experienced plenty of that back in New Jersey where there was a lot of show-and-tell in the areas we lived in. They take you as you are, and don't dress fancily. Maybe that's why there is no dry-cleaning service anywhere within a twenty-five-minute drive. I was shocked, as I thought the numerous hotels would need this service, but they all have their own laundry facilities. I presume most people simply get an iron out if they need a pressed shirt.

We also noticed that many people smoked, and when we read about the drinking in the local paper, we felt transported back into the 1970's again. That may account for the fact that the ambulance passes our house numerous times during the week.

Locals resist change on Chincoteague and in most cases, I agree with them. They prefer life to remain unchanged, so new ways of doing things are sometimes discouraged. When they tore down the once-popular Chincoteague Inn, it left islanders with no waterfront "spit and sawdust" bar to congregate in after work, a place where one could hang out with no pressure, open the windows to have a smoke, or simply watch the sunset.

The Jackspot (now the Ropewalk) had no such personality. It offered a very sanitized ambiance from the Inn it replaced, and that for some some is not what they wanted, so they gave it a miss.

We enjoy the food and atmosphere of the Chincoteague Diner where the familiar face of Stephanie always greets us when we enter. If a group of tourists comes in, she would of course cheerfully greet them, but if a local enters, Stephanie acknowledges them by name and makes sure they have a good seat. Her enthusiastic smile is always a joy no matter how badly her day might have gone.

When it comes to getting permission to construct or modify a property on the island, we have to be very careful. Kenny Lewis is the town code enforcer. It is helpful to be friends with him if you don't want trouble getting home improvements approved. Like him or hate him, I learned, as I heard both sides of people's stories, one had to consult him. Woe betide one if going ahead with something, particularly construction, without having run it by him first. He is simply doing his job. There is even a bumper sticker in town that asks "Who told Kenny?" which is funny given the power that Kenny has over decisions in the town.

Before we moved down to the island, we didn't realize how lousy the job market was. We were surprised to discover that most people worked paycheck to paycheck. They didn't put money into retirement, as they couldn't spare it. Also, some people become grandparents in their forties and often work several jobs to help their kids afford those children.

Since most island restaurants open only seasonally, they can't offer full-year employment. Many have a tough time recruiting chefs because they can't provide a yearly salary. Businesses seem to wash in and out of the town like the tides. A few have recently closed, even after many decades. As the owners grew older, they didn't have the energy to run a business; some got sick, and others missed their families who were off island.

Opening a business to sell my art was not something I anticipated years ago, but on Chincoteague, I found an opportunity to be a bigger fish in a smaller pond and carve out my own niche.

I named our in-house gallery "Tryfan" after a beloved mountain in Wales where I had grown up.

I painted a homemade art sign and erected it on the front lawn. Of course, I consulted Kenny to make sure it conformed to the size and placement laid down by the town code.

My First Art Sign

Using some of my paintings, I created outdoor vinyl banners to hang out on the front porch banisters, and I purchased a big sandwich board that read "Tryfan Gallery Open," for the front lawn. I was in business! I hoped the Welsh flag hanging on the porch provided an extra enticement for passers-by—or at least tickled their curiosity. Our house is not in the middle of town, so people have to make a decision to drive the short distance down Main Street to visit us.

Many people help each other out on the island. We were the recipients of that generosity several times. Whilst we were not considered part of their "inner circle," Teaguers would look after us if we were in trouble. Lin Mazza, the owner of Miss Molly's Inn, has been a great source of advice. "You will make lasting friends here," she told us once. "They are always willing to help, and they don't look at their watch." How correct she was.

After I brought my sailboat from New Jersey in the first year, I encountered a problem. The boat's cockpit had filled up with ice, and it had tipped up on its stern in the backyard. Fortunately, it was still on the trailer. I visited a local garage, Libertino's, and asked them if they had a substantial floor jack. Sure enough, they did, and I was surprised that they allowed me to borrow it without any hesitation. I used the jack to raise the sailboat and then returned it to Libertino's. The owner had never met me before, and it was the first example of generosity towards us on the island.

Such helpfulness later repeated itself with the loan of some rakes to help me complete our shell driveway. They mysteriously appeared at the back door when I had mentioned to our neighbor Anne Davis that I needed one. We also needed to find a chimney sweep to help us clean our chimneys before we could use them. The ladies at Debbie's swimming class recommended David Wiedenheft. He and his wife Barbara, who is from Leeds in the UK, run the very popular Channel Bass B&B in town. David gave generously of his time and came over to climb our steep roof to fix and clean our chimneys.

Joe, our neighbor two doors up, one evening brought over a bag of fresh tomatoes from his garden. He came over frequently in our early days to talk to us and asked how we were settling in and if we needed anything. Joe invited me over one evening to play pool after I had been here only a short while. He even offered me his truck anytime to put my boat in the water. He gave us some extra gravel to build our front wall. He is a regular guy who helps many people out—not just us. It was the first time in all my years here in the US that a neighbor did something generous like that. Maybe it was unfamiliar to me because I had lived in New Jersey, which is not representative of the rest of the US.

One of the most generous characters we met when we first moved to Chincoteague was Anne Davis next door, our connection with the Bunting past. Many locals affectionately knew her as Queen Anne. One summer evening when Debbie was away, there was a knock at the back door. I opened it, and standing there was Anne's medical aide from next door holding a covered paper plate.

"I just took Anne out for dinner," the aide said, "and she wanted me to bring this over to you. She knew you were on your own, so she wanted you to have this."

"Wow, that's so generous of her."

"Well, she knew you probably didn't want to cook for yourself or go out."

I uncovered the plate to peek. It was a plate of roast beef with potatoes, carrots, dumplings, and gravy.

"Would you please thank her from me," I replied gratefully, "and say that I look forward to talking with her again soon."

Anne's worsening health condition resulted in her transfer to a nursing home closer to daughter Bonnie and her family in Delmar. Sadly, she passed away within a year of our moving to the island, so we didn't get to know her well. Anne was too little to know Hattie Bunting, the first owner of our house, but Bonnie shared many photos of the past.

Anne's thoughtfulness was such an unexpected random act of kindness and very appreciated.

A friendly older couple named Jim and Virginia live across the road and two houses down. They had to move into their neighbor's trailer temporarily while their house was elevated above flood level. Virginia is Joe's mother-in-law, so Joe is always over there, helping them out.

The island is a place with many rumors and plenty of chatter. Some rumors we aren't sure of, but gossip frequently circulates about someone. Early on, we received advice to be careful about what we said and not offer any opinions about anyone. No different from life on any island, ours can feel like we live under a magnifying glass. Not only are events exaggerated, but there is no escaping the inspection and attention people give.

And they even make it public sometimes! It amuses us to occasionally read the Chincoteague Locals and Guests Facebook page.

Storytellers abound on the island. People have a lot to say and want to talk. Debbie was standing in line at the bank one afternoon and started chatting with someone. People seemed unashamed to tell us their whole life story in minutes, information one wouldn't think of sharing back in the UK until one knew them much better. I'm still not sure if this openness is because people sense our interest in their lives, or perhaps it is simply the way people are on Chincoteague.

We felt like we were under a microscope one Sunday when we chose to attend Emmanuel Episcopal Church. Debbie and I knew people who relocated here and attended Emmanuel. Debbie knew the Norrises, as Scott was Debbie's ex-husband's former boss. I knew Linda Scholer from St. David's in Cranbury, where I used to live in New Jersey. These coincidences suggested that we belonged here. We didn't have high expectations, coming from a rather more formal Episcopal church at St. John on the Mountain in Bernardsville, New Jersey. We expected the more relaxed island atmosphere would find its way into the local church services here.

Emmanuel Episcopal Church

It's a tiny church in a field in the middle of nowhere. Upon entering, we found it to be very cozy and tastefully decorated. It radiated an intimate atmosphere, with tall, clear glass windows with pointed arches on the sides. Decoratively etched glass globes, typical of the period, covered the beautiful rustic Victorian antique metal light fixtures hanging from the ceiling.

It was no surprise to see an aging congregation, mainly couples and mostly white. Since we were in our late fifties, we immediately brought the average age of the congregation down—into the mid-sixties. I was surprised that many of the men wore jackets and ties, given that most people were so casual on Chincoteague. The organist made me smile—he wore sneakers and chewed gum while playing.

When the service started, the organ dominated the singing, but that was okay, as the hymns that day were not well known. Passing the "Sign of the Peace" with other parishioners extended the service significantly, as everyone spent time catching up and sharing their stories. It seemed like everyone knew each other well—we stuck out rather conspicuously as "the new people."

Reverend Claire, the part-time priest, welcomed us. Afterward, when we talked to members of the congregation, we learned that many were well educated and some had naval backgrounds. They were the sort of people we liked mixing with—a microcosm of St John's up north, it seemed. They also held social events at people's houses, which interested us, as they sounded similar to gatherings in our previous church.

This was a tight, well-connected community of people rather like an extended family. For us, and for me in particular, it represented an opportunity to develop community again; similar to when I used to go to church in England. Perhaps here too, people might get to know my name. Everyone was welcoming and invited us to stay for coffee hour.

In the weeks that followed, we grew accustomed to the distinctive Teaguer accent and started to understand how Teaguers pronounced words. We lived on "Chincotigg," not Chincoteague. We saw a man wearing a T-shirt that read "Shinkatigg," the locals' phonetic way of naming the island.

Saying words like "fire" or "tire," Teaguers didn't pronounce the "R." They didn't say "ing" either. It wasn't Bunting Road; it was Buntin Road. Words were shortened. If a man traveled over to Assateague, he visited "der" and not there. Some words like "bar" were pronounced with two syllables: "baar," stressing the "a's." Locals pronounced house as "howse" and boat as "bowt." Julia Strain, my hair stylist, one day told me that even she couldn't understand a friend who telephoned her. The friend said he was on the ruff so couldn't come over to see her. When she questioned what he meant, he said he was on the roof doing some work.

The island's library oral history files have preserved this distinctive dialect as many locals share their stories about the past and what their life was like. Some deem it a lazy way of speaking—using the back of the tongue and lowering the jaw. It's an engrained accent, similar to the West Country accent that was familiar to me when I was growing up in the UK.

At times, the island appears to be twenty years behind present-day life, which is quaint. Those that know the history are dying off, so there is a lot of change taking place.

I asked local Teaguers the origin of the words Come'ere, the locals' term for visitors. Many couldn't offer a definitive way to spell it. I did glean that Teaguers use it verbally to distinguish themselves from the visiting tourists. Many agreed to its unkind use in the early days, as there was quite a bit of resentment toward the incoming visitors.

When we first moved down, a long-time Teaguer couple, Judy and Terry Howard, provided us with a better understanding of Come'ere. Terry remarked that if he wrote it in a letter, he would put a dash between the two words, and use quotation marks around it. Judy stated that since Teaguers talk so quickly she would write it as one word.

I could find no precedents for a phrase rarely written down. We visited Sundial Books, where we scanned various Chincoteague publications to check whether it existed in print. Over time more Come'eres have been moving to the island

and have added to the arts and cultural aspects of the island, whilst still respecting the culture of the Teaguers themselves. If it weren't for the Come'eres, there would be far fewer activities on the island and a less vibrant community.

Barbara Huffman Walker, who works on the front desk at the island YMCA, always greets me with a broad smile and 'Hiya Honey,' when I enter. A long time Teaguer with fascinating stories of the island, she told me she once had to sit on the roof of her house during a storm, waving a pillow at a helicopter and waiting to be rescued. Another time she shared the fun times she had waiting tables at the well-loved Pony Pines Restaurant.

Barbara tells me the Teaguers commonly call each other "Son," or "Honey." She explained that "Hiya, Honey" is a term of endearment and also used between members of the same sex. She often greets those who enter the YMCA with a "Hey, Son" or "Hiya, Honey." She also told me that oysters are pronounced "Arrsters."

One day in the winter I heard Barbara say, "I have been trying to get up with a plumber to fix my pipes." She told me it meant she was trying to make an appointment. Another time she told me a funny phrase. "Some days after eating too much, I am as full as a blood tick." It really gets across the feeling of being swollen but in a kind of gross way.

I was curious to learn more about the language, so Barbara loaned me a book by Arthur Fisher, *The Eastern Shore Wordbook*.

According to Fisher, there is no unique Eastern Shore accent. The accent is split into roughly three areas. The town of Painter, Virginia, is a rough dividing line, with the dialect below that being similar to the Tidewater area of Virginia. Above Painter, one hears the same dialect up the Delmarva Peninsula to Georgetown, Delaware. It's the watermen, however, who apparently share the similar use of words and expressions as described in Arthur's book. These words are passed down from generation to generation. According to Arthur, Baysiders lived west of the railway tracks that bisected the

Eastern Shore peninsula, whereas Seasiders lived on the eastern side of the tracks. If you went across the bay, it meant going down through the Chesapeake Bay Bridge Tunnel to Virginia Beach or Norfolk.

I often listened to locals talking at the local diner. One day I overheard the women in the next booth say, "She's never been a stewer, even though she's been stove up for weeks. I just hope she doesn't make a die of it."

I had to write it down to later consult the *Eastern Shore Wordbook* to see if I could make sense of it. I found that a stewer is a complainer. Being stove up means you have been ill and making a die of it meant an elderly person's imminent demise.

When I mentioned the sentences to Barbara Walker, she was not aware of the expressions except "to be stove up." She presumed the other terms were from the mainland.

5

ISLAND CHARACTERS

Some of the well-known characters on Chincoteague have taught me a great deal about the island culture and what life was like here many years ago. I met locals that I thought were Teaguers, but in fact, they are Come'eres from somewhere else. They integrated so well that they blended in and the Teaguers accepted them.

In the beloved Christmas special "Rudolph the Red-nosed Reindeer," the island of misfit toys received toys that were defective in some way, yet someone had loved them all. When I first met some of the more quirky Come'eres on Chincoteague, I wondered if they had succumbed to a similar fate, as they have their idiosyncrasies.

People choose to make Chincoteague their home for many reasons. There are those who moved to Chincoteague bound by similar motivations—to explore new horizons, a desire to start over, or to transform their lives somehow. For those who come from cities, a few seek refuge from crime and don't want their kids to go through metal detectors in the inner city schools. They are tired of overpopulation and the upwardly mobile pressure of urban life.

One of the most quirky, fun, unique, and passionate characters I have met on the island was Captain Barry Frishman. He could pass as a local, as everyone knows him, but he's a Come'ere. He drives around in a black jeep with all manner of paraphernalia hanging off it for conducting his boat tour business.

Captain Barry's Jeep

CBS News referred to Barry as the "Indiana Jones of Chincoteague," likening him, I assume, to the outgoing spirit and adventure played by Harrison Ford in the popular Indiana Jones movies. He doesn't do "all the pony viewing" as he referred to it, as the number of captains doing that had grown. Instead, Barry carves out his unique niche with his Backbay "Get Your Feet Wet" cruises, which "he has been running for twenty-seven years," he said. His pontoon boat is a "floating classroom" that accommodates only six people at a time.

Now there are the larger twenty-plus-person pontoon cruises on the island. They tend to be less personalized and compete with the smaller operators like Captain Barry and Captain Spider.

Barry prefers to keep his business small and very personal, rather like a well-known restaurant whose proprietor greets you when you visit. As Debbie pointed out, he was an educator like us, and he runs his trips with such passion that it is hard to forget one of his tours. He compares his environment to a Broadway play, telling us his stage is the landscape and wildlife the players for his show.

Captain Barry loves to have kids on the boat and sometimes he has to tell parents to be quiet when he involves the kids with tour activities. The kids get covered in marsh mud, and from my point of view, this is the perfect experience for them.

Barry believes it was important that kids get dirty and learn about nature. The parents often give him cursed looks as if he was ruining their children's' lives.

He makes a difference in their kids' lives. His Facebook page shows pictures of kids who come back twenty years later still affected by one of his trips. Many have gone into marine biology after the initial spark of interest he generated in them during his boat tours.

Captain Barry conducts five trips a day, seven days a week—he really doesn't have a life from June to September. "You have to love what you do!" he told us.

Barry is from New York and doesn't suffer fools lightly. It was reassuring to meet another "tell you how it is" person. In that way, he is similar to Lynne Ballerini, with no frills. We watch him drive by our house many times a day, coming and going to take his trips. At the end of the day, Barry still has the energy to talk to us at the Ropewalk even after a long day's work.

Captain Spider

Captain Spider's Sign

Since I owned a sailboat and intended to use it, I investigated the Island Marina and met Captain Spider, as he likes to be called. He was in charge of the marina, and since he lived close by, he could watch over the boats. From the moment I spoke to Captain Spider, I could tell he was a gentleman. A tall, slim, politely spoken, and confident man, he reminded me of a smart British naval captain. I could tell he had served the U.S. Coast Guard in some capacity. He, too, offers boat tours—but with a special touch. He not only can captain a scenic cruise, but is authorized to marry you on the trip! Captain Spider has seen a lot of change on the island since he started his business way back when there weren't as many boat captains as there are now. He is a great source of advice for me about the local waters around Chincoteague, and there is always something new to learn from him. When I drive down Main Street, I wave to Captain Spider most mornings as he strolls with his dog along Main Street.

Roe "Duc Man" Terry

When I sought out the wonderful carver, Roe "Duc Man" Terry, I assumed he was a classic local, but I was in for a surprise. I pulled up to his home on North Main Street with a large workshop behind his property. His red Toyota truck parked out front bore the license plate "Duc Man." I immediately noticed a wooden plaque hanging on the outside railing with a funny phrase handwritten on it: "Open when I'm here. Closed when I ain't."

It was a simple message, but it gave me a sense of the experience I was about to have.

I knocked on his workshop door and heard a call from somewhere inside. I paused and opened the door, and I immediately smelled the fragrant white pine from the wood.

"Hey Roe, are you in here?"

I heard a muffled reply off to the right. I entered his small showroom with a table in the center covered with magazines, books, and a large swan decoy.

I followed the voice past shelves of carved decoys all neatly laid out by their species and down the hall. The corridor led to a spacious workshop, where Roe sat buried behind a desk surrounded by walls of tools and decoys. My eye scanned his busy work area and all the artifacts hanging on the walls. There was hardly room for a coffee mug on the desk where he worked. He didn't stop applying white paint to the underside of a hollow pintail duck. I recognized his long grey hair, mustache, and beard from when I saw him for the first time a few years earlier. Back then, I thought how cool he looked with his headband, cutoff shirt, and multiple tattoos up his arms. I thought he would have fitted in perfectly with a heavy metal band. He could have been the lead guitarist for Metallica.

This was a different Roe though, at work in his own comfortable workshop. No headband or cutoff shirt this time, just a lot of tools and an apron covered in shavings and paint. I introduced myself and recalled our last meeting at the Chincoteague Fireman's Carnival.

My first question was how he got the name "Duc Man." I was always curious about that.

He replied, "When I was six years old, my dad was an Aviation Ordnance Chief in the Navy. I wasn't born here, but I am as close to a local as is most of the locals."

Roe was born in Whitby Island, Washington State. His dad was in charge of a squadron and was transferred here. Roe told me that his dad, sadly, contracted Lou Gehrig disease and died when Terry was only nine. So Terry didn't have a dad from that point on.

Terry lived down South Main Street near an old carver and waterman called Doug Jester Jr., who was his neighbor. Over time Doug's son, Donald Jester, became Roe's adopted dad.

At that moment Roe's phone uttered a loud duck quacking sound, which made me laugh. *What a fitting ringtone for a carver,* I thought as he silenced it.

Terry told me he watched Doug Jester carve, and at age fifteen, Doug showed Terry how to make a basic little duck. Roe then explained why he is called "Duc Man."

"Back in the days of the CB set—Citizen Band set radios—everyone had a call name like Bulldog or Rocketman. There was a duck carver on air called Ray Walker whose nickname was "Duc Man." I wanted to be the Duc Man, but I had to wait for Ray to die so I could become Duc Man."

I asked Roe why there was no "k" on "duc."

"Well that's because back in the old days they only gave you six letters on the vehicle license tag," Roe replied.

Roe told me more about his working life. He served in the Navy and went out on a nuclear submarine once for its sea trials, which he thought was pretty cool. When he came out of the Navy, he didn't have a job. Since he had served in the electronics field as a radioman, he said to his friends and wife that he was going to seek work with the National Oceanic and Atmospheric Administration over at the nearby NASA Wallops Island Navy Base. He declared he would earn two hundred dollars a week, but most people didn't think he could do it. After all, they figured he was destined to be a hunting guide on the island. Terry applied to NOAA several times, but there were no jobs. He persisted, and eventually, a position opened up, so they hired him. Part of his job involved using a computer to move the big dishes around on the base to track the satellites.

"I stayed four and half years, and after a while realized I hated the work, so I quit," Roe said. "The clean clothes, computers, and AC drove me mad. I told them I was going to carve ducks for a living."

Roe told me his wife said she was going to leave him if he quit, but she didn't.

After leaving his NOAA job, Terry carved ducks for nine years and nine months, he told me, and of course I noted his precision on the timing. He also knew exactly how many ducks he carved.

"I made 5,751 pieces, traveled all over the place, did shows, entered and judged contests, won over three hundred awards and over a hundred blue ribbons."

In 1986, he was featured along with Cigar Daisey in a leather-bound book, *The Making of Hunting Decoys* written by William Veasey. Roe pulled the book from his shelf and read a few lines to me.

Roe told me that after the nine-year (and nine months!) stint of carving he got bored with it.

"I wanted a good cushy job and to be bored again doing nothing and getting paid well," he said.

"So I went back to NOAA. If you worked in civil service within ten years, you were reinstated if they had an opening," Roe told me. "You don't burn bridges." He was thirty-seven at the time. His hands hurt after all the birds he had made. There wasn't any opening, so Roe told them he would work for thirty days without pay, and if they didn't like what he did, they could fire him. He was lucky and got rehired at the same GS7 level he worked at before and stayed there eighteen more years. In 2013, he was a senior technician.

I was impressed with Roe's work ethic. He never gave up the carving. He worked twelve-hour shifts and would do three days on, two off. He would go to NOAA at 7 p.m. and come back the next morning at 7 a.m. He would sleep for four hours and then do eight hours in the shop. He repeated this every day for eighteen years. He told me he learned to adapt, but he was like a zombie back in those days.

Roe switched subjects and asked me, "Do you watch the 'Swamp People' TV Show?"

"No, but I know about it," I replied.

"Well, I go down and hunt with the Swamp People. Every year for a week in September I travel an hour and a half below New Orleans to kill alligators with them. People ask me if I'm afraid, to which I say, if I am going to die, I would rather be eaten by an alligator than die in a nursing home. It's much more cool going that way than waiting around to die."

The biggest alligator Roe killed was almost eleven feet long.

"They are like dinosaurs," Roe explained. "They have small brains, so you have to shoot a spot the size of a golf ball to kill them. If you graze their brain, you stun them, and their eyes close. You pull them in the boat, and an hour later the eyes suddenly open, and they start crawling around the boat. You have to shoot them again while they are in the boat. All they do is eat, sleep, and reproduce."

Roe has even applied his carving skills to alligators. He didn't just hunt them. He made things out of them when they were dead. From a side drawer, Roe pulled out a knife made from the jawbone of an alligator. He showed me how the two jawbones joined at the front and explained how he used a band saw and a drum sander to file the bone down.

"The hardest bone you'll ever work with," he said.

Roe learned how to make his homemade fighting knives from the Native Americans in Louisiana. He invited me to feel the tip on it and explained that he gives some away to Boy Scouts. The raw teeth are shipped up to him, which he cleans up. He explained the gator's tooth is hollow.

"The only solid part is the very tip. I fill them, sand them, drill holes, and then I make necklaces." Roe picked up two buckets of gator teeth from near his chair. He's been doing it for almost ten years.

In my head, I started to think that if Captain Barry is the Indiana Jones of the island on the water, then Roe is the land-based equivalent of Steve Irwin, the late crocodile hunter.

I asked Roe about the tattoos up his arms, which comprised various sharks and ducks.

Roe said, "I was raised shark hunting, I speared them and used bows and arrows. I used to kill sharks by the hundreds, but they have all gone now. I still have my old arrows and spearheads from when I was a kid in the other room."

In a way, Roe reminded me of the character Quint, played by Robert Shaw from the movie *Jaws*. In the movie, Quint and Hooper compared scars from sharks while on the boat *Orca*.

"What you see in here is not decoration," Terry said. "This is my life."

He stood up and showed me his clamming tools. A two-prong gaff hook, oyster tools, and various other tools hung on the wall. He picked up an alligator head and showed me exactly where he shot it. He pointed at eight Shoveler hunting decoys on shelves.

"These are thousand-dollar birds that I am going to use for hunting and are actually going to be shot over. They are my own personal birds. One of them sold at auction for $4,700."

"You are willing to put that much money into the water?" I asked, amazed.

"It makes me feel good," he replied."

I asked Roe what he thought about the Come'eres. He had an interesting viewpoint.

"You can be a Come'ere, and if you act right, it doesn't take the Teaguers a long time to warm up to you. But don't try to change it, don't try to change us. Don't make this place where you came from. Because where you came from evidently you didn't like the place good enough to stay there."

I agreed with his advice.

"The people who come who want privacy," he continued, "who put fences up, and don't want people on their land are in for a shock. When a storm comes, they'll regret not meeting their neighbors to help bail them out. If a tree falls on your house, I can get my chainsaw out and fix your house for nothing. You want to be a local or good old guy on this island.

"Also, don't offer an opinion unless you have walked the walk and talked the talk. You can have your opinion if you have been here, and been through everything like the mayor and council and boating, etc."

"What about all the recent changes that have occurred on the island?" I asked Roe.

"When I grew up here there were changes. It is free enterprise if a waterpark comes here. If someone comes here and fixes up a house and wants to live here then great. We are going to need a bigger police force as time goes by, though. The town is already starting to outgrow the fire company."

Roe is a straight shooter who doesn't hold back. Whether you like it or not, you are going to get the truth—or at least his version of it. As Roe put it, "I am not sugar coating nothing." Terry told me he keeps his word; otherwise, he doesn't tell you.

Roe's favorite saying on Facebook is "Nobody gave me shit and I don't take shit." Roe worked for everything he has. His dad died young, he had a very strict Polish mother, and was raised hard.

"If you want something," his mother said to him, "get your ass out and work."

Terry treats his kids the same way. They know he will give them anything if they have to have it. I liked Roe's work ethic, his perseverance with his NOAA job, and his dedication to carving. He has the right values in a changing world.

We talked about his workspace again. A friend of Roe's tells him that his shed is like a museum. Terry states that he adds to it as he does things. He has his big screen TV and a radio in there and puts in about 10 hours a day.

Terry is now at a point where he can command a thousand dollars a piece for his work. He is well known in his field with a large following.

Roe continued to work on the hollow pintail duck. He applied the white paste on the bottom to create texture, like feathers.

These days Roe is investing in himself. "This is my stock market," he said, pointing at thirty-six brant geese stacked on shelves. He uses everything for hunting. He said he wants three hundred of his own birds before he quits. Now he tries to find his own birds to buy back. Years ago he made them for twenty-five or fifty dollars a piece; now they are worth at least five hundred.

"I will come in here after dinner, and this is my slowdown time," Roe said. He showed me a bucket full of half-finished white pine duck heads. He also works with cedar and cottonwood. "I'll take this, and when I am done it will look like this." He picked up two completed duck heads.

He used a knife to finish the duck heads up.

"Right now I am working on twenty-one heads," he said. "In the morning I'll use the bandsaw to cut the blocks out." He took me into a small enclosed room that housed his bandsaw. He explained how he starts on the band saw and does all the rounding up and chopping with a hatchet. He then uses patterns to cut out the bodies. Even though he has had rotator cuff surgery on both shoulders, Roe is still chopping.

He is even doing demonstration carvings at the world carving championship in Ocean City, Maryland.

I asked him how long it takes to complete a duck.

"I can turn out a duck in a day," he said. "That is twelve hours—and fifty years of learning." He showed me shelves of rounded up wood drying out, with the duck species listed in pencil at the end of each one.

"I don't know how you do it all, Roe!" I said.

He replied, "If you want a bit of money you got to keep busy."

As we walked back out to the salesroom area, Roe pointed out completed green-winged teals sitting neatly on shelves. Roe gets five to seven customers a day. He also pointed out Cigar Daisey's works on a shelf, listed at nine-hundred dollars apiece. Roe handed me some drink cozies. "Nobody ever throws a coolie cup away," he said. I immediately noticed on the cozy the copy line repeated from the outside of his shop. "Open when I'm here. Closed when I ain't."

Roe pointed out some sharks' jaws he shot hanging on the walls, including a two-hundred-fifty-pound lemon shark. He showed me the homemade spears and arrows he made in high school. He explained his line was attached to a jug with a big round ball just like in the *Jaws* movie. "The sharks would come into Toms' Cove to spawn where we would shoot at them." Roe couldn't afford brass arrows, so he fashioned his arrows with a piece of copper tubing welded to a length of fiberglass. Roe taught his son the old ways using the very equipment he made himself.

It was time to leave, so I shook hands with Roe and thanked him for a very entertaining hour.

JJ on his Scooter

Occasionally I notice a man riding his scooter along Main Street with a cigar horizontal in his mouth. A woolen bobble hat in the Jamaican colors with a crash helmet over the top, dreads flowing in the wind, make him easy to spot.

He introduced himself one evening at AJ's, a local restaurant, and stated he was an electrician and actually from Jamaica. He preferred we call him JJ or "Jamaica John." He has lived on the island for twenty-three years and is probably the only Jamaican for a hundred miles around. While chatting over our drinks, JJ offered to bring some skinned ducks around to our house.

He remarked, "It's best to marinate them in milk for two days to get the gamey smell out." After our first meeting, we didn't see him for a while, so we never did take him up on his offer.

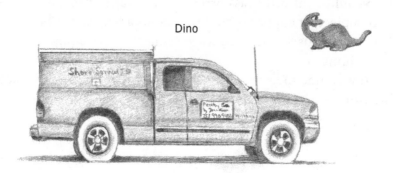

Dino

I met Dino at McDonald's on the island. When I arrived, I noticed his iconic turquoise truck parked outside with a unique dinosaur logo on the passenger door. A stocky gentleman with curly grey hair in his early seventies, he had a face full of character and a wry, almost cheeky, smile. Dino wore his work clothes with splashes of paint randomly splatted across them. I asked him if he just came from work. He replied, "yes" and continued enthusiastically in a very thick Teaguer accent that I found hard to follow. He was enthusiastic about his painting career, telling me he could roll a whole house in one day. I had to listen hard, as Dino's accent was far more pronounced than Barbara Walker at the YMCA.

Dino is the only painter in his large family. He learned the trade from his father who told him he could do what he liked, but he should enjoy it.

"Back in those days, they didn't have rollers, just brushes," Dino said. Dino had two sides of a house done when his father came back one day and asked him how he finished it so quickly. Dino has painted ever since for some sixty years. He proudly said, "I can tell which paint is which by just smelling the lids."

I noted that at least he wasn't having to deal with lead paints these days. He recounted a time when the fumes from one paint job did affect him.

Dino likes the variety his work offers. He told me of meeting a woman in passing.

"You don't remember me do you?" she asked.

"No," he replied to her, "but I remember what color I painted your house."

Dino uses Benjamin Moore paints because they last longer.

"You get what you pay for," he said.

According to Dino, everyone has a nickname on the island. Dino has over six thousand pictures of Teaguers which he has collected as a hobby over the years, some in thick folders. He doesn't charge people for copies if they want one.

I asked, "How did you get your nickname, Dino?"

Dino was always fast on his feet, he told me, so his friends just called him Dino. I am not sure I understood the reason as dinosaurs are slow. In school, he used to jump the high bar. He then ran races and tried to come in first or second. His lucky number is 12, which he says stands for first and second place.

I could tell Dino wanted to talk more about his love of painting.

When the paint brands change labels, Dino looks at the cans to see what they took out of it or added to it. "When you put paint and primer together it doesn't work," he said. "You can't mix them together."

Dino said he doesn't use a drop cloth. He can roll a ceiling without a single drop of paint on the floor. He discussed the techniques he uses to avoid any spillages and how to cut in ceilings and leave a 1/16-inch gap. Dino once dreamed he was painting ceilings all night long. When he got up the next morning his arms hurt.

"If I quit working I would die in a month," Dino said.

"How do you think the island has changed?" I asked him.

"The old timers didn't like the tourists because they saw them as coming in and taking their business." Dino acknowledged, however, that he wouldn't have much of his business without the tourists. "To me, the Come'eres are into more stuff. They keep the place going, and I think they have respected the island traditions."

Dino told me he likes antiques. "I have a house full of things," he said. Dino has lighthouse journals displayed at the island museum. He also has a hand stamp he found on the beach, a tobacco cutter, oyster cans, an old hand pump from a home, and smoke pots he found on the side of the road. He's around a lot of older people, and they don't want stuff, so Dino ends up taking it from them.

Dino has an interesting perspective on life. "You can laugh about life or cry. I laugh" he said. "You can't take nothing with you so enjoy it while you are here."

I had certainly enjoyed my chat with Dino, even if the McDonald's background music was not ideal.

Helen Merritt

The Breyers Beautiful Breeds Ornament

I enjoyed another wonderful visit with Helen Merritt, whose calendar was hard to get on. At ninety-one, she is still busy on the island, doing a lot of work in the community and for friends. She lives in a wonderful, cozy little home with a bright red door on busy Maddox Boulevard, the main road through the island. When I arrived, her door was open, so I could see through the screen door into the main reception room. A petite, slim lady with beautifully coiffed hair, Helen immediately appeared at my knock, greeting me with: "You're a big tall guy, and I'm a midget compared to you." We laughed as she welcomed me into her home.

I immediately noticed her love of the Assateague lighthouse, as there were lighthouses everywhere: lighthouse lamp stands, lighthouse paintings, lighthouse designs on the cushions. When I commented on her extensive collection, she told me she had an old, hand painted lighthouse in the Chincoteague museum display. I told her about my recent lighthouse painting class and how the students had enjoyed creating their own versions of the iconic building.

I asked Helen about her family history on the island and how life used to be for her.

Helen was raised in the days before *Misty of Chincoteague*—a children's award-winning novel—brought worldwide fame and tourism to the island. She has lived on Chincoteague her whole life, and she's seen a lot: the Ash Wednesday storm of 1962, the rise and fame of the pony Misty, and the birth and sale of her family's pony farm, to name a few events.

"I have been here ninety-one years," she said. "I don't know how or why. My family don't live this long."

I guessed she was lucky, as her husband Paul and son Greg had both passed. Her son Greg was a sports editor and loved baseball. Her husband was a politician and island supervisor for thirty-two years.

"Raising Greg was my biggest accomplishment," Helen said proudly.

"Folks worked on the water when I was young. Not many people had money back then," she said. "We didn't have a lot when I was growing up, but we had the best of life. We were never hungry. We had plenty of seafood. A lot of people did the chicken business. There were very few rich people around. We had plenty to eat, plenty of warm clothes, and plenty of heat in the house. We didn't have no fineries like you can get today. It was just good living.

"Sometimes when you turn the TV on today, the world is so terrible. I feel so sorry today for young people coming out of school and having to face this world. There is so much bad things going on. So many bad things that we never had to think about in our day."

I agreed with Helen and asked her what she thought of the island these days.

"We have to have tourism now because that's what our people are dependent upon. My granddaughter has a business, and it's a good business, but it's not the living like I was used to living.

"You see, I used to know all of my neighbors," she lamented. "I don't know any town now that really has neighbors. I like the motel next to me because there are lights all the time and I am alone. A lot of people complain about tourism, but I enjoy seeing the families walk by my house. I'd rather see people than see nobody.

"Some of the change is good, and some of it is not good. Most people are good hard working people, and they have made their own way," she said. "The Navy base came over here, and that was a big thing for Chincoteague. My husband worked over there and my family. It's getting bigger all the time. My grandson works there now."

While we talked, a radio scanner interrupted us with call-outs from the police and fire service. I asked Helen why she had it on.

"I like it. It tells me what's going on," replied Helen.

Helen told me that one of the big problems is that the older Teaguers are dying off.

"Here I am at ninety-one, and I know I haven't got much longer," she said. Her friends, she said, are all dying in their seventies and eighties. Then Helen told me the only surgery she has ever had is cataracts, so she has been lucky. She said she isn't happy with the healthcare on the Eastern Shore. "We don't have enough of it," she said, "and it takes a while to get an appointment."

"How is your business doing these days?" I asked Helen. I knew she ran Pony Penning Enterprises where she sold the Breyer model horses. Breyer is a manufacturer of model animals. The company specializes in model horses made from cellulose acetate, a form of plastic, and produces other animal models from the same material as well.

"I have the largest selection of Breyer model horses on the Shore," she said.

Helen walked to her display cabinet in the corner and brought over a model pony in a display case. "They came out with a Chincoteague pony this year. My people are crazy for them, but I can't get any more of them. They just let me have a dozen."

I could tell that she was upset. She had taken people's money in advance for the pony. "Everyone on the island wants one for their family for Christmas," Helen said. I suggested that maybe because she hadn't committed to a big order, they weren't willing to make that many.

"I run the shop all by myself," Helen said. "I have a little help in the summer, and I meet some of the nicest people. Horse people are such nice people."

I was curious to know about Helen's hectic social calendar.

She told me she helps her sister, who is sick, and takes her in the car to get groceries. "I guess I am good for something," she said. She also helps a nephew who is alone. He can't drive, so she takes him to the store as well.

She is active in the Union Baptist Church, where she works with a group of ladies whom she often meets for lunch.

"I'm not a person who can stay in the house all the time," said Helen. "I have girlfriends, and they're widows, too. We do a lot of things that girls still do. We try to do a lot of good work for the community."

I told Helen where I lived down the marsh, and she knew our house. She knew of the Buntings and how wealthy they were, but she immediately mentioned the name Shake Bunting. I had heard about him, but not in a nice way.

"Talk about a character nobody liked," she said. "He was like the devil. I never knew him to do a kind deed in his life. The kids were scared of him. You couldn't walk across his yard or anything like that."

When I asked Helen why people say she is one of the island characters, she told me she was really timid when she was young.

Helen was always the smallest one in the class. She was afraid to say anything or do anything.

"I began to wonder why do I have to be like this," she said. "I have a right to my opinion as well as you do. Now they tell me I am feisty."

"You sound like somebody who speaks her mind," I replied.

"I do," she said. "When it comes to politics, they know where I stand. I'm not going to change for them. We don't want to offend people, but we want them to know that everyone has the same privilege."

"You must have some interesting stories to tell," I hinted.

Helen left the room for a moment and returned with a drawing created by Roy Jones.

"Did you ever see the map that Roy Jones made?" she asked. "It shows all the homes on Assateague with a list of who lived in each house.

"He is pushing a hundred now, and the oldest resident on the island. He don't come out much, but knew a lot about Assateague. He lived on Assateague for ten or twelve years. My father was a foreman for the watermen, so I lived on Assateague for the summer. The waterman had to pole over to Assateague. They had it hard." Helen used to get her girlfriends to come over and "they had a ball," she said.

"Well," I said. "I have to get going now, but I must thank you for your time. I am sure you'll make it to a hundred."

Helen chuckled, "If I do, I want you to come back."

Helen used to be outside in her yard a lot of the time, but she can't do that now. "It's hard to accept that you don't have the strength to do what you used to do," she said. "I do everything for myself. I never even have a neighbor who can come over and pull my trashcan out. My family are never here. They are all at work."

Helen is proud that she can do everything for herself. "I am going to keep plugging," she said.

What an amazing lady. I am sure she will reach one hundred with her resolve.

Throughout the year, I see all these people going about their work on the island. A great sense of humor is present in all of them; so is the fact that they tell you exactly how things are—they don't embellish things.

Many have faced hardships in their lives and are therefore quite resilient. They don't complain and are direct and honest. I wish I had the space to include many more stories, as there are many.

When I visited the YMCA one day, I mentioned whom I had met to Barbara Walker, who added one crucial thing.

"It's okay for us Teaguers to talk about each other, but it's not okay if you talk about us."

I had to laugh.

The people Debbie and I met in that first year were kind and generous. For me, it was the first opportunity to feel at home in the US. It wasn't just because my interests existed here, but people slowed down to talk, and they really cared. Initially, these heartfelt encounters came from the Come'eres, but soon we began to get to know the Teaguers.

One day I had the pleasure of visiting Cork McGee, one the classic old timers on the island. He gave me an excellent account of what it was like to live on the island back in the 1930s and '40s.

6

A STEP BACK IN TIME

A Morning with Cork McGee

I visited Cork on a cloudless sunny day with a slight breeze. Finding his home was quite easy since he had a lane named after him off East Side Drive. I turned left onto McGee Lane, an undulating dusty dirt track that led back into the woods. I passed some modern houses, which ended as the track led into the woods. "*Where is his home?*" I wondered. The track split as I entered the woods; I took the left fork, which brought me into a clearing. There stood Cork's house—a doublewide home with multiple sheds in back, sheltered in a tranquil oasis of mature trees and stands of bamboo. It seemed a very quiet place, far away from the tourist hubbub of Maddox Boulevard.

A gentle breeze blew through his silent paradise with the occasional sound of birds. As I stepped out of my car, an old man wearing a baseball hat and Cabella's t-shirt sauntered over to me from the far sheds.

"Cork McGee, I presume," I asked.

"I sure am," he said. He asked me to speak loudly and stand close to him so he could hear me.

He motioned me over to sit under a shaded picnic structure where an assortment of old chairs lay scattered around. Cork pointed to his workshops in front of a tall stand of bamboo. Through the open door of the far right shed, I could see carvings and a vast collection of tools and other interesting items I wanted to visit. Various metal signs adorned the outside. One had his name in blue with the words "ducks geese decoys and shorebirds." Another looked like a road sign with the words "Old Hunter Xing."

Against the shed lay an assortment of old tools, a net, old plastic decoys, and a bleached white deer antler. To the left of his carving shed was another shed that housed his band saw to cut his wood. He laughingly declared it was "spotless in there."

After a short while, Amy Lewis, his daughter, arrived in her car and came over to greet me. She promptly excused herself to put away his groceries.

I began by asking Cork about his family history on the island.

He was born in 1931 and grew up on the east side of the island with two brothers and three sisters. Amy came out of the house and joined us. She told me that Cork was lucky to escape some early scares in his life. When a youngster, he contracted typhoid fever but survived it.

Then, at age six, he had an accident with a car—one of the few that visited the island back then. While waiting for the school bus, Cork and his friends would play chicken if a car came by. They would cut across in front of the car just before it got to them. One day an old scrapple man drove past the kids in an old Model T with a rumble seat.

"Well one day the scrapple man struck Cork," Amy said, "and dragged him by his sheepskin coat up the road for at least two houses."

In addition to typhoid, he survived that as well with some minor cuts and bruises. Cork laughed it off with a smile as Amy spoke. I could tell from our early discussions that Cork had a wicked sense of humor.

I asked Cork if he enjoyed school. "I didn't want to go to school," he said. "I can read and write, and I don't do too bad. I have got by all these years."

Cork checked out of school after seventh grade and got a job locally to earn some money.

"How was life years ago?" I asked him.

Teaguers used kerosene lamps, as there were no electric lights or running water. According to Cork, East Side was once known as Dodge City because it was so rough.

"Other boys wouldn't go over there," he said. "The town area was known as town rats." Cork continued, "You knew everyone on the island, so you were suspect of anyone new. People very rarely left the island, and if they did, it was a huge deal to go to Pocomoke City. There were very few cars in those days, and life was simple."

He told me everybody was self-sufficient back then. They had plenty to eat, but people were poor. In their backyards they raised pigs and chickens for eating. While life was much simpler back then, it wasn't easy, as they really lived off the land. There were few grocery stores or markets, so islanders hunted or produced their food from their gardens.

Cork recalled spending a lot of time hanging around a small, brightly colored yellow store down the road from him where he would meet his friends.

I was shocked to learn what Cork ate.

"You didn't turn down much. You'd eat just about anything that crept or crawled," he said. "We would make a tasty Sunday dinner out of a snapper turtle. In the winter, though, diamondback turtles were a delicacy and much tastier."

One of his uncles was an expert at "progging" or "munging" for diamondback terrapins, an edible turtle that lives in and around the Chesapeake Bay's brackish tidal waters. Cork referred to him as a "munger," someone who scavenged the marsh, picking up anything edible. First, his uncle would look for the turtle's air bubbles rising from the mud below, and then he would use a long stick to prod down their air hole and dig them out of the mud.

Cork, too, was a bit of a munger himself back then, and his nickname was Scavenger. He was also referred to as a mud turtle because he loved to wallow in the mud in the creeks. That made me wonder what he did for fun. When I asked him, he told me a series of amusing tales.

"Our Saturday evening entertainment involved going around the island tipping over people's outhouses," he said.

Apparently, the latrines were common. Heaven forbid if someone was in there at the time. Very few homes had indoor plumbing.

"You didn't open and look. You just dun it and take off running."

On Monday mornings they would help set the outhouses back up.

Cork got up to further mischievous deeds with his friends by throwing stuff on people's roofs like tin cans. They would also "tick tack" the outside weatherboarding, as he called it. The kids would rake a stick down the side of the house, knock on the door, and run off.

Amy jumped in and said, "Tell him what you did to your grandfather."

Cork explained that he once put roofing tar on the toilet seat for his grandfather.

"Grandma had to use kerosene to clean him up," Amy said.

Once again, Cork laughed heartily, proud of his fun times.

I asked Cork how he made a living.

"I went out on my own, and it wasn't long—when I was twelve or fourteen years old, I caught almost as many clams as the grownups. Stuff was more plentiful back then."

When he was fifteen years old, he joined his dad on the boat down at Hog Island and learned clamming from him. Ironically, the boat belonged to William C. Bunting, who originally owned our house.

"We'd go away for two weeks at a time," Cork said, "and would have to kill something to eat or eat a slab of bacon or beans. A fifth of what I made for clamming I gave to the boat. Gas and my food came out of the rest. You were lucky if you made twenty-five dollars when you came off the trip. During the signing season, four or five of us would go down to Hog Island Bay and bring over a hundred thousand clams in a week. I asked Cork what he meant by signing season. He replied, "The signing season is when the warmer weather arrives, and the clams are closer to the surface giving off signs of their presence. Once I caught over seventeen thousand clams in five days with my feet! I made some soft moccasins to wear so I could detect the clams."

Clams used to cost eight dollars for a thousand back then, Cork said, but recently his son-in-law told him he brought some to the flea market at fifty cents apiece.

"In the fall we harvested seed oysters. Christmas it froze, so we hunted after Christmas to get by. In March, we clammed down the bay and learned the signs for clams by looking for small slits in the mud."

He tried everything that could earn him some money.

"You adapt to what works," he said.

He ended up carving and taking people out for hunting. He guided hunting parties for nearly sixty years.

"Nowadays you do whatever income you can get, especially as no one can make money off the water unless you are a boat tour operator."

Cork learned to hunt from Charles Clark, his wife's daddy. Cork used to hunt for survival. "We brought home what we could eat, or someone else would eat it. We'd sell it for extra cash."

Cork then asked me an interesting question. "You never saw a "mile or more" bird? It's a right pretty bird. It's got a little longer bill than the rest of the birds."

I had no idea what he was talking about, so Amy jumped in. "You might as well go ahead and tell him."

"It's got a different habit than most of the birds," Cork continued. "He sticks his bill in the ground and whistles through his butt so you can hear him for a mile or more."

I laughed, at which point Amy stated the obvious.

"He's a jokester. He's always trying to pull something on you."

The mischievous trickster from when Cork was a boy has never left. Recently he painted a lifelike bird in bright colors and placed it in his yard. A friend came over and took pictures of it, thinking it was real. Amy pointed out another uncannily lifelike bird behind me near the trees. I could see why the friend mistook it for the real deal.

I asked Amy and Cork about unique Teaguer phrases...

"Instead of sit down it used to be 'sot down,'" Cork said. "If you climb a tree you 'clim up a tree.'"

"How about a "winder pane" for window pane?" Amy asked.

I asked Cork if I could have a look at the decoys in his shed.

"There's a lot of history in that carving shed," Amy said.

Walking over, I noticed a handwritten chalk sign hanging outside. It spoke directly to Cork's sense of humor. The headline read: "Old Chincoteague Barometer." Below that it read: "Rope moving = Windy, Rope Still = Calm, Rope Wet = Rain, Rope White = Snow, Rope Invisible = Fog, Rope Gone = Hurricane."

Entering his shed, I found a compact rectangular space jam-packed with everything Cork used. It struck me as a cross between a natural history museum and schoolboy's treasure trove. A fan wedged in the side window ran continuously. A simple chair and working area stood to the right as one entered.

A bird book was opened at the page for shorebirds and propped up on his bench. His sold carvings were perched on the top shelf, ready for collection, and the completed bird carvings sat neatly on a shelf with white price tags. I asked him which bird he enjoyed most to carve.

"The marsh hen (clapper rail) or the curlews." he replied, "I mostly does the sandpipers though." Noting he is eighty-seven years old, he added, "I don't do many of the large birds anymore. A good friend brings me a truck of basswood every memorial holiday from off island. I repay him with some birds. I am getting old, and the big pieces of wood is harder to work. As to the time to create a decoy, the greatest time is the painting of the bird."

He pointed out various artifacts that hung above his desk. A long metal flashlight he's had since he was fourteen took six batteries. He used it to locate deer's eyes in the dark. He showed me a strange-looking tool for scraping the hair off hogs. Above my head, I saw wedged into the rafters a large assortment of knives he used to kill hogs back in the day. An old oyster tong hung from the center beam along with various oyster-shucking blades. I turned to my left, where a large stuffed Canada goose hung ominously from the ceiling.

Old tins, bottles, and a feast of knickknacks, including binoculars in their cases, filled various shelves. A license plate propped on a shelf read MCGEE L. On the top shelf, Cork pointed out an old hummingbird nest still attached to a branch.

During Cork's long life, many changes have occurred on Chincoteague. I asked him what he thought about them. He replied in a melancholy tone.

"When it was cold, seven or eight of the local guys would come and sit around my wood fire. Now, most have passed away.

"As far as on the water, I don't see anything that would be good for me for being a waterman. If I was going to start over, there's ain't no way that I could make it. On East Side there used to be seven shucking houses, now there's one. Ninety-five percent of the clams these days is raised in cages. They are not local clams. There's a different texture to the farm-raised clams. I can tell it."

Amy said, "I am afraid that Burbage will come in and buy everything up and make the whole island a little Ocean City."

Jack and Todd Burbage of Berlin, Maryland, own Blue Water Development Corporation and are developing tourist properties on the island.

Cork replied, "I used to start out and name everybody from Snug Harbor and up to Piney Island. I got a map and draw it. I made a little circle and names all the people that owned the home and all their children. Now I don't know ten people that live on this side here. This is where I stay. The only time I leave out is when I go to church Sundays and Wednesdays."

He offered me one of his carved birds, but I refused. I would rather come back and buy one, which I did later. Before I left, I was treated to Cork's infectious sense of humor once again.

Amy told Cork that she had got him a Stouffer's dinner to which he replied with his usual fast wit.

"Or I could just eat a frog or something."

7

IF OLD SHEDS COULD TALK

After I published my memoir, *The Come'ere*, Captain Spider stopped by one afternoon to share some of his memories on the island. He wanted to discuss some of the old-timers and brought over some framed mementos and booklets about the people he missed.

We sat on the front porch where he began by saying, "I like to kick myself because I have run into so many neat stories about people on this island. Do you remember the old shed that used to be at the Island Marina?"

"Yes," I said.

"Well, a treasure trove of information passed through that shed," Spider continued. "It has a lot of history. A great number of my friends used to meet every week in that shed to discuss life in general. Well-known names like Bill Tom, Ed Lewis ('Popsicle'), Weldon Bowden, Ed Bowden, Chet Williams,

Derwood Hall, and Spike Spidel ('Spangler'), the boat builder and boxer. Some had nicknames like 'Bullet,' who was a fighter or scrapper, and 'Taterbug.'

"You know, every little town has a little fabric. Chincoteague has its own fabric. If you created a patchwork quilt and stitched it together with all these old names, it would be pretty cool right?"

"I agree," I said.

"The story I want to tell you about relates to Ed Lewis, or 'Popsicle,' as we called him," Spider said. "Popsicle earned his lifelong nickname by selling the cold treats offered by his parents at their ice cream parlor on the corner of Cleveland Street.

"Well, one day I was sitting in the shed with Popsicle and a few of the others when Popsicle started to recount his war days. In July of 1944, he was assigned to a Navy amphibious group at Little Creek, Virginia, to serve on an LST. [These Navy tank landing ships in World War II were nicknamed "large slow targets."] These ships carried tanks and other large vehicles and had huge bow doors that opened with a ramp for them to unload. Ed's crew picked up their LST in Pittsburgh, did some trial runs, and then sailed to the Pacific in late 1944. Ed told us that his ship was involved in the invasions of both Iwo Jima in February 1945 and Okinawa in April 1945. He recalled that he was lucky not to have any kamikaze hits at the time.

"Well, Ed started talking about this thing about a flag that was raised on Iwo Jima in 1945, and I am thinking he is now embellishing his story a bit here. I think Ed didn't think me or any of the others believed him, so he quietly got up and left. Fifteen minutes later, he came back with this black and white ledger book and some old books from the Coastguard. Ed comes in, sits down, and says, 'Now I want to show you all something.'

"Ed started by telling us he was the ship's clerk or supply officer on the LST-758 that was anchored off Iwo Jima. At eight in the morning on February 23, 1945, Ed said, a patrol of forty men from the third platoon, second battalion, 28th Marines assembled at the base of Mount Suribachi at the end of Iwo Jima. The platoon's mission was to take the crater at the peak and raise the U.S. flag.

"The platoon slowly climbed the steep trails to the summit but encountered no enemy fire. The Marines surrounded the crater watching for pockets of enemy resistance while others looked for a pole or something to raise the flag on. Somehow, the message reached the LST that Ed served on. Ed was taking a steel pipe out of service off the boat at the time, when he realized that the pipe could hold the flag. So Ed's pipe was brought ashore and used for the first flag raising on Iwo Jima. It was captured on film.

Here is the famous photo many people have seen.

"I just said 'holy mackerel!'" Captain Spider said. "Everyone else fell silent. Many of the others had war stories, but nothing compared to Popsicle's.

"According to Popsicle, three hours later, another patrol was dispatched to raise another, larger U.S. flag on Mount Suribachi."

Captain Spider sat back in his chair.

"You know it wasn't just the stories that were told in that shed. It was the things on the wall as well. When you walked in, there was a picture of President Kennedy. Also, a picture signed by Gregory H. "Pappy" Boyington, the World War II flying tiger ace. History lined the walls of the shed.

"You walked in," Spider continued, "and to the right was a long Formica countertop with an opening to get behind it with a walk space. There was a counter behind that with a grill, cooking stuff, and the pie case. The pie case is wooden and has two doors that open in the front with a shelf inside. I have that today, so it's a nice memory. In front of the counter were low, leather art deco swivel stools. Also a couple of chairs in there. From the outside, it looked like a modern shed, but inside it was another world."

Captain Spider continued: "A photo of the shed's interior appeared in the local paper showing how it looked in about 1920 or '30. The building was originally downtown and served as a breakfast shop. It was brought up to George's Island Marina around 1959, and after it was moved, it was used as an office at the Marina. There was a gas line into the building.

"When I entered the shed, I thought: these boys have it made here with all this stuff inside. When the Marina Bay Hotel was under construction, the developers wanted to get rid of the shed. I told them, 'You can't crunch it up. This is history.'"

The developers gave Captain Spider eight hours to get it out of there. Spider said that it wasn't enough time, so he pleaded for more. The developers were out of Ocean City and didn't care about some old shed lying in the way of their build. They had a schedule to keep to and just wanted it out of there so they could break ground.

Having made numerous phone calls, Spider said, "I finally called Dean at Barry Fisher. He had the equipment like a lowboy trailer and other things we needed."

Captain Spider then relived the amusing story of how they eventually moved the shed.

"First of all, we jacked the shed up to get the lowboy under it. Dean got a pole and rode down Main Street on the lowboy, measuring to see if the shed would clear the overhead wires. It wouldn't clear under two, so they made a long fork. Mackie sat on the hot metal roof of the shed with the fork and lifted the lines up as they went down the street. The town was concerned that it would block the road, so we chose a time when there wasn't much traffic. It was pretty late in the evening if I remember. It's now down on Mackie's property overlooking the bay.

"Do you want to go see it?" Captain Spider said.

"Sure," I replied. "I'd love to."

"I don't think Mackie will shoot me. Jump in my truck, and we'll head down. Someone might say something, but we won't be a minute on the property."

It was a quick, five-minute ride up Main Street.

As we drove, passers-by waved or beeped their horns, as many people knew Captain Spider.

The cherished old shed from the island marina faced out to the bay. It had a green metal roof and from the look of the outside didn't appear historical. For some reason, beer cans were strewn around the lawn. Maybe someone had partied recently, or the recycling had turned over in the wind. As we strode over, I thought we might look like town inspectors—I wore my work clothes of a button-down shirt with khakis, and Spider was dressed smart casual as well. I carried a clipboard ready to make notes, which no doubt completed the look.

Captain Spider yelled out "Mackie" as we got close to the shed. No one answered. He yelled again, "Mackie, you in there?" No answer. We approached the shed.

"Look in here, through the screened side window," Captain Spider said.

I immediately saw the old counter. It was quite a sizeable space.

"Do you see the old chairs and stools?" he said, peering through the window with me.

"Wait, wait, a minute. Some of the stuff is still on the walls," he said. "Is that cool, or what?"

I walked to the far end of the building to the entrance door. The torn bug screen allowed me a less obstructed view inside. I noticed an old ships steering wheel hung on the far wall.

"Is the old telephone still on the wall?" Spider asked.

"I can't see it," I replied.

"I think it's under that shelf in the far corner," said Spider. He spotted an old cabinet covered in papers that he recognized on the far wall. There were framed photos along the left wall, but from my restricted view, I couldn't make out what was in the frames. Maybe President Kennedy, or Gregory H. "Pappy" Boyington.

Captain Spider said, "I'll have to call Mackie to come over for you to go inside." Before we left, I noticed the old charter cruise signs on the outside wall, one that read "Spider's Explorer."

Captain Spider dropped me back at the house afterward. I could tell he was very emotional about the shed. If the characters who frequented it were alive today, they would speak volumes. He also told me one last funny thing about Popsicle.

"You know, he had a train whistle hooked up to an air compressor in the basement of his house. Every day at twelve o'clock, he went to the basement to pull it."

SPRING

8

THE WATCHMAN'S SHACK

Watercolor of the Watchman's Shack

Each year Chincoteague witnesses a rebirth of the marsh. The dull, murky brown stalks, flattened from winter's high tides and winds, are pushed aside from beneath or float away on a spring tide.

Our first year on Chincoteague, we saw the emergence of bright, light yellow shoots coming from the bases of the reeds, which turned into a gentle greening of the marsh. At first, it was simply flickers of life here and there, and then the color started to rise like a curtain of green from the raw umber darkness. A great transformation occurred, blossoming into an emerald green carpet, which when caught in the sun displayed a shimmering multitude of greens and gold hues across the landscape as far as one could see. As our year unfolded, we learned how to adapt to the seasons and the changes that occurred.

As the landscape changed in May, we could sense a noticeable change in the number of people on the island. It was the build-up to the first major holiday, a time when the tourists came back. Most tourists were just regular people who loved the island like us, but some chose to bring some unwelcome behavior to the island way of life.

As the Friday of Memorial Day weekend progressed, the traffic increased. I could see tourists weighed down on the causeway bridge in monstrous rumbling trucks, decked out with window and bumper stickers commemorating past visits. Huge RVs thundered past our house, as did a fleet of SUVs loaded with bikes, canoes, and children. Many of the RVs were bigger than some of the trailers people lived in on the island. On they came, and how busy it suddenly became. A plethora of images streamed by: a swaying convoy on Maddox Boulevard, the trailer tide spilling onto the island, adolescent girls in bathing suits screaming out the back of pickup trucks. Most of the incomers passed by us to go south to the Inlet View Campground, or they made a left towards the Tom's Cove Campground.

It was easy to spot the newcomers with their unmuddied cars, untanned skins, and perfect hairdos. The party house catty-corner to us and the house to the left of us erupted into life. Numerous families arrived with teenagers, who hung out on the porches with their iPhones.

Tourists coming back across the causeway

Dusk was falling as I looked out of the window across the bay, but I still heard hundreds of laughing gulls way out in the marsh. Maybe they were having the last laugh to welcome the incoming tourists. One thing was for sure—too many gulls would become road-kill victims from the speeding vehicles on the causeway in the coming weeks.

Bright car headlights streamed across the causeway, evenly spaced, like the steady rhythm on a heart monitor. Lights switched on in formerly dormant houses, animating all the homes that had been unoccupied for the winter. The island trolley and open-sided electric cars passed our house almost soundlessly, while the occasional lines of rented scooters sharply interrupted our peaceful world. I was amazed at how often people stopped to say hi on the corner or waved as they drove past our house. It happened all day—an endless display of pleasantness, mostly from the locals and repeat family visitors.

The island was coming to life, and it was time for the local businesses to make their money. The window of opportunity was here and now; everyone had their chance.

It was 2:00 p.m. on Sunday during the Memorial Day weekend. I had been working hard for three days on our new shell driveway as well as installing our mailbox when I decided it was time to take a break and walk on the refuge. I was on my own, as Debbie was back in New Jersey. I wanted to find the Bivalve Trail that had recently opened on the Chincoteague Wildlife Refuge. I grabbed our trusty homemade witch hazel bug spray that had worked well so far and set off in the car.

On crossing the bridge to the refuge, I noticed a line of cars leading to the entrance booths, most no doubt headed straight for the vast beach. I had not seen this before, having always had the opportunity to drive straight through the booths, generally only manned in winter on holidays. I shouldn't have been surprised to see so many visitors this weekend. The Chincoteague National Wildlife Refuge is one of the most visited refuges in the country. I probably owed my fair share of entry money. Debbie and I hadn't purchased a thirty-dollar yearly pass yet, which was something very worthwhile for residents like us, who visited the refuge often.

The booth attendant had to ask a colleague in the adjacent booth how I could get to the trail I came to discover. I parked and headed to the Woodland Trail, which was in the shape of a loop. The Bivalve Trail cut off sharply from it once one was about halfway around. As I strolled alone through the woods, the silence engulfed me. All I could hear was the wind rustling through the tree canopy above and the chatter of birds further down the trail. A hot early summer's day in the pine forest brought out a rich, spicy smell of pine. It was a sharp, intense, resinous, and somehow sweet scent; with the pleasure of the fresh fragrances in my nose, I walked and listened to the gentle breeze making the pine needles "rush," which was at once refreshing and soothing.

While I ambled along the silent path in this vibrant woodland, I knew that cars poured in through the Refuge entrance gates and mostly headed straight for the pristine ocean beach. A sudden noise interrupted my silent world like an express train about to pass. Loud chattering reverberated through the woods, and a group of people ambled along the trail without seeming to notice the natural glory around them. When they passed me, I didn't see them savoring this tremendous environment—instead, they strode noisily with their iPhones out and earbuds in, chatting loudly. I gratefully heard their voices fade away as they continued further along the path.

Tall loblolly pines with poison ivy growing up their trunks punctuated the deep thickets from which numerous birds flitted and stretched all the way up into the canopy. Their huge, notched trunks bore thick, chunky plate-like scales that evoked the formidable breastplates of Roman armor, ready to defend the tree against the voracious pine bark beetle. Some trees were snapped in half and stood splintered like those from a World War I landscape, a few with a beautiful semicircular orange fungus called a "mock oyster" growing up the trunk like embedded gold coins. The loblolly pines formed a crown shape at their tops, rather like an impressive head of broccoli. Some of this broccoli had turned a rusty brown color, however, as the pine bark beetle had ravaged substantial stands of the trees.

The health of the trees reminded me of Peter Wohlleben's book, *The Hidden Life of Trees*, in which he invites us to share in the joy that trees can bring us. I read how social they are, how they communicate, and how they care for each other.

The trees here on the wildlife refuge are so vulnerable. As the pine bark beetle has felled so many trees, gaps in the forest allow the hot sun and winds to reach down to disrupt the wet climate below. Consequently, the protective closeness provided by trees standing together is compromised. The tall loblolly pines with top-heavy crowns present a wide cover to catch the wind, and their towering trunks intensify the pressure. Add to that the sandy soil they stand in and their shallow root system, and it is easy to understand why winter storms create such havoc.

I rounded a corner and saw a small clearing to my right, with a single tree in the center. A melodious song came from the tree, and I caught sight of a male rose-breasted grosbeak going about its business as if he didn't notice me. Close by, the female did her own thing while the male sang his heart out.

The sweet song was the only sound I heard combined with the wind symphony from the pines above.

Then came another sudden interruption from a family on bikes as the kids hollered to their mother if dinosaurs lived in the woods. Despite my feeling of annoyance, I couldn't blame them for shouting and being slightly scared, as any kid might be. At least they were outside and not in front of a computer at home.

I sauntered further and nearly missed the unmarked Bivalve Trail off to my left. With no sign, this thwarted the casual walker, who might be reluctant to be drawn down the dark tunnel of pines. Tiny white shell fragments lined the secret path, decidedly narrower than the asphalt trail I had been on, and led me into a silent wood of closely planted pine trees. I no longer heard my footsteps as I left the gravel to walk deftly on soft pine needles lying on top of the white shells. The twisting path was dark, somewhat claustrophobic, and yet strangely comforting as the mysterious tunnel led me somewhere through the trees.

I strolled along this path in complete calm and contentment. I felt gently jolted from my current existence to savor a connection to something more immense than the mundane elements of my life. The silence and warm ocean breeze soothed me, lulling me into a sense of wonder of the raw connection to the living, breathing world around me. I felt suspended in a weird, calm void as if I had left the world behind and entered a "thin space."

Experiencing a thin space is supposed to disorient us, make us confused and lose our bearings. The veil that separates heaven and earth lifts, and one is reputedly able to receive a glimpse of the glory of God. It wasn't like that for me, but it was a unique spiritual serenity.

It is no wonder that thin places are most often associated with wild landscapes and islands, which often means traveling to a place where we have less control and where the unpredictable becomes the means of discovery.

Many writers have declared their love of paths and trails. In Robert Macfarlane's book, *The Old Ways*, he discusses various writers' love of pathways.

John Clare was fond of footpaths because they were "rich and joyful to the mind: ways of walking that were also ways of thinking." To William Wordsworth, long-used paths were routes to adventure, leading into "the recesses of the country."

The American historian and geographer John Brinckerhoff Jackson wrote,

> *"Over thousands of years for men and women, the path and road stood for some intense experience: freedom, new human relationships, a new awareness of the landscape. The road offered a journey into the unknown that could end up allowing us to discover who we were."*

The breeze made the hairs on my neck prickle with the anticipation of seeing something greater than myself. The whole canopy swayed. I heard the faint roar of the ocean waves a mile away, crashing on the Assateague shoreline. I focused on the tunnel of trees in front of me that twisted, rose up and turned, leading out to Tom's Cove. I looked up through the canopy and caught sight of an enormous bald eagle. His bright white head illuminated in the afternoon sun as he glided with straight flat wings over the treetops. An excerpt from a poem by Stacy Smith, titled *From an Eagle's View*, makes one wonder what it must be like to be an eagle:

> *Have you ever wondered what it's like to fly free,*
> *To see the world as far as the eye can see,*
> *To view the surroundings from high and from low,*
> *To hear only the sound of a distant echo,*
>
> *If you were an eagle you would wonder no more,*
> *For it can see things you have never seen before.*
> *Next time you look into the sky of blue,*
> *Think of what it's like from an eagle's view.*

I liked that the trail was hard to find, since it made it more special and secretive—like I was going to my own enchanted place. Since the pines were so close together, they became a dark sound trap with bird songs amplified. I heard the distinct *sip* of a cardinal as he called from somewhere in the understory.

Light appeared ahead in the tunnel of trees, which I assumed was leading me to Tom's Cove. Dappled sunlight shone on the shell pathway when suddenly I broke through the trees to see a classic watchman's shack standing firm in an idyllic setting.

The woodland curtain had been pulled back to reveal a glimpse of the past, a very real working past, where men who have gone before had pulled up their boats to maybe take a short rest from the water, sort their catch, or simply hang out. I felt I was viewing a landscape painting from an old master.

The reality was that someone had stayed out there to watch over the oyster beds. The owner was Tommy Clark of Don's Seafood in town. He reputedly used to pay someone to stay in the shack and sit with a gun to watch over the oyster beds, but that was many years ago. Beyond the sand of this remote beach, the shack stood as a significant feature out in the bay. A line of dark weathered posts, evenly spaced, led out toward it from the shore.

An enormous osprey nest was perched on the shack's roof, with its two birds settled on the gable at the far end. Modern shingles covered the roof and looked well maintained. The shack, a typical rectangular house shape, didn't look that old, unless the pale blue vinyl siding covered an older part. It had windows on all sides and a small extension off to the side. I questioned the angled supports beneath it that were dark and twisted. Some posts leaned at a precarious angle, and I wondered how stable the building really was.

I emerged onto a silent, deserted shoreline by the cove. As I strolled out on the short beach, I looked left to see hundreds of cars maybe a mile away parked on the visitor beaches facing the ocean. All I could think of was how lucky I was to have my own quiet beach to myself.

Sun-bleached and bruised driftwood had been randomly cast up on the shoreline, alone and without purpose. Weather-beaten ridges and grooves etched into the driftwood, the hallmarks of its resistance against the forces of water. Most pieces were a subdued grey color, twisted and gnarled from years adrift in the salty brine that had washed the very color from them. Some made me think of a well-loved T-shirt that had been in the machine a few times too often. Maybe some fragments would tell me the tales from storms and giant waves they had been through. I picked up and examined each piece of wood, hoping it might have come from some ancient shipwreck, or it might contain a few nails or inscriptions etched into it.

I knelt down and gently dipped my hands into the still waters of the cove. The water swirled slowly and lazily near the shore, the way cream in morning coffee curls on the top as one pours it. When I lifted my hands again, a gust of air made them feel cold, yet the afternoon sun warmed my back. When the ocean breezes momentarily stopped, the air grew hot and still, reminiscent of opening an oven on baking day.

When I looked over to my far right across Tom's Cove, I could see the Wallops Flight Facility buildings in the distance. It was possible to see mirror images of the Wallops base shimmering in the heat out on the water. Here I could have sat all day were it not for the rumbling of my stomach and the need to get back to my chores at home.

I noticed piles of cordgrass washed up on the shoreline from previous high tides. The bay was not very deep, maybe six feet at the most, but it looked deep enough from where I viewed it. To the left of the shack, I noticed the obsolete Tom's Cove Lifesaving Station on the far shoreline. It stood out with its brick-colored red roof, white façade, and various rusted antennae. The aerials used to be in service many years back to save those shipwrecked on the shore.

The gentle, salty ocean breeze picked up again, drawing a steady rhythmic sloshing of short waves lapping up gently onto the sand. I knew that others would find my secret place soon as the trail became better known, but for now, this had been my special find on a glorious early summer's day. It provided the perfect peace to end my few days alone on the island.

As I was about to leave, I heard other people who had also discovered this trail. Noise traveled quickly on the breeze so I could hear them—a family of four on their bikes, parents and two teenagers—chatting loudly as they got closer. A reminder of the real world again, the busy world of people and cars. The teenagers decided to sit on the beach—with their iPhones, unsurprisingly. I doubt they noticed much about the shack or the view beyond.

I took many photos of contrasting views of the shack and planned to create some watercolors. A camera would become necessary every time I visited the refuge.

It was time for me to go. If only I could preserve this beautiful scene and freeze it in time, like roses that kept their scent for a week.

As I trekked back through the wake of many voices, I held that time and place in my mind. Such sites are private respites where one can go to retreat, to re-energize and gain a different perspective on life: a place to renew the spirit on an early summer day. I felt blissfully reinvigorated, rejuvenated and delighted, having celebrated the wonder of this particular time and place.

The English landscape expert W.G. Hoskins once wrote: "Few people in this overcrowded country have not some favorite heath or common or moor to which they retire when they need solitude, or unpolluted air, the glimpse of wildlife, or the sound of water falling over stones."

Hoskins understood that humans will always need special places where they can contemplate the natural world.

9

IMPATIENCE

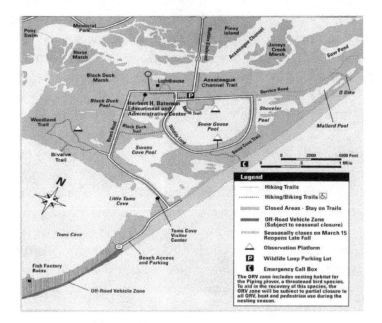

The Chincoteague Wildlife Refuge

S pring was in full swing, and more visitors arrived on the island. Some took days to slow down from their busy worlds to absorb the ways of the island. For those who embraced what the islanders call "island time" and paid attention, the rewards were immense. Those who did not and avoided the refuge missed out.

Patience is the one thing many people lack when they visit the island. I once witnessed a phenomenon while watching fishermen at the New Jersey shore. To improve their chances of catching a fish, the locals posted their fish catches on Facebook and let other fishermen know where to find the fish on the beaches. There was no patience or time to stop and savor the process.

Debbie and I have experienced this impatience on the Wildlife Loop, a place where one should be inclined to take one's time to relish nature, but we live in a restless world where instantaneous entertainment is supposed to materialize when requested on our televisions or handheld devices.

Quite a number of visitors "bird plow" onto the island from their busy urban lives. Jon Young explains the "bird plow" in his book *What the Robin Knows,* noting that bird plows are more disruptive in areas where nature is not used to man.

> *Consider the plow mounted on a huge truck barreling down the highway in a heavy storm, shoving aside the snow and anything else in its path. It doesn't slow down. It has no respect. Out of the way! In the wild, the birds are the first creatures that flee an invaded scene, and they proclaim the alarm for all to see and hear. We call this the bird plow, and it's why Native American scouts could pinpoint the location of invading cavalry troops from two miles away.*

When cars are permitted on the refuge's Wildlife Loop in the afternoon, some cars speed around, causing birds to rise up quickly in alarm, and the area is then disturbed: bird plow. Some days there are so many cars following each other around the drive that it's a wonder anyone sees anything. People drive too fast to notice anything and sometimes come up quickly behind you, pushing you along. Some drive around as if it were a racetrack loop and not a scenic wildlife journey.

The cars lead to opportunities for "wake hunters": those birds that prey on those that get disturbed or flushed. Fortunately, the egrets and herons on the Wildlife Loop are used to cars, but there still can be upsets. If a flock of snow geese is feeding on Swan Cove Pool, the slightest disturbance can set them off.

A passing bald eagle might spring into flight to pick off an injured bird because of the disruption.

Jon Young further explains, "The natural world is a culture of vigilance based on carefully tended relationships and connections maintained through recognition, mutual respect. Joe the hiker or Jill the jogger throws it into disarray."

Debbie and I have learned to slow down and move slowly within the landscape. Merging into the scene is crucial to see more wildlife. You have to get out on foot and immerse yourself in it.

In early May, we took walks on the loop before the refuge opened it for cars in the afternoon. These walks allowed me to examine the LBJs (little brown jobs) more closely as the birds were too hard to identify from the car. The warblers were coming through. Grand yellow thistles rose from the grass verges on the side of the road. It was heavenly to have the place to ourselves except for the odd biker.

Since fewer cars drive the Wildlife Loop when the weather is rainy and cold, those are the best times to visit. We often turn the car engine off to hear the birds around us and the ocean roar in the distance. Taking the car is second best though, as it doesn't allow one to see and hear the intricate side of nature that lies within the marsh. When the weather is inhospitable or buggy, the car is the only way, even if it is a bit like armchair birding.

10

NO LAUGHING MATTER

I didn't think that one bird species I enjoyed watching on the refuge would become an annoyance during my first spring on the island. It was early May, and for several days the laughing gulls outside my open bedroom window woke me very early with their distinctive screeching call. Debbie and I enjoyed meeting a host of characters in our first year, but the one thing we didn't welcome around our wonderful home were these "Cachinnans," a word that comes from Latin and means to laugh heartily. Linguists believe that the name came about because it sounded like they were laughing. When I first heard the supposed laugh, I did not agree!

Their early morning call was not the flock call that was kinder on the ears, but a call that intensified as predators or other gulls came by. It was a raucous "Get out of my face, mate" call—definitely not a laugh, but more of a nasty scream. Composer Frederic Austin, the arranger of "The Twelve Days of Christmas" created a bird theme by naming calling birds, turtle doves, French hens, swans, and geese, but I now understand why he perhaps changed his song and jokingly removed the five laughing gulls screeching in favor of some random gold rings.

The laughing gulls decorated us from above with their bird droppings and stole our food quickly out of our hands on the beach. They were loud, greedy, invasive, polluting, and aggressive. They ate anything that moved and many items that didn't. Some locals referred to them as flying rats.

Hate them as I chose to that first summer, I had to admit those seagulls were one hundred percent badass, though they weren't as huge as the harassing herring gulls that plagued the promenade back in Llandudno in North Wales, where I grew up. I was convinced that the Welsh gulls doubled in size from when I was a boy. They, too, acted with attitude, and maybe they were worse.

In some coastal towns in the UK, herring gulls are considered public enemy number one. They swoop down on young children and pensioners out for a quiet Sunday afternoon walk. On occasion, they even snatched children's ice cream cones from their hands. The fact that fish and chips is quite common in the UK doesn't help matters, as they will follow unsuspecting eaters until they get some, too.

Beware of the Gulls

Despite the annoying gull noises, when we could, we chose to sleep with the windows open so the cool breezes could waft through the house. The problem with that was we invited other noises to come in as well. The house catty-corner to us used a sprinkler system, which, after running for a while, deposited a pool of fresh water on the side of the road for the birds to drink. Since it was the only freshwater pool around, it became a common meeting place for the gulls.

One morning at 5:40 a.m., I ventured out to investigate the cause of the latest gull social. A small flock was at their watering hole when I ambled over to gatecrash their party, threw some shells at them, and told them to shut up. It was probably a foolish thing to do, as they menacingly hovered above me as if to say, "Who is this idiot?!" At 6:30 a.m., they flew off to annoy someone else.

As I strutted back inside the house, the workers arrived at Loraine's construction site opposite. They too started early with their lifting tractor, as if the gulls weren't enough of a noise already. After lifting a few stacks of wood, the contractors discussed the day's work. Afterward, a heavenly silence reigned that should always exist in a place like this.

I decided to put the morning's seagull confrontation behind me and do something positive on such a bright start to the day. It was still early, and the sun hadn't risen above the pines in our backyard. The blackcurrant bushes were still in shade, so I gave them a drenching with the hose as they yielded so much fruit in their first year. Then I watered the fresh herbs we planted and the lone cucumber plant we decided to try.

Our so-called "farm" at the rear of our property, was like a mini nature reserve. A cool stand of tall pines grew beside a gut (small stream) that ran behind them. The fruit on our fig tree was ripening, so the birds gathered on its branches probing the juicy fruits. Some of the laughing gulls waited below for easy pickings. Our backyard was a haven for many kinds of creatures.

After I shut the water off, I was surprised to see one of the laughing gulls standing at the bottom of our driveway. These gulls held themselves distinctively from other gulls with their more upright, cocky stance. They also shuffled with an attitude—with deliberate, well-placed steps as they strutted about. This bird gave me an annoying stare with its head cocked to one side. A distinctive white patch above his eye made him stand out from the other laughing gulls. Maybe it was a battle scar or a mark in his feather. Given his dark hood, he looked like he wore a mask, which added to his badass appearance. Perhaps he (or she) decided to come around to "flip me the bird" and check me out or even to make peace after I previously lobbed shells at them.

I won't venture to suggest these guys have personalities, but there appeared to be a smirk on this gull's face as he looked at me. He didn't come too far up the driveway, as he knew I would fire another shell at him, so we engaged in a standoff. A short staring-down contest followed, and then he flew off. He knew I meant business and wasn't standing for any more antics.

The rest of the morning was quieter, except for the morning flow of trucks pulling boats to the launch ramp or runners puffing on the sidewalk. Families were learning to ride a bike again, often on the wrong side of the road, teenagers looking down at their phones while they rode along… agh!

Each day we got used to the daily dawn kerfuffle of laughing gulls greeting their pals, but thankfully it died down after an hour or so, and then the birds hung out on the rooftops preening and watching each other in silence. They uttered a few last calls to remind us how annoying they sounded, and then flew off to the marsh opposite for the day, or to annoy the tourists on the beaches.

In the evening, the gulls returned and gathered again on the rooftops opposite our house to talk about their day and preen. Then they flew back to the marsh to roost for the night in their colony.

Despite my dislike of the laughing gulls, every evening we watched many flocks of egrets, herons, and ibis fly over our house to roost opposite. The smooth convex lines of the ibis, in particular, were a delight to watch. There were two kinds: the glossy and the white. The white stood out more in this landscape.

Watercolor of White Ibis

Iridescent coppers and fluorescent, metallic greens swathed the glossy ibis. When viewed in the best light, the birds positively glowed with color that adorned the marsh. It's no wonder monarchs and kings idolized the bird as this poem, *Ibis* by R.A. Marschall states:

Idolized by pharaohs, monarchs, and kings;
Bird of the wetlands, marshes, and swamps.
Interesting forager with long bill and stilted long legs;
Sacred icon of the dynasties of yore.

If we worked in the garden or casually looked out through a window, we couldn't anticipate what magnificent birds might appear. A bald eagle flying low over the house with a fish wriggling in its talons, brown pelicans showing off their flap-and-glide technique, one behind the other out in the bay. A flock of white ibis flying in formation, or the appearance of hummingbirds at our feeders. It was an amazing place to live, despite the intrusive calls of the laughing gulls.

To operate my home business, we laid a shell driveway in early summer to comply with the town's requirement that we have space to park four cars. It was much cheaper than laying gravel or cement. Many of the moon shells still had their sea snails inside. The smell from the discarded half-dead sea snails grew overpowering when the hot sun roasted them. I decided to walk around the driveway with a hammer and break the shells open, hoping that the laughing gulls would swoop down and feed on them. My theory was this would eradicate the smell more quickly than merely leaving the snails to rot in their shells. The feeding didn't happen immediately, so I waited until a few laughing gulls flew close by and attempted to entice them by throwing some of the shell contents their way.

I recognized by the narrow white dash above his eye the very gull that stared me down a few days earlier at the end of the driveway. He noticed my offerings from the top of a nearby telephone pole. He might have wondered why I offered him delicious shell contents when previously I threw those very shells at him in annoyance. I threw some snails his way on the driveway and on the road. After a while, he circled down to pick up a piece, which he quickly gulped down. Then he picked at some more.

The following day he was back in earnest striding around the driveway tugging at the discarded shell contents and selecting his choice of morsels for breakfast. When I left for work, surprisingly he didn't fly off. Instead, he gave me a sideways stare and ambled over to the side of the driveway, while I slowly backed my car out. When I returned later in the day, there he was again in the middle of the driveway as if he owned the place. I drove in gently, pushing him off to the side.

I stepped out of the car, whereupon a ridiculous thought entered my head. I felt like saying, "How was your day? Did you enjoy the shell offerings?" as if he were a member of the family. Was I actually making friends with one of these noisy, arrogant birds, the very birds that disturbed my early mornings for weeks?

One morning I couldn't believe he was actually perched on my car hood waiting for me when I left the house. This back and forth exchange continued for a week or so, and we became accustomed to seeing each other. I told Debbie one evening that I was naming him "Gustav." He simply looked like a Gustav. I am not sure why, but the name instantly came into my head. The name Gustav is associated with Swedish royalty, and this bird certainly had a majestic aura. The fact that laughing gulls walk with such a proud, upright stance made me think that they believe they are more upscale than other seagulls.

In the coming weeks, Gustav enjoyed his sushi shellfish buffet and put on weight. I broke open a few shells every so often, and Gustav took out the rest of the contents during the day. It was a relationship built upon cooperation. He helped me clean up the driveway, and I fed him in the process.

One afternoon when I returned from school, a lady companion—a "gull-friend" from the marsh—joined Gustav. She merely stood bored and uninterested at the edge of the driveway while he sauntered over to feed her with various pieces of moon shell. I couldn't see what he saw in her, as she had no personality. She did none of the work and blankly stared at him for his efforts. I guessed it was their courtship ritual.

The marsh now heaved with laughing gulls. One morning as I drove to work, I observed a mass copulation of gulls in the grasses on either side of the causeway. It was as if everyone agreed this was the day to have sex at the same time. When I returned home, Gustav decided to join the day's orgy but in his novel way. Rather than doing it like everyone else out in the marsh, he perched on top of his mate at the top of our telephone pole to have a grand old time. What a show-off! Later, after copious screeches and calls, both gulls stood exhausted on the driveway enjoying a cigarette... just kidding. They fed each other more stringy bits of shell contents for the rest of the evening.

In the weeks that followed, I didn't see much of them, so I presumed they were off raising their growing family out in the marsh. I observed the laughing gulls on the cultivated fields on the mainland during inclement weather. They stood in their pairs, madly in love and staring at each other. They also engaged in cooperative feeding with the egrets in shallow pools. The laughing gulls paddled about stirring up the pool, while the egrets perched around the edges snatching up the disturbed creatures. It was about the only generous behavior I noticed from the gulls.

One sunny day, Gustav suddenly appeared back in the yard alone. I was sitting in the kitchen looking out the window when he flew down below it and gave me his usual hello gesture with his head cocked to one side. He then walked about on the driveway, casting the occasional stare my way. *Why is there no food waiting?* I presumed he thought. There was plenty still there, but he apparently expected tasty contents that I extracted for him from the shells. He had grown meticulous and wanted the best and most accessible pieces like before. He didn't want to have to work at it—prying contents out of shells, banging shells on the ground, or dropping them from great heights like his herring gull cousins. I could tell by the way he looked at me that he was frustrated, as his food supply dried up and no doubt he needed to feed his family back on the marsh. The day after, he didn't hop onto my car hood as usual, but he did do something unthinkable.

I noticed through the corner of my eye two adult mallards who waddled into the yard with their two very pint-sized chicks. Gustav noticed them too, and immediately approached them gingerly but stayed a few feet away. The adults instantly closed ranks around their two tiny chicks, but the fledglings didn't heed their calls and wandered away. I sensed something terrible was about to happen, so I stopped eating breakfast and banged loudly on the kitchen window, shouting at Gustav to not interfere. I could see that Gustav was trying to force the two adults apart so he could get access to the chicks.

It happened so quickly and rather violently.

Gustav suddenly darted forward, his wings spread out, his red beak flared, gaping wide open. He chased one of the wee chicks into the long grass and closed his beak swiftly around its neck. As I bolted out of the back door, Gustav flew up into the air with the tiny helpless chick dangling and wriggling pathetically in his beak.

"Damn you, Gustav," I shouted, but he was gone.

It was then that I realized something profound. I had been lulled over the weeks into thinking Gustav was a pet. This was no pet, but a wild creature, an experienced opportunist, driven by his primal instincts to feed his family.

From that day on, I stopped calling him Gustav. I felt foolish to have allowed him to affect me that way. He was simply like all the other gulls that frequented our backyard, yet something struck me about Gustav. His personality made for a unique encounter. He had used me to procure choice snails just as his squawking relatives preyed on innocent children's casually held sandwiches. Perhaps Gustav meant no malice. Nevertheless, I felt used.

A few weeks later, a laughing gull dumped on me while I was on my boat. At feeling the pattering sensation of splatter on my Aussie hat, I looked skyward; the gull looked down as if to say, "Gotcha now!" Something told me it was Gustav.

11

THE TEAGUER'S TUMP TOUR

The Tour Van

I have taken a few boat tours around Chincoteague Island, but I wanted to make a land tour of the island to learn more about it. Who better to do this with than a fifth-generation Teaguer?

Denise Bowden invited us to meet her in a parking lot behind the village shopping mall, which was a curious start to the trip. I imagined I was about to conduct some clandestine deal with a dealer. When I arrived, I noticed other people, mainly seniors, sitting in their cars, peering out at each other, wondering if we were on the same tour.

Denise arrived in her bright white ten-passenger van emblazoned with her logo and phone number. The bus side displayed the slogan: "Discover Chincoteague Island in a Whole New Way." She hopped out wearing a Saltwater Cowboys t-shirt; the silhouette of the island tattooed on her left bicep.

She opened the side doors for us to board and introduced herself. There were eight of us, mostly older retired couples. Noticing my long legs, Denise asked if I wanted to sit up front. When I commented on my height, Denise remarked that she was twenty-three inches long when she was born.

"I only grew another 3 feet," she added jokingly.

The van was a snug fit, and once everyone was on board Denise said,

"You don't have to put your seat belts on back there as I don't drive over eighty on Chincoteague."

Someone behind me laughed.

Denise asked where everyone was from (Virginia) and if they had visited the island before (no). She explained that her family went back on both sides.

"I am a twenty-nine-year member of the Chincoteague Volunteer Fire Company, where I have served in numerous capacities. Right now, I am the public relations officer for the company. That can be a good thing and a bad thing depending on what's happening. I also serve on the town council.

"I am doing this tour because listening to my parents and my grandparents all these years and doing my own research on Chincoteague, I realized we have lost a lot. We have gained a lot, but from where we started out from it is not what we have now. Seafood was king, and we had a lot of industry on here. So today we are going to talk about those things.

"We are going to talk about some colorful characters we had around town over the years," she said. "You'll hear me talk about my grandparents quite a bit. I was very close to both sets. I was smart enough in my teenage years to write things down. It's so important to me. It's about keeping things alive so the next generation can know what goes on. You can't go where you're going until you know where you've been."

Denise handed everyone a little booklet to look at. The front cover read:

"We hope you enjoy taking a peek into our past! Use this booklet to help you follow along with the tour route. What you are about to see no longer exists. It only lives in our minds and memories." The booklet contained old and present-day photos of most of the stops on the tour.

"Not every stop we make has a picture," Denise said, "so don't try to get ahead of yourselves. I know it's tempting.

"At the end of the tour, we'll come back here, so let me get out and come around to get the stool out for you. You can just leave your booklets right on the seat."

One of the passengers asked if we got out of the van while on the tour. Denise said no.

I replied jokingly, "Unless you get thrown out."

Denise said she has had the odd person she had wanted to kick off in the past but didn't go into details.

Noting my Welsh accent, the passengers asked where I was from. Denise just said, "He's from down south. You can hear his accent."

Denise told everyone that her accent wasn't as thick as her parents. Then she turned to me and asked, "What about Barbara Walker's accent then?"

I agreed, as Barbara always made me laugh when she greeted me at the island YMCA with "Hiya, Honey."

Denise asked everyone to silence their cell phones, and we were off.

We stopped at a ramshackle building on Willow Street that looked like it was about to fall down.

"This was the office of our famous and most beloved doctor called Doc Amrien or as Teaguers say 'Amron,'" Denise said. "He was a wonderful, good old country doctor that came from the city. You didn't have to make an appointment. You might have to wait, but you would be seen that day no matter what. He did not believe in sending people off to specialists like we do these days. The days of Doc Amrien are sadly over with. He was an excellent diagnostic doctor and knew the human body very well."

Denise made everyone laugh when she said, "His X-ray machine looked like it came over on the Mayflower."

Many elderly Teaguers wish Amrien were here today, she noted.

"He had one big, bad drawback," Denise said. "He had bottom-of-the-barrel bedside manners. Not a drop. He would enter the examination room with his glasses down, always a cigarette in hand, and say, 'What the hell's wrong with you today?'"

We turned and drove down Cleveland Street. Denise slowed down as we passed a driver who rolled his window down to hand Denise a package. She seemed to know what it was, as she said thank you with a laugh, and then turned to us.

"That's how it's done on Chincoteague," she said. "You often stop in the middle of the street and say how are you doing." This became a recurring theme on the tour as everyone beeped or waved at Denise.

Denise asked us to turn in our booklets to a picture of what is now the Island Value grocery store as she turned into the parking lot. This was the location of the very first pony corral, which paved the way for the annual Pony Penning event that takes place every year on the island. Many of the homes shown in the booklet are still there. Our perspective from the bus was the same as in the old photo—we could compare the past and present simultaneously.

Shortly after, we stopped at the old town jail, marked by a sign outside. "You were brought here for something minor," Denise said, "drunk in public, a fist fighting, or petty theft. You never stayed more than two nights. Anything bad, you went to the county jail. Nowadays you go there for everything. It's referred to as the Accomack Hilton." She turned her attention back to the old town jail.

"It's a small two-cell jail with a bathroom. That's all it was. An employee of the town, Clifton Reed looked after it. He came over daily on his bike and fed whoever was in there."

Denise explained he was a quiet character, and locals called him "Titty Wee." She had no idea why. Denise recounted one amusing story about Titty Wee.

"One day he came by, and a female was in the jail. She asked him for a Kotex. Titty replied, 'You will get Corn Flakes as everyone else does.'"

Denise pointed out where the old bridge used to come into town and discussed how much damage the 1962 Ash Wednesday storm—one of the top ten of the twentieth century—wrecked on the downtown. Some ninety percent of the island flooded, and more than a hundred of the Chincoteague ponies died. The most famous, Misty of Chincoteague, survived when she was brought from the flooded barn into her owners' kitchen, where she stayed for three days.

"Have any of you seen the movie 'Misty'?" Denise asked my fellow tourists. None of them had. Denise encouraged them to do so.

She pointed out Wallace's Barbershop in our booklet.

"It was right there where the medical center is and featured in the movie. Today it is known as the library, and it was moved seventy-five yards north."

Denise drove further south along Main Street and pulled up on the left side of the street.

"How can you pull up on the wrong side of the street?" one of the passengers asked with a concerned voice.

"I only get cussed out a couple of times," Denise calmly replied.

Denise pointed out the Coast Guard buildings and explained that all the life-saving equipment was housed there, as opposed to the old Coast Guard building at the end of Tom's Cove (now decommissioned and part of the Assateague National Seashore). Denise remarked that before 9/11 anyone could go through the gates of the coast guard and potter about. On 9/11, Denise saw armed guards for the first time on the gate.

We traveled a little further down South Main Street and parked opposite the carnival grounds. It gave Denise the opportunity to tell everyone how important the ponies, owned and managed by the Chincoteague Volunteer Fire Company, are to the town.

"We put a lot of money into these ponies because they are our bread and butter here. Everything on Chincoteague is centered around the ponies. The high school mascot is a pony. The elementary school mascot is the colt. We love these ponies. During the pony roundups, they are given their vet checks and inoculations.

"Outside of saving lives and property, they are our number-one priority. It's not just the financial benefit for us. It's because the volunteer fire company are animal lovers. We want to make sure they are healthy. The pony committee determines which ponies are sold every year. Not only do we come by your house to put out a fire or to take you to the hospital, but we also give away eight scholarships a year to high school seniors. We do a lot of fundraising for different things around the island such as Little League baseball, football, and Beta Club sponsorship. We want to give back to this community as much as people have given back to us."

Denise drove further down Main Street and approached our house. She directed our attention diagonally across the street.

"You are looking at Clark's Corner," she said. "Owned by Mr. and Mrs. Ed Clark. They had a love for animals. They came into ownership of Cloudy, who was Misty's grandson. They spoiled Cloudy and kept him very well at the house. They even taught Cloudy how to do tricks, such as kneeling down or how to stand up on a stool. If Mr. Clark took a sip of Pepsi, so did Cloudy. If Mr. Clark belted a shot of whiskey, so did Cloudy. When Mr. Clark passed away in the early seventies, his wife was unable to care for Cloudy."

After we passed J & B's Sub Shop, Denise told us the area we entered, including Debbie's and my house, was what the old timers referred to as "Down the Marsh."

"Every house on the left feels the need to have a pier out on the right," Denise said. "These things are expensive. You have to have a lot of permits to go with them. If you see an aerial shot of this area, it looks like a ladder going up and down the shoreline.

"This part of the island is a beautiful place to watch the sunsets, watch the boats coming in, and the dolphins. My favorite thing is to watch a good thunderstorm," she said.

We arrived at the southern tip of the island at Merritt Harbor. Denise noted that the island is seven miles long and a mile and a half wide.

"If you stand here at Inlet View Campground," she said, "you look out to some of the prettiest views. If you own a boat looking in, however, it's best to turn your head and look somewhere else. The owner doesn't have a good reputation for taking care of his property here."

When Denise was growing up, the harbor was just one big marshy swimming hole. There were no docks, paving, or boats. Her mother forbade her from coming down and swimming by herself for fear she would drown, but she snuck down every chance she could.

"If you make a left out of the harbor," Denise said, "it takes you right out to the Atlantic Ocean. Make a right, and it takes you right up the Intracoastal Waterway all the way up the East Coast."

She pointed out the Waterman's Memorial up a slight rise, from where one can watch the NASA rocket launches from Wallops Island. "It's a nice, quiet, serene place to be," she said.

I pointed out all the old boats in the harbor and how I came down to paint them on occasion.

Denise drove down to the far end of the harbor to see what the watermen were bringing in. Two brawny men added ice to their recent catch.

"These are some of the hardest working people you'll come across in your life," Denise said, "They fish the tides, and most of the time it's the tide coming in."

We returned to Main Street and headed back north to pull into the Ocean Breeze mobile home park. Not a sign at either entrance announced it. Denise told us that every road in the park begins with the word Sea.

"You have got Sea Bass, Sea Horse, Sea Breeze, and Sea Shell, and wait till you *see* how bad the roads are," she said jokingly. The bus erupted with laughter.

"It's also one of the first areas that will flood. The post office will not deliver mail down here. However, if I am driving the ambulance and you have broken your leg, I can't say, 'How about you come out front, and I'll pick you up.'"

After driving through the mobile home park, Denise said we were back on town-owned roads and asked us to turn the page in our tour booklet.

"You are looking at the Beebe Ranch house location where this double-wide trailer now is. When you do watch the movie 'Misty,' during the flood of 1962 Grandpa Beebe brought Misty into the house. Misty lived for three days in the kitchen until the floods went down. Tragically, around thirty years ago, in '92 or '93, the ranch house caught fire for no apparent reason. Arson was suspected. You can now see signs erected in the pasture around this location stating that this was Misty's pasture."

Traveling further north on Ridge Road, we came across an unusual home owned by a well-known person called Star with a giant Viking statue lying on its side beside the house. Denise told us the Viking was worth a lot of money. Not much was said about the crazy-colored home and its littered belongings. Denise just said, "It's a mess."

Denise pointed out Pony Swim Lane where the ponies come up out of the water when they swim them across the Assateague Channel in July.

"Everyone waits for a four and half minute swim which is about seventy-five yards," Denise said. "If they do it on a low slack tide, the ponies can almost walk across part of it. Sometimes some even swim over during the year. There are four boats, two on each side, to keep them in line when they swim across. The cowboys have already got their horses over on a barge."

When Denise has people ask her at the Carnival grounds what to bring for the swim, "I tells them bring your patience.

They might delay when they come over. People have to be ready to wait."

"The mud will wash off, but those memories will last forever," Denise said, recounting the thunderstorm when the ponies came across in 2013.

"We have never lost a pony in a swim," Denise proudly said.

Denise asked us to turn the page in our booklets again. "You should have a picture of Floyds Drive In. This was owned by Mr. and Mrs. Brasure who would bring food out on a tray and set it on your car window. Bob and Tina Zoller bought it eventually and ran it as Mr. Baldy's until Bob fell ill with his heart."

As we drove further north along Ridge Road, Denise pointed out that the road was one of the highest places on the island.

Someone in the back of the van asked: "Are you going to tell us how Chicken City Road got its name?"

"Oh, yes," Denise assured him. But she was saving that information as we approached the end of the tour and the spot itself.

We came upon Mechanics Cemetery, curiously named after the junior order of American mechanics when, in the 1870s, there were no cars or trucks. Denise wasn't sure what they were doing mechanics on. She told us she had a lot of family in the Mechanics Cemetery. It is the largest cemetery on the island with fifteen hundred graves. All told, there are about five thousand graves on the island.

Later on, Denise told us that during the great storm of '62, flooding caused many vault lids to come off the graves at Redman's Cemetery on Taylor Street. Once the waters subsided, everyone pitched in to meticulously replace the lids. As a consequence, some people now have a cement slab put over the top to make sure they don't reappear in inclement weather.

We drove on East Side Drive, and Denise recounted the days when there were forty-three shucking houses on the island.

"There are now only two," she said, echoing the demise Cork McGee shared with me. "Chincoteague Shellfish on the left is the largest supplier of shellfish to the Harris Teeter grocery chain. Huge quantities of shellfish pass through here. The other shucking house is Tom's Cove shucking farm owned by Tommy Clark of Don's Seafood. He supplies the Grand Central Oyster Bar in New York City.

Unfortunately, a decline in seafood production and an increase in regulations have impacted the industry on the island.

"It will never be what it was," Denise said.

Denise stopped her van opposite a field that contained some old skiff boats.

"I would not be a good Chincoteaguer or tour guide if I did not stop at this stop. This piece of land right here was the home of our most famous, most beloved Pony Pines Restaurant and lounge. If you turn your page, you'll see what it looked like back in the 1920s and early '30s. It was referred to as The Pines. Everybody wanted to be at The Pines. It was the place to dance, drink, and eat fabulous seafood. There were three dining rooms. When you walked in, it had a 'Mafia feel' to it, thanks to the red sconce lights and the dim lighting. Talent came here from all over the place.

"Barbara, who I mentioned earlier and who works at the YMCA, apparently has in her last wishes that her funeral procession will ride by here on its way to the cemetery. She worked at The Pines for over twenty years.

In the '90s the then-owner, Theresa, suffered a bad stroke and that signaled the end. After her death, her family tried to run it, but it had to be torn down after outside investors failed to save it.

This was another place loved by Teaguers, just like the Chincoteague inn that was torn down in recent years. "I am a collector of Chincoteague history, so when they tore it down, I went over to see the people doing it. Since I know them, they cut out a big section of the dance floor for me. I have that piece inlaid into my hardwood floors at my home. Now I can dance anytime I want to at Pony Pines."

We returned to Willow Street and pulled to the side of the road. Off to the right, I asked about a brick building mostly obscured in vines. I had always wondered what it was. Denise told us that at one time the building housed a big, full-service bakery that made cakes, breads, donuts, éclairs, and cookies. Denise described the heavenly smell that would linger in the air.

"Inside the area where the old ovens can be seen, the chimneys used to be visible, but they have long gone."

We turned onto Church Street, where Denise talked about the much-loved Salyer Funeral Home, a third generation business from back in the 1940s. Amanda "Mandy" Betts, the granddaughter, runs it today. Ninety-five percent of those living on Chincoteague use the funeral home.

"We have the only funeral home on the shore that still puts out the name of the deceased out front," said Denise. "When you ride by, you can see who has passed away, depending on the color of the wreath out front—blue for men and pink for women.

"On Chincoteague, if you have been away for a couple of days or weeks, you don't go straight home until you ride by to see if anyone has died. We are nosy people," said Denise.

We finally made it to Chicken City Road.

"There is not another boulevard, road, or cul-de-sac in the world named Chicken City Road. In the Depression, the watermen took a hit financially, so they looked to their mainland counterparts to see about raising chickens. It became a huge industry on the island. At one time, seven million birds were produced a year. In 1962, the great storm destroyed them all.

"Little did the islanders know that when Marguerite Henry wrote her book in 1947 and the movie 'Misty' came out in 1962, that it would lead to tourism."

We arrived next at a simple white building on the right where Denise announced another industry that was popular—for all the wrong reasons.

"This was our brothel," Denise said with a smile on her face. "It was called the Virginia Inn. You grabbed your two-dollar bottle of whiskey from a bootlegger across the street and then came over to the brothel. The lady that owns the house still has the original sign. A bunch of us have begged for her to sell it, but she won't."

As we drove back to North Main Street, Denise asked,"Do you remember the actress Linda Lavin from the TV sitcom 'Alice'?" A few in the back replied yes. "Well, Linda got on her bike one day and rode back into the woods around here and found an old, beat-up house."

Denise asked us to turn to the page in our booklets, which showed the original dilapidated structure, now known as the Lavinder House.

"She fell in love with this house, bought it, restored it, and had it moved across the street here. It's a great little place with a unique tower, and it is now a vacation rental."

We drove south on North Main Street past the main bridge into town. Denise explained that the body of water to our right was part of the Intracoastal Waterway. Not once had Denise taken us on Maddox Boulevard, the town's current hub of commerce. Instead, she focused on Historic Main Street, back roads, the harbor and old buildings. Denise's warm personality enhanced the experience as she told an entertaining mix of funny, dramatic, and heart-warming tales about the island's past.

"If you turn the page, you will see why I am so grateful that Linda Lavin saved that house." She pointed out the old Lighthouse Inn that used to sit where a current modern structure is. "It was wonderful, but the owner tore it down and rebuilt it."

Another beautiful home, the Whealton House, existed on the site where the Shore Stop gas station is today. Denise has one of the bricks from the hearth of the house.

"Have you thought of starting a preservation society or something on the island?" one of the passengers asked.

"I am working on creating a Chincoteague Historical Society," Denise replied. "That's on my radar."

It is no surprise that many Teaguers are surprised when Denise reveals historical facts they've never heard before.

"Turn your page," instructed Denise. "We are near the end now. This is Miss Molly's Inn where Marguerite Henry wrote the book *Misty of Chincoteague*, and they have the Marguerite Henry room. I am not sure if they will let you go inside and look at everything. It's a beautiful original home. Everything is as it was for the most part."

As we looked at an old photo of Main Street, Denise mentioned that on the right side of the street, the flood destroyed everything. On the left side, everything is pretty much still there, except the beautiful Redman's building that was where the post office is today. The old Marine Bank, which is now Taylor Bank, has been renovated to look like it did in the early days.

Driving back through downtown, Denise recounted what each store used to be and a little history about it. We noticed the Island Library, which was originally Wallace's Barbershop. Sundial Books used to be Flicks Restaurant, and then it became Tull's. Denise showed the location of the old swing bridge from where you used to leave the island.

After pointing this out, she said, "And folks, that wraps up the Teaguer's Tump Tour." Everyone gave rapturous applause. "When you come back next time, you are going to ride by and say you know what each place used to be." Denise was very courteous when we arrived back to the original parking lot. She reminded us we had been sitting, so she retrieved the footstool. She asked us to leave our booklets on the seats.

"Good luck with the historical society," an old lady said as she exited the van.

"I don't want to make it complicated," Denise replied. "It would be nice to have some pictures outside with a little history of when places were established."

"Wasn't that an excellent tour?" one of the passengers said.

I wholeheartedly agreed as I jumped back in my car.

SUMMER

12

THE MAGIC OF OUR FRONT PORCH

Our previous owner gave us an old black and white photograph taken at the end of the nineteenth century of the Bunting family, the original owners of our house. I can imagine the family sitting on our front porch and chatting with the locals who strolled by. The American front porch once represented the ideal of community in America, where we shared interactions and discussions. It was a zone between the public community outside and the private sanctity of the home.

Traditionally, the great American front porch was always there, open and sociable, an unassigned part of the house that belonged to everyone and no one, a place for family and friends to pass the time together. It connected the home's interior, where human control prevailed, to nature and the wilderness outside it. It served as a vital transition between the uncontrollable out-of-doors and the cherished interior of the home—a place where one could safely view nature without immersing oneself in it and a sanctuary for reflection.

Over the years, so-called "progress" resulted in people preferring to stay indoors. Automobiles became popular, so people chose to drive rather than walk places. The noise from cars also meant families preferred the quiet inside of a home to the busy outside. (We certainly can relate to this on some days.) The popularity and increased sales of televisions also drew people inside, further diminishing outdoor social interaction between people. Today, of course, our preoccupation with technology, including smartphones and widescreen televisions, has doomed porch time in favor of screen time. Air conditioning has also become commonplace, keeping people inside to avoid suffering the often brutal heat and humidity. Due to these changes gradually taking place, the iconic front porch has virtually disappeared from modern house plans, replaced with patios, decks, and hot tubs designed to be enjoyed in the privacy of one's backyard.

Debbie and I are thankful we still have the original front porch on our house. We consider it the best room in the house. The previous owner left screened wood panels in the back shed to seal the porch off against mosquitos, but we haven't used them, preferring instead a seamless view of the world outside. We purchased comfortable wicker chairs, and Debbie made custom cushion covers from some pony-themed fabric she bought from a store on Route 13. As soon as the warm weather arrives, and before the mosquitos are a nuisance, we venture outside.

Our front porch offers a front-row seat to the constant hive of activity from May through September, where we watch the world go by, and others see us, too. Friends honk their car horns as they wave and turn the corner. It does have its annoying days when there is too much noisy traffic, but we wouldn't trade it for a quiet porch in the back any day.

Patricia Neely-Dorsey's poem titled *Front Porch* describes how the porch is the center of hospitality.

> *Just the spot*
> *For taking in a cool breeze*
> *And watching the world go by*
> *Friends and neighbors out*
> *For a leisurely stroll*
> *Stop and sit a spell*
> *"Lemonade"?*
> *"Iced Tea"?*
> *"Co-Cola"?*
> *"Did you hear about ..."?*
> *"Do Tell!"*
> *"You Don't Say!"*
> *"My, how the time flies"*
> *"Y'all come back, now"*
> *"You hear"?*

From our porch, we listen to the daily music of the island, such as the duck noises, or willets settling on the clam beds out front at low tide with their distinctive *"pill-will-willet"* calls. We breathe in the sulfurous smells of marsh as they drift into our noses from time to time or the occasional whiff of fried onions from J & B's Deli. We occasionally rush inside if the town mosquito spray truck makes its rounds and the wind is likely to push the insecticide our way.

While drinking my early morning tea, I watch various runners and bikers coming down the street. Sometimes the Coast Guard takes their morning run past our house, waving and shouting *hello!* as they round the corner.

Watching people in motion from the porch as they stroll by, with subtle and unsubtle movement of legs, arms, knees, shoulders, and hips, provides endless enjoyment.

I find it easy to distinguish the Come'eres who pass, as they appear unrecognizable and look markedly distinct. Often I see adolescent runners with their music plugged into their ears, wearing the latest athletic gear and sporting immaculately clean brand name shoes. Apparently, they want to keep up their fitness practice while away from home. Distinct groups of people park their cars and trucks out in front of our house and then walk back to visit J & B's Deli. Often they wear T-shirts, cargo shorts, and flip-flops; quite a few smoke; and some are overweight. Then there are what I termed the chatterers—middle-aged women walking in pairs. Often, one wears a visor and sips non-stop out of a cup as they loudly discuss their relationship issues. I mustn't forget the old-timers, a group of senior men who jog past the house around 6 o'clock in the morning. They must not realize how far their voices carry, stirring me from my sleep.

Some days our porch serves like a parade reviewing stand as the procession of characters walk, jog, cycle, and drive past the house. We love it!

When you are on an island, you tend to notice exactly where the sun sets every day and how it moves across the horizon from week to week. In mid-May, the sun moves further north, so it sets exactly between the party house catty-corner from ours and Loraine's new house directly across the street. We can watch it dip below the horizon from our comfortable wicker chairs. A sense of calm hangs in the air before the island becomes busier on Memorial Day. The laughing gull colony chatters noisily as they settle for the night in the marsh. They create such a din—like the sound of a cheering crowd from a stadium in the distance.

In our first June on Chincoteague, we were astounded to see dolphins from our comfortable porch chairs chasing the newly arrived croaker fish up the bay. The locals call croakers "hardheads." The dolphins' unmistakable leaps were a marvel to watch as a whole pod passed by. I would scarcely have believed we would see such a sight sitting on our front porch.

In mid-July, more traffic passes by: lines of annoying scooter renters, cyclists who don't signal correctly, and drivers who constantly hit the curb. Can the drivers not see the road from their gigantic trucks, or are they merely bad drivers?

An amazing range of music blasts from vehicles, with the bass sometimes cranked up so loud that the whole car shakes as it makes the turn. One night one person's truck blasted a country song with a lyric that exclaimed: "the grandfather hit the bottle again in '64." The driver made the turn so quickly we didn't hear the line after.

Our conversation was silenced by the rumbling noise of a pickup truck towing a sizable boat bejeweled with twelve fishing rods sitting at attention in their holders. No doubt the two hefty outboard motors strapped to the back delivered far more power than that particular boat required.

We welcome the pleasant interlude when the island trolley passes by, hardly noticed, or the virtually silent open-sided electric cars as they slip past the house. A charming exception was the evening six youthful ladies enjoying a bachelorette night rode by singing one of the Flintstone songs in a six-seater electric vehicle.

The trucks that drive by are not typically the ones that city folks drive with their immaculate back beds. If they don't contain fishing equipment, they might have the contents of half a house piled up in the back. We find it a matter of curiosity to try to identify the contents of trucks as they slow down to make the turn.

No wonder we yearn for the less busy months. When we left New Jersey, I thought we left the crazy drivers behind, but unfortunately, they are everywhere these days, even on an island.

In the afternoons, neighbors visit our porch to tell us their stories or something exciting that occurred in their lives. Conversation with these ordinary people bearing no airs or graces is seldom quick, though, as no one is on the clock; it is like that here.

Some of Anne's family next door, Justin and Ron, came over one afternoon to visit us. It was as if they needed to unload their burdens and frustrations with life. Ron shared the time he knocked his teeth out while up a tree using his chainsaw. Little Karma, Ron's granddaughter, was thrilled to hang out with us and tell us about her new teacher.

One evening a family walked by on their way to the carnival with their excited kids dressed up in patriotic red, white, and blue. When the children spotted us out on the porch, they sprinted up, unprompted, to join us like family for a chat. They didn't know us, which was sweet, but their actions startled their parents, who quickly apologized.

Most afternoons it gets sweltering around 4:30 until the sun sinks below the party house opposite, so we installed two bamboo screens so we can sit in more comfort later in the day. The blinds allow some light through and offer more privacy from the house opposite.

On days when it is too hot to be on the porch, we retire to our couch inside. From there we have a clear view through the dining room window out to the bay, and we can watch the boats go by in the channel.

One summer's day the heat and resulting humidity built up so much that a thunderstorm came marching across the bay. At first, it looked like a typical storm with dark grey cumulonimbus clouds forming in the distance but then changed dramatically, growing wider and longer and stretching across the entire horizon. It developed a scary looking rolling carpet shape and headed toward us. We hadn't seen anything like it before and watched it creep slowly from the mainland across the entire sky like a vast, end-of-the-world airborne tsunami. I learned later that a shelf cloud is a nasty looking, low horizontal cloud formation and not an everyday occurrence. This one definitely meant serious business, so we waited to see what would happen.

Strangely, there was no sound as the dark gray carpet roll unfurled directly over our house. Dangling below were substantial spiraling grey strands that looked like the evil Medusa's hair from Greek mythology. The cloud strands twirled ominously underneath the leading edge of the storm, pulling back into themselves, and re-emitting even longer twisting sinews. There was still no sound, no wind or rain—just a slanting curtain of gray coming at us quickly. It was slightly eerie, as the sky behind the roll was a strange greenish turquoise color, swirling in every direction, as if right out of a Disney horror movie. Then suddenly, as Medusa's snakes passed silently over our house, the wind raced in ferociously, lashing our porch pillars and the small roof above with a deluge of warm rain.

The ozone smell reminded me of words from the environmentalist John Muir.

> *Winds are advertisements of all they touch, however much or little we may be able to read them; telling their wanderings even by their scents alone.*

We stayed on the porch to watch as full rolls of thunder boomed in the bay, immediately followed by a whip crack of lightning that thumped directly into the marsh opposite, shaking the ground. It sent the entire laughing gull colony, petrified, into the air. The gulls flew around aimlessly, calling to each other in a confused state, not knowing what to do. We were sure a few laughing gulls got fried up that day. The storm served to remind us who is boss, and that nature is in charge.

It also reminded me that we are fully human and need the weather to remind us of that. In our enclosed air-conditioned lives, we sometimes forget this. The English writer John Ruskin wrote of a horrible thunderstorm he witnessed in August 1879 at his home, Brantwood. I like the way he compared it to trains and artillery, adding a sense of drama to the event:

> *The most terrific and horrible thunderstorm, this morning, I ever remember. It waked me at six, or a little before—then rolling incessantly, like railway luggage trains, quite ghastly in its mockery of them—the air one loathsome mass of sultry and foul*

fog, like smoke; scarcely raining at all, but increasing to heavier rollings, with flashes quivering vaguely through all the air, and at last terrific double streams of reddish-violet fire, not forked or zigzag, but rippled rivulets—two at the same instant some twenty to thirty degrees apart, with grand artillery-peals following; not rattling crashes, or irregular cracklings, but delivered volleys.

There is no better place to see the ensuing day's weather. In addition to watching storms from our porch, we also notice advancing weather systems and fronts long before they arrive on the island. We guess as to what each cloud formation means— is it fine weather or bad? Many times a broad cerulean swash brushed across the far evening sky foretells sun the next day.

Some days we don't know if we would see a great sunset until the last moment of the day when a stage curtain partially lifts on the horizon for the parting show. Sometimes after a day of torrential rain, a bright sun emerges, offering a spectacular sunset display of soft pinks and golds that melt away like butter. Often heavily laden rain clouds travel up the mainland instead of coming over the bay toward us. It is as if the wind holds them in suspension, glued over the land so they cannot travel over the water. I suspect it is due to the relative heat of the land versus the cooler water. No doubt we have a separate microclimate on the island.

Most evenings the sight of a bald eagle impressed us, flying directly over our house, sometimes with dinner in his talons, which consisted of his six-piece "Chicken McLaughing Gull" meal after his raid over at the colony. He flapped and glided with straight cardboard stiff wings like an airborne torpedo, direct and with purpose, confident and determined to reach his roost for the night. On one evening in mid-August, four bald eagles flew over the house within minutes of each other from the marsh. *How often do people see that?* I wondered. The eagles had startled the entire laughing gull colony into the sky while they hunted for their evening meal. As the sun disappeared below the far trees, skeins of white ibis in their families flew over the house to roost in the marsh, their streamlined bodies and long beaks, like elegantly pointed arrows, crossing the sky.

Many nights after dark, a loud, steady buzzing in the distance, like a huge nest of stirred-up bees, comes from the engines of the E-2 Hawkeye and C-2 Greyhound Navy planes warming up to practice their night flying exercises from Wallops Flight Facility on the mainland.

The E-2 Hawkeye

On various nights, we can watch the Navy flyers perform their "touch and go" aircraft carrier maneuvers in the distance. They fly in low to the runway, touch down briefly, and then climb up sharply and circle back around again to repeat the procedure. One afternoon I counted as many as five planes circling continually around, performing their maneuvers. Sometimes they fly at night, and with their lights blazing, they can provide quite a scare when coming in low and buzzing us unexpectedly while we cross the causeway.

In our first June on Chincoteague, the Blue Angels Naval Display Team arrived to use Wallops Flight Facility as their base for the Ocean City Airshow in Maryland. For a few days, five immaculate, shiny blue F18 Hornets crisscrossed the skyline in front of the house, giving us a private show. They fanned out, banked steeply up, and twisted and careened around the Chincoteague sky.

After dark, the Wallops Flight Facility sparkles like a giant Christmas tree in the distance opposite our house. Flashing red and white lights emanate from various giant white radar dishes and other pieces of naval equipment. In the fall, I always look across to the base before turning in for the night. If I can't see the lights, I know it is foggy, and we might have a delayed school opening the next day. If this occurs, it affords me the opportunity for an occasional much-loved breakfast treat: two jumbo boiled eggs cooked to perfection, the yolks not quite set, and served in British eggcups—special holders to hold the eggs that you don't see much over here. It takes me back to special memories when I was a child. My mother made what she called "little soldiers," strips of toasted bread covered in butter that I dipped into the runny yolk.

During weekends in July, we watch people walk by on their way to the carnival six houses up from ours, and then return, often laden down with strange, gaudy-colored plush animals they won on the games, an odd assortment of creatures that I think no one really likes to cuddle. One night an older couple in their open-sided electric car parked right in front of our house, unfolded some tinfoil, and ate their oyster fritters, happily chatting away.

Debbie's brother Dave came to stay with us one July week and enjoyed checking out the carnival. He hung out in one of our comfortable wicker chairs on the front porch watching the world go by. One evening we walked out to join him, but he wasn't there. We thought he took one of his frequent walks up the street, but then we got a surprise phone call. It was Dave.

"Hi," he said. "I am on the bus, in case you wondered where I am. I was over the road taking a photo of the bay when the bus came down the street, so I hailed it."

We chuckled, as it was typical Dave. We knew he meant the island trolley and not an actual bus. In fact, our Pony Express Trolley is the easiest and cheapest way to get around the island. The trolley has twenty-four stops across the island, but at the driver's discretion for safety, you can flag down a trolley anywhere on the route. Each elevated vehicle is red and bottle-green with decorative gold stenciling around the windows and along its sides. The interior has a wonderful, old-fashioned atmosphere to it with decorative wood trim and a polished wood floor. The floor is so clean and free of marks that it's a pleasure to ride—it takes one back to a more genteel time when riding a vehicle was a pleasure. Being higher up also offers excellent views of the island.

When Dave returned, we bellowed even harder when we noticed he still wore his slippers.

"The driver didn't even flinch when I boarded wearing them," he remarked.

"If you ask for a trolley token after getting your ice cream at the Island Creamery," he added, "it gives you a free ride back home. How great is that!"

The Trolley Token

We sat laughing with Dave on the porch and watched the cars that parked on Main Street cough up their occupants in a myriad of forms. Some were filled to the brim with nubile teenagers who managed to exit the vehicles with perfectly brushed hair while looking down at their smartphones. One car door opened, launching a screaming child into the evening air to be quickly strapped into a stroller. Various trucks emptied out tattooed groups of students, some of whom were overweight and struggled to clamber out and plop themselves onto the sidewalk. As the performances showed up, it was quite a show most nights.

Debbie and I fall into a regular schedule by mid-July. School is still out, and we are enjoying the final days of every teacher's most precious benefit—a long vacation with lazy summer mornings. But not in our case. The pesky flying rats (aka laughing gulls) wake us every morning at six o'clock with their attempt at the dawn chorus. Unfortunately, the only song they could provide sounded like nails on a chalkboard, not even a lousy choir.

Later, sipping my tea on the front porch, the day's routine begins. I can recognize which boat tour captain is already out taking visitors on a trip by the color of the awnings or the decals on the sides on their pontoon boats. Captain Barry accelerates his pontoon boat into hyper speed out in the bay, taking his eight o'clock tour to get their feet wet. Miss Chincoteague, a fine bright-red bay boat, slowly cruises by, carrying her first charter passengers to try their luck on a three-hour fishing trip.

Walkers pass our house cradling their precious morning coffee as if it were grandma's ashes. One wears headphones while singing the words "little baby" over and over again, aloud and off key. (If only people knew how stupid they sounded when they did this.) Occasional runners jog by, immersed in their music, clutching their precious phones. A massive Sysco delivery truck grinds its breaks to make the turn and haul its bulky length around the corner like a huge white slug, thankfully out of sight. As nine o'clock approaches, the gulls' interrupting ruckus moves further away in the marsh, and I savor the beauty of this place once again.

The dock opposite casts a gentle, rippling shadow on the water beneath it to welcome the day. In the mornings, the bay tends to stillness—flat as a pancake with an oily calm and bathed in indigo blue—ready for boaters to churn it up and try their luck at flounder fishing. Pudgy ducks waddle from side to side as they lead their chicks across the road to chew on what must be a greener patch of fresh grass.

The late August sun rises quickly to soak into the wooden framed houses, melting the tarmac on Maddox Boulevard, splitting the earth on the dried-up refuge ponds, and searing the grass in our backyards.

"Down the Marsh," what Teaguers call our end of the island, we don't notice from our porch the cars backing up on the causeway, eager to get to their parking spaces on the beach. We also don't see the cyclists streaming over to the refuge with their beach chairs hung awkwardly on their backs. Every kind of vehicle makes up the busy corridor of traffic along Maddox Boulevard, which carves a straight artery out to the beach. Many incoming visitors stop at Funland Amusements to enjoy the various rides and the mini golf course surrounded by enormous plastic African animals and the myriad T-shirt shops along the way.

Later in the day on their way back, folks fill their hungry stomachs with a variety of BBQ and taco options while standing around applying Aloe Vera to their sunburnt bodies. Most beachgoers stream off the island at the end of the day, while others travel back to island hotels, B & B's, or summer cabanas. Debbie and I settle into our usual evening routine, sitting on the porch with a glass of wine, especially after the dinner traffic dies down.

As late August approaches, the traffic isn't as heavy on Main Street, and evenings grow quieter. The sun gradually moves south, so we can't see it set directly from the porch anymore. We savor the silence of the bay as twilight slips into night.

Darkness falls quickly on Chincoteague compared to the UK, where I grew up. Chincoteague Island's latitude is thirty-seven degrees, whereas London is fifty degrees, allowing for a more protracted twilight. Locations at latitudes between fifty and seventy degrees, such as in the Scandinavian countries, enjoy the finest twilights.

By this time in late summer, the laughing gulls stay in the marsh with their infant families rather than annoy us with their raucous calls from the nearby rooftops. From the porch, we watch a solitary egret patrol a sandbar that is gradually disappearing with the rising tide. Families once again pass by on bikes and wave at us. As the light fades, I anticipate the arrival of my nemeses: merciless mosquitos that seek me out for their evening meal. Perfectly formed flocks of geese and ibis cross over the house, heading west to settle in the marsh opposite to spend the night. The water in the bay calms and settles into a glass-like surface, mirroring above a cerulean blue sky with fading greys and soft rose madder pinks on the horizon. The channel buoys take up their night-time roles, flashing red and green to guide the fishing boats in for the evening. Captain Barry cruises by in his pontoon boat on his sunset trip—a faint chorus of laughter echoes from the revelers aboard. The garish bright colors of J & B's Deli off to our left reflect in the wet tarmac of their parking lot.

I gaze back at the silhouette of that solitary egret, still waiting for his dinner out in the bay as patiently as ever. He's less visible now, the clam bed below him but a mere sliver of black, as the soft orange evening light that previously highlighted him disappears. Birds fly with a purpose straight to their destinations over into the marsh to settle down before darkness falls. A line of pelicans floats along lazily, their wings undulating smoothly up and down in the distance, one behind the other, with their familiar flap and glide technique. A lone bald eagle heads toward me, moving effortlessly with its heavy, methodical, regular wing beats, his unmistakable white-shell-bleached head catching the sunlight. Most evenings I recognize him as the same eagle, but sometimes a few others join him.

Then suddenly something catches my eye—a stabbing motion from that egret, set against the silvery backdrop, as he finally catches his dinner with just enough daylight left to see what he is about to eat. He had toiled patiently, waiting to snag his sole morsel in the time it took for me to polish off my easy-to-serve ice cream. The details of the egret slowly faded with the light—his form dissipating and melting away. The pillars under the docks dissolve into darkness, the clam beds lose their shape and disappear, and everything grows vague and unclear as the shapes and forms gently fuse and fade into the pinkish grey backdrop.

The author Peter Davidson explores the moods and emotions we sense at twilight in his book *The Last of the Light: About Twilight.*

> *Evening with its ivory rose, smoke grey and washed yellow, cobalt and diamond, until the lights come on in the windows. These are the territories of melancholy and revenants, longings and regrets, 'tranquility shot through with sorrow,' homecomings and serenities.*

As darkness draws on, a steady stream of cars traverse back across the causeway, headlights illuminated like an EKG monitor with bright white blips equally spaced apart along the straight route. The brightest star, Venus, makes her appearance high in the sky.

I sense a tickling of the hairs on my legs, like a breeze brushing them, but it is the damned mosquitos gently probing for a juicy landing spot. Their unmistakable whine follows soon after. As D.H. Lawrence once wrote about mosquitos when the sun set, *"It is your small, high, hateful bugle in my ear."*

It is time to go inside. I do so reluctantly.

13

THE CAT LAIR

One night something unusual occurred while we sat on our front porch. We witnessed straggly, undoubtedly feral cats coming and leaving from a large hole on the side of the party house catty-corner to us. It seems a cover had come loose, permitting any critter to enter the crawlspace.

For a few weeks, I had heard cats wailing in the middle of the night and wondered what was transpiring in our neighborhood. On this particular night, we noticed a considerable ginger alpha cat leading a parade of darker cats, including one we had dubbed "Socks" because of his two white front paws, through the opening and into the dark recess of the empty house.

The well-to-do owners of the house probably wouldn't notice even wild cats lounging around their house given the way they left everything when they departed. They visited mostly on major holidays and tended to stay in their house, becoming very loud when they drank on their back porch. The children's play toys were strewn all over the place. They left crab cages and canoes along their boat dock, bikes out on the front porch, and back porch furniture with drinks on the tables. Once, they even left on the outdoor patio lights in the back. Their air conditioning ran at full pelt even if the weather was cool, which wasted so much energy.

After they left, we joked that the cats probably came out and sat on their furniture on the back porch drinking the remaining cocktails and having a blast. They probably found a way in and helped themselves to the drinks cabinet.

We knew that some neighborhoods on the island unwillingly harbored quite a few feral cats, and we certainly didn't want that to happen around us. Debbie's brother Dave was still with us, and he and I decided to take action. Fortified with the courage to face a legion of wild cats and carrying a gigantic cinderblock and a chunk of wood, we marched across the street to the party house and placed the square wooden cover back into its place on the side of the house. While replacing it, we feared a rush for the exit by scared cats, but our surprise mission stirred up no activity. We didn't have nails to secure the cover, so we propped the cinderblock and the chunk of wood against it to hold it in place, preferring not to think we had just sealed an indeterminate number of cats inside.

From then on, the daily cat noises stopped, and we didn't see them anymore.

The party was over for the moment, but we had a hunch the cats would return.

THE PARTY CATS

There is a funny piece of folklore concerning cats on the Eastern Shore. Many years back when a farmer who was not near the water wanted to find out whether the tide was high or low, they looked into the eyes of a local cat. If the cat's pupils were oblong, straight up and down, it was high tide. If their pupils were round and full, it was low tide. The tide was up the day that we sealed the hole in the side of the house. I wondered how the cats' eyes looked.

14

THE SMELLS AND SOUNDS
OF SUMMER

Watercolor of the Fireman's Carnival

E ach day in summer, the myriad activities tease the ears, while the increase in odors both delight and offend the sense of smell. Both provoke speculation as to where they have come from. Some are welcomed, others not, but that is what makes Chincoteague interesting. We are continually deciphering the sounds and olfactory messages conveyed to us across the island.

I often awake early to the loudspeaker of the natural life that surrounds us, a time when the world still belongs to the birds. From the front of the house come the distant calls of the enormous laughing gull colony in the bay, like the noise from a thousand squeaky trollies. In the rear of our property, we hear the calmer flute section of the dawn chorus: the cooing duets from mourning doves, interspersed with the harsh rusty gate sounds from grackles. The house sparrows bring violins to mind as they constantly chatter away in the background.

Because our house is on a busy corner lot, we are prone to island vehicle noises, especially during the summer season. Some drivers—tourists and locals alike—seem to take pride in how much annoying noise their vehicles make—as if they are in the final stages of bronchitis and can't make it to the end of the driveway. Many vehicles sound as if they could die any minute. The grinding brakes, souped-up engines, and other strange sounds coming out of these vehicles continue throughout the summer.

The noise from humans in their machines drowns out the sounds of early morning birds. Surveys have found that the sounds produced by human activity in natural areas like Assateague are often much louder than the native music from the elements like wind and rain. The voices from nature on the island are the best sounds to listen to, and many visitors only come to soak up these sounds and relax. Those who engage with the landscape enjoy a full orchestra from melodious song-birds, crashing waves, neighing horses, ringing willets, and the chirrup from insects. The challenge is to obey the deliberately low speed limits and silence a noisy smartphone; this makes an enormous difference to the wildlife and to the enjoyment of others.

The unpleasant odor of sulfurous rotten egg from the marsh at low tide pervades the island off and on throughout the year. Thankfully, we don't smell it constantly. I was curious about what caused this nasty smell, so I did some research. I found that because salt marshes contain lots of decomposing material, oxygen levels become low, leading to dead zones. These dead zones grow bacteria, which cause this stench. A tempting smell, on the other hand, that sometimes wafts across our porch is the pungent and aromatic scent from J & B's Deli across the street of fried onions added to the various subs they make for their customers.

As summer picks up, we get used to a seasonal smell from the visitors that invade the beach—the invasive whiff of sprayed suntan lotion, mainly the pungent coconut bouquet that blows up your nose from the people upwind, with no idea they are spraying everyone else, often in the eyes.

To take a break from the beach odors, one day Debbie and I took a drive around the wildlife refuge to find the red-headed woodpecker we had heard we could see in late spring. Our field guide said they are common, but we hadn't seen one of these amazingly colorful birds yet. Other birders recommended we start at the Wildlife Loop in the woodland area near the parking lot, a habitat with numerous dead trees that woodpeckers explore and excavate. Just as I discovered on my walk on the woodland trail in the spring, the pine bark beetle ravaged this area as well. At least the woodpeckers assist the trees in eating quite a few of the beetles.

The bird apparently makes a hoarse 'tchur' sound, sort of like a crow, as it flies laterally, but our first attempts at listening for it were unsuccessful. We met some walkers who had seen one, and they told us they identified them easily, as the bird looks like a flying checkerboard. Various field guides confirm this.

We first sighted this stunning bird when it appeared as a blur of flashing white, undulating in flight from tree to tree further out in the woods. When the woodpecker finally came to rest, we trained our binoculars and examined it closer, immediately noticing its rich, ruby-red head and well turned-out black and white attire. It looked very regal, like the peers' robes worn by lords at a royal wedding, exactly what people told us, a marvelous-looking bird.

Red-headed Woodpecker

To celebrate our sighting, we drove out to the mainland to have dinner at Ray's Shanty, a favorite seafood restaurant and noticed that soft-shell crabs were back on the menu. These tasty crabs are available in May for a month or two and are delicious—or so I'm told, as I can't eat them because I have a shellfish allergy. Instead, I savored the wonderful mako shark steaks that Ray's Shanty serves to perfection.

June is full of intense colors, notably punctuated by the ruby-throated hummingbirds that arrive back at our feeders at the end of April in a sudden burst of iridescent color crossing the yard, virtually radioactive in its luminescence.

Emily Dickenson's poem *A Route of Evanescence*, captures the sudden appearance of this bird.

A Route of Evanescence,
With a revolving Wheel—
A Resonance of Emerald—
A Rush of Cochineal—
And every Blossom on the Bush
Adjusts its tumbled Head-

Untroubled bright cobalt-blue skies and electric green grasses sway in the breeze, with early summer rains contributing to the luscious growth as the sun beats down. The marsh is full of life, much of it hidden. A drive on the Wildlife Loop yields a tiny gem from the orchid family. A plant called Ladies' tresses growing by the side of the road displays spikes of twisted small, white, fragrant flowers growing up its stem.

In the evenings, we hear coming from the bay a distinctive "w-a-a-ah" sound that lasts about three to seven seconds with periods of silence in between. We learned it was the mating call of the Fowler's toad, and we found it a soothing sound to fall asleep to. Fowler's toads are one of only four toads and frogs commonly found on Assateague Island. They frequent sandy or forested areas near freshwater pools and ponds where, from April through July, the male toad calls as he tries to attract a suitable mate. We also heard gray tree frogs, which get pretty raucous at night when looking for love.

One night while having dinner on the porch, we heard a high-pitched continuous whirring coming from what sounded like a motorcycle. It turned out to be a town pickup truck spraying for mosquitos. The sprayer mounted in the bed of the truck belted out a fog of permethrin insecticide, which wafted onto our porch for a few seconds as it passed our house. It was an annoying sound that we became accustomed to every night for the rest of the summer season. We tried to time our dinners so that we finished our meal by the time it came by.

Most summer nights we fall asleep to a background symphony from the calls of willets, frogs in the marsh, or the occasional hoot from a great horned owl back in the woods.

It was a beautiful evening for the first night of the carnival, located six houses down the road from us. The Chincoteague Volunteer Fire Company holds it every year to raise funds, and it is open every weekend through July, culminating in Pony Penning. The carnival is Chincoteague Island's showcase event, guaranteed to attract most of the locals.

A cool breeze started to waft through our yard after a hot day, which was typical on the island. In the distance, I heard country music from the first band of the carnival season, and the aroma of fried fish filled the air in our backyard. The fried fish vapors pervaded everything—heavy and thick, salty, enticing and greasy.

The breeze was comfortable and warm as the breath of tree swallows arced and wheeled through our yard catching the dying rays of the sun. The sun caught the laughing gulls on the wing and bathed their underbellies in a soft orange glow. Their tail feathers fanned out like scallop shells. The night was, thankfully, bug-free with low humidity, but we knew later in summer this wouldn't be the case.

Every so often, we heard screams of delight echoing in the air, coming from children enjoying their first carnival rides. From the back of our yard, Debbie and I could see the brightly colored lights on the paratrooper ride, a popular colorful metal monster that gyrated smoothly up and down in the distance. We could hear the occasional hard metal clink of the hi-striker hammer, a game the huge strong lads played to show off their strength.

Just as the carnival grew busy and traffic slowed for cars to park along Main Street, our backyard ducks decided to lead their brood of seven across the road. The parade, led by Crackhead, halted the traffic. Diane, Anne's aide next door, named this duck for the white stripe down the back of her head.

Debbie decided to strike up her bagpipes, sending a Celtic tune into the evening air, which no doubt left some people wondering where the sound was coming from.

We decided to take a walk to the carnival to check it out. It didn't take us long to get there. We entered up a few low red painted steps, above which hung a generous red banner that announced "WELCOME" in giant letters with balloons painted on either side. A multi-colored information booth was to our left, and to the right a life-sized statue of the legendary "Surfer Dude" pony rearing up on his hind legs. Greeters handed us a free Gideon Bible, which they gave out every year.

We strolled over to where the five flags of the armed services flew on their poles. The carnival grounds spread out either side of this central meeting point, with low, whitewashed buildings organized in curved rows and some buildings scattered on their own here and there. The buildings housed booths with flipped down wooden panels, or metal panels that pulled upwards like garage doors for quick set up.

Young girls and boys entered the grounds with their parents, excited to go on their first rides and taste the unique deep-fried delicacies. Older couples sat on the picnic benches, legs bouncing to live music. Families wandered around the different booths and rides, chatting and acknowledging each other. The carnival crowd, some tattooed in a tide of ink across various body parts, was a gigantic social gathering primed for fun, with no dress code, where everyone checked everyone else out, but not in a comparing way. Youths gathered on the corners to chat or waited, laughing, in lines for the rides. Girls proud of their early tans wore their cutoff jeans, checking their smartphones for messages. A sizeable group of slim teenage girls from out of town checked out the booths and looked out of place in their denim daisy dukes.

A lot of unhealthy eating was in play—but it all tasted so scrumptious! The elixir of scents made everyone hungry. A glow of insipid yellow lighting from inside every concession stand cast the servers in a familiar nuclear glow. They say the color yellow whets the appetite, and it sure worked for everyone that night. The crowd was drawn into the food offerings. The servers wore red T-shirts to complement the yellow lights, attracting attention and stimulating the desire to eat. It is no wonder the golden arches of McDonald's feature a red and yellow logo.

Even after dark, a substantial flock of laughing gulls gathered well past their bedtime on the roof of the concession stands. They, too, enjoyed an evening feast and swooped down for the occasional fries dropped by those leaving the booths below.

One of the summer rites of passage featured the season's first deep-fried oysters and clams, a fine island tradition. However, there was also something the crowd craved that was even more indulgent.

We knew the carnival served deep-fried Oreos, but we could not have imagined vendors offered deep-fried Twinkies. For those that do not know, this quintessential junk food treat is a cream-filled, one-hundred-fifty-calorie sponge cake. A single Twinkie, according to the label, contains thirty-seven ingredients, but only five of them are what most would consider "recognizable": flour, egg, water, sugar, and salt. Each Twinkie contains fourteen of the top twenty chemicals made in the U.S., which might account for the speculation on how many decades a Twinkie can sit on a store shelf before consumption.

I cannot imagine why anyone wanted to eat one of these so-called treats, let alone one that has been deep-fried. The sign in front of the Twinkie booth was warning enough, as it depicted a nasty pale blue Twinkie. Even more worrying to me was that Twinkie booth formed the longest line of the concessions stands.

While many fried foods at the carnival were traditionally unhealthy for us, one treat attempted to be healthier—the "Pony Fries," which I thoroughly enjoyed. Cooked in soybean oil, they weren't as greasy as other offerings, and when one added malt vinegar and salt, they tasted simply delicious. I would rate them right up there with some of the best chips from the UK.

We sat to eat our fries with strangers at a picnic table, while a band called Virginia Creek struck up a popular Johnny Cash song, "Folsom Prison Blues". Everyone at the table began nodding their heads and tapping their thighs. Couples stopped on the grass in front of the band to dance, twirling around in time to the beat. It was the perfect evening for the first night of the carnival.

Passing the luminous booths, I recognized a man from previous years serving at the clam booth. He wore a distinctive cream-colored cowboy hat and a white wife-beater T-shirt stained with grease. He was evidently one of the regular yearly fixtures. Someday I wanted to find out more about him.

While walking the grounds, one could not escape the distinctive smell of fried fish. Soft yellow lights illuminated those concentrating on their Bingo boards in the spacious, open-sided hall in the center of the carnival. The players listened intently to the numbers shouted out by the MC, fried fish sandwiches and giant sodas positioned close at hand.

The younger members of the crowd roamed the carnival grounds carrying token grand plush trophies won for their girlfriends and an assortment of gaudy colored snakes, monkeys, and Pokémon characters.

A few booths, often run by Teaguers putting in their carnival shift times, offered a chance to win a rifle or boat. If you were lucky, you won both and gained the essential equipment to be a hunter.

There was nothing formal or structured about the carnival; it was merely pure, relaxed fun with no preconceptions, a family night, with the raucous echoes of laughter ringing around the grounds from those who shared similar experiences on a warm night. I spotted the glint in a teenage girl's eye as she giggled at a friend's joke and the smile from a wife as the husband tried to get her to dance to the blues.

The colored lights from the rides shone into everyone's eyes that night. We experienced a carefree, low-key carnival, Chincoteague style.

Debbie and I headed home early, leaving the festivities to the youthful crowd. Falling asleep with the windows open, we could hear the shrieks of kids enjoying themselves as they rode the rides late into the night. We would be treated to the sounds from the carnival every weekend night for the rest of July.

As the Independence Day holiday approached, we braced for an island invasion, but instead of amphibious landing craft, we were treated to RVs. Giant and imposing vehicles such as Cyclones, Pumas, and Heritage Glens streamed down Main Street to claim their holiday spaces. The summer visitors we saw for the Memorial Day weekend now returned *en masse* since schools let out in June. Ironically, a town street cleaning vehicle spent the day sweeping the roads just as the onslaught of visitors arrived to mess things up again. After the July Fourth holiday, the protracted procession of RVs would once again pass our house to return home.

Most of the RVs were what we expected for their size, but then we noticed the beast of them all, the Raptor Velocity towing an SUV behind it.

The Raptor Velocity

The Raptor had a sleek black and white curvaceous body with striking Star Wars-like graphics emblazoned down its 40-foot length. These immense travel trailers came fitted with the latest entertainment extras and pulled additional vehicles from which the owners could launch themselves into the surrounding area. The combined sound of the RVs and the rental scooters was considerable for a few hours.

Even the shorebird community grows noisy on certain nights out in the marsh. The night after Hurricane Arthur brushed us was the Buck Moon (the July full moon), and the Gulls were particularly loud. Maybe the birds needed the social connection to confirm their status and overcome insecurity within the colony.

While Debbie and I may have found the island nights noisier than usual, our visitors living off-island remark how they enjoyed a great night's sleep on Chincoteague thanks to the silence. The first early morning sounds tend to be the "get out of my face" calls from the laughing gulls, followed by a sweet catbird singing from Anne's apple tree in the adjoining garden. Human-made sounds follow soon after.

On July Fourth, the town held a fireworks display in front of the carnival, so we benefitted from seeing everything from our front porch. While we enjoyed the Independence Day celebrations, I considered how disparately America and Britain approach celebrations. Americans are excellent at creating parties, whatever they might entail, but Brits, I believe, excel at pomp and circumstance (in other words, an ostentatious display of ceremonial grandeur). One only has to view any of the royal weddings to see how well-timed events are, always displaying the "correct" protocol and traditions. In many ways, I prefer the American way of holding events, especially when it comes to celebrations. Here on the island, the Teaguers know how to have a good time.

Before the fireworks began, a police officer coordinated the traffic on the corner in front of our house and stopped the traffic on Main Street after nine o'clock. We got a kick out of hearing some of the bogus excuses people gave to the police officer in hopes of slipping through the barricade to get a closer viewing spot.

Eventually, a sudden burst of light flowered in the northern sky over the water. Giant chrysanthemums of rosy light bloomed above the bay, and we watched a stupendous American firework display.

One fine Thursday evening, we enjoyed another display, but this took the form of a free movie in the park organized by the Chincoteague Cultural Alliance (CCA), an organization that promotes and presents arts and culture in many forms for residents and visitors to Chincoteague Island. They showed the film *The Secret of Roan Innish*, a story about a girl named Fiona who goes to live with her grandparents on the tiny island of Roan Innish on the west coast of Ireland. Fiona hears stories about her ancestors, tales that involve mythical creatures called Selkies who can shift from seal to human form.

Movies in the Park

Sitting on folding chairs in the park, we were well into the film when we noticed lightning jigs off to our right in the distance. We presumed it was some heat lightning, present most evenings out in the bay. When the ensuing flash of lightning lit up the sky, darker clouds moved closer. We heard no thunder, so we didn't think much of it. In the movie, Fiona was looking for her brother while a storm brewed. The wind and sound of the ocean played on the screen, masking the sound of our very own storm brewing close by.

I looked up to see dark clouds marching over the moon directly above with a determined demeanor, like a pony intent on breaking out of the refuge fence. Rain suddenly fell in buckets over the unsuspecting viewers, as if someone abruptly turned a shower on, full blast, in a wind tunnel.

Panic ensued as we hastily folded up our beach chairs, and everyone made a mad dash for the closest cover. Fat raindrops pummeled us as we ran to our car, getting thoroughly soaked in the process. While I sprinted, I looked back for an instant and glimpsed John Beam, the president of the CCA, grabbing the projector equipment and running to the covered picnic area, holding it close to his chest to shield it from the deluge. I hoped he unplugged it first and then thought to myself that there was no way it survived the downpour.

While driving hastily back to our house I remembered that we had left our front windows open, so when we arrived, the interior floors at the front of the house were thoroughly soaked. We mopped up the water with beach towels and spent at least an hour cleaning up. Our wet chairs and carpets air-dried over several days after that storm. The amazing thing about that storm was there was no warning, no sound, until the very last minute when the stealthy wind and rain hit us.

A week or so later John Beam invited us over to his house to watch the rest of the movie with a glass of wine. We enjoyed a much better experience, and unbelievably he set up the same equipment from the park. I laughed when he told us that he left it out to dry completely before trying it again.

Typical of July weather, the heat, and humidity built up over a week after the holiday. There was a stillness in the air—I felt as if I were trapped inside a Ball jam jar. I sensed a storm was imminent. Sure enough, one afternoon a series of squalls came marching across the bay. The force of the wind broke up the organized flights of geese that attempted to reshape themselves, achieving only broken, outstretched wavering strands across the sky. The wind worked its magic, buffeting each bird in advance of the rising cloud heads. The enormous puffy thunderheads strode their way over the bay, fattening themselves up in the process, growing quickly like expanded spray insulation. As the winds picked up, I sensed a sweet, pungent zing in my nostrils, the sharp aroma of fresh ozone.

This air came fast across the open water, followed by sudden rain that lashed our house sideways and sounded like a drum on the siding. It was just like the tropical downpours we watched on TV, refreshing and warm, which temporarily removed the heaviness in the air. The storm drenched everything and everyone in its path, leaving a fresh, clean scent in the air. Australian researchers in 1964 named it "petrichor," that earthy ozone fragrance, a combination of plant oils and the chemical compound geosmin released from the soil when it rains. A lot of rain and dirt regularly carried in the wind causes algae to grow on our house siding. We have to powerwash our house frequently, especially the north side that doesn't get as much sun.

A steady clearing toward evening gave way to the bright reddish-orange orb of the sun slipping down beneath the far woods. The following day we awoke to a gorgeous, crisp, clear, breezy morning—one we wished we could have every day, with not a bug in sight. We saw the distant woods clearly for a change behind the Wallops Flight Facility. Fortunately, we didn't have to run the air conditioning much in the summer, as the bay breezes coursed through our windows, and the house breathed from every side, given its classic Eastern shore design.

The bay that morning after the storm was a deep indigo blue, set against a clear cerulean blue sky. A bright red fishing boat emblazoned with the name The Instigator plowed a gentle white wake across its bow as it returned lazily with its catch from the sea. Outside our house, I hoisted the American flag on one flagpole and the Welsh flag on another. Both wafted gently in the breeze as I sipped my freshly made tea from the porch. Walkers chatted as they took their morning exercise on the sidewalk outside, and families of bikers confirmed directions as they rounded our corner.

Later that day, we strolled across Main Street to stand on our neighbor's dock to look out at the bay. It was low tide, and a pungent, sulfurous, salty fish smell wafted into our noses. The twice-daily comings and goings of the tides are constant reminders of the pull of the moon, the gravitational forces that drive our solar system, and the ecosystem of our backyard. Nature's impeccable timing in the ebb and flow of tides and the changing light that runs birds' internal clocks never ceases to amaze me

We heard the instantly recognizable calls of willets in the distance, watched a graceful flight of egrets cross the horizon, and admired the gliding of a slender, great egret, reminiscent of a prehistoric ancestor, as it alighted gently on a clam bed. We noted a marked absence of great blue herons at this time of year, as they spent the summer somewhere else in a raucous nesting colony. In their place, other species of heron predominated, particularly the green herons, which look perpetually angry with their bright yellow eyes.

In the distance, we could see white caps cresting on the waves in the bay as a stiff wind came in to whip them up. We were delighted to see a pod of dolphin chase the croaker fish up the channel.

In mid-July, we didn't know what to expect when we witnessed our first rocket launch from the Wallops Flight Facility. For Debbie, the launch brought back childhood memories from 1969 when her mother gave her permission to stay up late to watch history. Her mother stated, "You need to be awake to see this." Back then her entire school came together in the gym to watch every rocket launch.

We drove down to Merritt Harbor at the southern end of the island to see the launch of Orbital's Antares to resupply the International Space Station. From here we had a great view of the launch pad from across the bay. A vast sheet of water stretched out before us; the tallest buildings on the horizon were the Wallops rocket towers rising out of the glass gray mirror in the distance.

We had plenty of company. People brought various viewing scopes, radios, and their smartphones to observe the activity. It was quite surreal to hear the countdown banter going back and forth over at the launchpad from our spot across the water.

I heard the word "nominal" used several times as Wallops carried out their checks and wondered what it meant. A person beside me commented that using a distinctive word like nominal precluded any possibility for confusion, especially over a poor, lousy connection. The launch team selected terms used in the context of space operations so that they didn't sound like any other word, and therefore, were not mistaken for any other commonly occurring word.

I heard the launch team carry out a sequence of more than four hundred checks. This was quite a checklist to ensure that everything was okay.

As launch time approached, the control tower counted down to lift off with the memorable words, "T minus thirty seconds on my mark."

The launch director then asked, "Trina, status"?

"We are go for launch," replied Trina.

Then we heard the final words spoken by the Launch Director.

"This is LD, launch director, go for launch."

An immediate bright flash of white light on the horizon accompanied a puff of smoke as the rocket lifted. It rose soundlessly until suddenly we felt and heard the enormous roar that followed from the rocket's engines. The mighty rumbling and shaking only hinted at the incredible force that drove the rocket up. The ground beneath our feet trembled. It was all about the sound.

That unique roar as the rocket drove its upward course will always stick with me. The crowd craned their necks back, and some used binoculars to follow the white contrails until the rocket eventually disappeared into orbit. A sense of awe and jubilation followed—some clapped, while others stood still in amazement at the whole incredible experience they witnessed. Debbie was slightly teary, marveling at the technical ability for man to carry out such a feat.

Antares Lift Off

For both of us, the unique sound left its mark in our memory. I later might awake to the distinct rumbling roar of smaller rockets launched early in the morning, but nothing like the Antares sound that lasted a minute or two until it finally petered out.

After the launch, we retired to Steamers Restaurant on the island to watch some of the FIFA World Cup. Various Orbital employees stopped in, wearing Antares launch T-shirts, some with their name tags still hung around their necks, so we assumed they were part of the team that made the launch possible. Drinkers at the bar congratulated them on their hard work, many no doubt oblivious to the work involved in preparing and launching such a rocket.

By mid-July, immature laughing gulls were everywhere, identified by their dull brown plumage and a distinctive black band across their tails. Their horrible high-pitched screeching calls were even worse than their parents, so the combined calls of both made for a boisterous unwelcome morning alarm call. Either the adults brought their offspring over from the marsh, or the young gulls followed them over, begging for food. I am not sure which. We wished the RVs would take the gulls with them. Eventually, the gulls left to harass the beachgoers. The birds couldn't fly very well, so they often became the victims of traffic out on the causeway, with their battered bodies lining the grass verges alongside the railings. (It occurred to me that the numerous families of bikers could soon be traffic accidents as well, given that some hadn't ridden since they were children and were not familiar with the rules.)

July was the peak of activity in the marsh. Shorebird numbers declined as many were up north breeding. Egrets gathered early in the morning for socials in the marsh before dispersing for the day. Plenty was in bloom—pink and white hibiscus burst open on the marsh trails, as well as mimosa trees and trumpet vine. A lone Orchard oriole sang sweetly from a bush on the Wildlife Loop, and grasses reached their maximum height for the season. The period of harvest and decay was imminent, and then dormancy and renewal once again.

Life seems held in suspension for a moment in July as each plant that blooms holds its breath for changes that would come. Winds become more northerly with a subtle cooling of the nights. Later in the month, greater yellowlegs—the harbingers of seasonal change—arrive in more significant numbers. This shorebird is nicknamed the "Tattler," as it continually raises the alarm with its high-pitched "tew" calls. They are the first on the marsh in the spring and one of the last birds to leave in the fall. They tend to linger until the first frosts when the frozen pools restrict access to their food supply.

So overwhelming is the accumulated evidence of growth on the marsh—newly born chicks, clouds of pollen, dust blown around by the wind—that the entire motion combines to create an uninterrupted purr, the ambiance of summer.

At sunset, from our house, we can see the colossal gull colony gyrating in the distance, many birds putting on an acrobatic show as they pause in mid-flight to shake their legs. Every night before darkness falls, the ibis and egret families fly over our house from the wildlife refuge to the marshes opposite to roost.

In mid-August, we visited Swan Cove Pool and observed some interesting birds. A variety of terns, specifically Caspian, Royal, Sandwich, and one lone black tern, rested on the mud flat nearest the beach. Also, we sighted red knots, black-bellied plovers with their black bibs, and marbled godwits. The area is a fantastic haven for birds, and we are lucky to see such a variety year round.

The hummingbirds were now back in earnest at our feeders, no doubt fattening up for their long flight south to Mexico and beyond. They attended our feeders frequently as if they were ravenous, craving the sweet nectar they needed for their journey south.

As August wears on, the deeper greens of the marsh grasses fade and turn a more yellowy color. They sprout seed plumes that shimmer a golden color when caught in the evening light. The laughing gulls begin to lose their distinctive black hoods and sport half-menacing-looking masks instead as they change into winter plumage.

The intensity of the mosquitos hit a peak in mid-August. We were able to sit out on the porch after dark most evenings until the end of June, but after that, most days make it impossible to do so. As the light fades, a familiar, ominous buzz fills the air as they drift in from across the marsh to have their evening meal. They swarm at dusk, venturing up onto our porch for my freely donated European blood. I recognize the slight tickle on my legs as they seek me out.

Inevitably, the islanders begin to beg on the locals' Facebook page for the mosquito plane to spray. Early one morning I was startled from my sleep by a low-flying prop plane buzzing the house to dust for mosquitos. It sounded like we were under attack by a foreign enemy, but with no firepower. When I ventured outside to catch a glimpse of the plane, it buzzed again, about fifty feet above the pines in the backyard. The dusting worked for a few days, but it didn't kill green flies that patrol the yard and take a chunk out of us. They bit through a thick shirt, and surprisingly one day, through my sneaker. The greenhead horsefly or salt marsh greenhead is common around coastal marshes of the eastern United States. They sport an oversized green head—as shiny a green as you have ever seen—and will pop you in an instant and draw blood. The sensation is as if an ice pick has hit you.

Toward the end of August, we have a few days of relief from the bugs when cool air blows in. We immediately throw the windows open and escape from our housebound air conditioning to the front porch. The sun moves further south to set behind the houses opposite, rather than baking us directly. We missed watching it slowly sinking into the distant trees. The gulls grow quieter, playing in the light breezes with their young. The ibis in their characteristic V flying formation make their usual fly-over to roost, soon to be off with the black-necked stilts who gather in the marsh with their young for the journey south.

The unique and pleasant sounds from summer still echo in my head from the carnival, the NASA rocket launch, the fireworks, the calls from willets and red-headed woodpeckers. The sounds that annoyed me faded—the crickets, the screeching laughing gulls, the town mosquito sprayer, the rumble from noisy engines and annoying buzz from mosquitos. What remained were the pleasant memories of the smell of ozone rain and the background music from tree frogs, Fowler toads, great horned owls, and swallows.

Slowly every island sensation, its smell, and sound became well known; the familiar became precious. Omnipresent is the constant endearing smell that pervades the air year-round—that of the marsh.

15

HOUSE INVASION

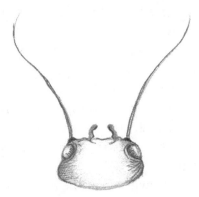

Earlier in spring, a nasty six-foot black snake surfaced from a huge rock pile on the side of our house. Evidently, the rock pile was its home. Loraine, the previous house owner, told us the rocks were from ships ballast deposited many years back. Rather than invite any more snakes to our yard, we decided to remove the rocks, which also prevented us from landscaping the side of our property. I didn't relish the task of moving them. As I gingerly lifted each rock, I expected to find another serpent beneath it. I removed the last two rocks, and there they were—two snakes writhing around and hissing unhappily when I disturbed their safe home. I retrieved a long garden rake and gently shooed them away into the grasses. The rock pile also contained a massive quantity of crickets that scurried away through the grasses to find a new home.

I felt a sense of relief. Over the following weeks, we moved the large rocks out to the side of the road with a sign that said

FREE. Rocks are valued on the island because people use them to support their bulkheads. In a month, they all disappeared.

Debbie and I enjoyed the peace of our new home. We made plans on how to organize the garden now that the snakes and crickets had gone. We sat on our front porch enjoying the view, drinking a glass of wine.

The first signs of a problem occurred in our kitchen. A single chirping "cree" progressed into two more. I sauntered into the kitchen to find out what the sound was. When I flicked the lights on, six enormous crickets stared back at me from the hardwood kitchen floor. Each was ugly—a nasty shiny black color with twitching antennae that looked menacingly up at me, so I immediately whacked them with a fly swatter. This proved useless, as their armor-plated backs shielded them, and I swore they snickered as they scurried away behind the cabinets and appliances.

Summer was in full swing, and the homeless crickets infiltrated the yard. Every day we found more in the flowerbeds, the grass, and on our back porch. Apparently, the crickets sought a living space as comfortable as the rock pile. Unfortunately for us, our house became the main attraction.

The next evening I captured some under plastic cups, slid cardboard underneath the cup to pick them up, and took them outside where they could watch the Persied Meteor shower instead. My patient approach quickly progressed into giving no mercy, or no quarter, as the British say. The crickets emerged in greater numbers in the family room and from behind the couch, often freaking us out as they sat quietly on the arm of the couch or on the floor beneath our feet. Debbie found them on the third floor as well, having scaled the interior joists that ran up from the crawlspace below. Unbeknownst to us, the crawlspace under our house wasn't sealed, so the crickets easily found their way into our home.

It was a horrible experience—just like one of those sci-fi movies on TV. We had no idea how to deal with them. When we retired to bed, their incessant chirping throughout the house made it difficult to sleep, and when I visited the bathroom during the night, one was even in the light cover above my head. Such were the numbers entering our house and appearing when it got dark that we needed to attack them head-on with some drastic treatment.

The next day I purchased twenty aerosol cans of expanding foam insulation and squirted it into the numerous external and internal cavities around the house. I moved room by room, sealing every hole and crevice on the first floor. The imperfect seals between our first floor and the crawlspace required painstaking effort. Some of the gaps were two inches wide, and I am sure I didn't notice all of them. The twenty cans emptied quickly, requiring the acquisition of a further ten cans.

The staff at Ace Hardware suggested that I might need an insulation company for my project. At one point, I asked Gary at Ace if they had any customers with cricket issues. He answered simply, "We all get a few now and then. It's what you expect living on the island." They had no idea how many we had.

Some online forums suggested that we use duct tape turned upside down and fixed to strips of wood to capture the crickets. We tried this in the attic, as it was cheaper than the store bought treatments, but this proved to be an extremely disagreeable solution. It was gross to deal with, the bodies piled up so high. They tried to get away, often leaving a leg or two behind on the tape. The famous lines from Shakespeare's poem, Henry V came into my head:

Once more unto the breach, dear friends, once more; Or close the wall up with our English dead!

In our case, the cricket dead. The dead crickets would have fed many a household reptile pet.

We replaced our motion-activated outdoor white security light with a yellow incandescent light bulb, hoping it would be less of an attractor.

We tried another treatment, a sweet mixture of one part molasses and ten parts water placed in a shallow bowl. Apparently, this enticed the crickets to drink, fall in, and drown. And they did. I subsequently filled numerous plastic containers with the mixture and placed them inside and outside the house to lure them in. It worked quickly, but left me with another repulsive job—every other day I emptied the dead bodies into the flowerbed. To take my mind off this disgusting task, I created a nicer, and if there is such a thing, a more humorous way for the crickets to die with their friends. Instead of providing them with a mere plastic bowl, I built them a disco.

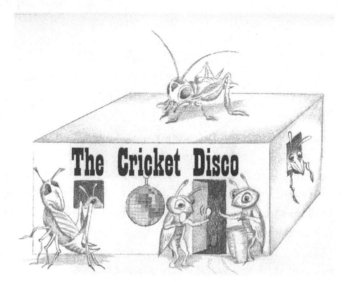

The Cricket Disco

Creating the Cricket Disco provided me much-needed amusement after weeks of aggravation and annoyance of stamping, swatting, and spraying. I like to think it gave the crickets a fun time before they expired. I housed an extra-special plastic bowl, "aka deluxe swimming pool" inside an upturned cardboard box, into which I cut holes in the sides for windows and a door for the crickets to enter. On the exterior of the box, I drew pictures of crickets enjoying themselves in the windows, and I even drew a sparkly disco ball on the outside. We all remember those iconic 70s disco balls, right? It needed no publicity to attract partygoers and filled up quickly once the word got out. It became the hottest cricket club in town. Crickets entered via the main door or any window, chatted with their friends, and then leaped headlong into the sweet pool of death to taste the nectar before drowning. I swore we heard them laughing and partying themselves to death some nights. Emptying the swimming pool the next morning was gross, as the bodies lay stretched out in the hot sun stinking up our shell driveway.

We considered opening a chain of Molasses Cricket Discos around our property to cope with the infestation, but fortunately, as the summer wore on, the numbers slowly died down. We were, at last, winning the onslaught using a combination of duct tape, diatomaceous earth powder, molasses, and old-fashioned bludgeoning, which, frankly, felt the best.

Appointing a contractor to encapsulate the crawlspace under the house solved the problem, once and for all. One of the workers remarked that, as they sealed up the crawl space, he saw vast numbers of crickets fleeing the scene, carrying their suitcases through the crawlspace door.

The number of crickets died down considerably; nonetheless, a few persistent ones still found a way in. It became an ongoing project, just like the annoying ants that made their way into our kitchen from time to time.

16

A TRIP WITH CAPTAIN BARRY

Captain Barry's Pontoon Boat

In mid-July, we took a boat trip with Captain Barry on one of his "Back Bay Cruises." We had wanted to go for a while, and since friends were with us, it was the perfect opportunity. Captain Barry is what I call a live wire, always upbeat no matter what the weather. Whenever I see him, he is enthusiastic about life and his work, and so generous. He rarely complains, and if he hints at any dissatisfaction about his day, he always accentuates the positive. He is not a man of great stature, but his infectious personality and wicked sense of humor make him larger than life. He sports an outdoor beard and would fit in perfectly on board a pirate ship.

His trips require active participation. He strives to get everyone on his boat trip involved by teaching them to use their senses and learn what it's like to work as a waterman.

And he likes getting kids into the mud. He also tells the kids not to whine. They are lucky, he tells them, compared to some of the kids he has helped on his overseas disaster relief trips. During his downtime in the winter, Captain Barry travels to places like Haiti to help people or North Carolina to assist in rebuilding after the hurricanes.

In effect, his boat is a floating classroom and research vessel, not unlike the wonderful work undertaken in the bay by the Chincoteague Bay Field Station.

Once we boarded his well-organized pontoon boat and settled into our orange plastic chairs, Captain Barry showed us an instant pop-up toilet that materialized from nowhere. Standing near the back of his boat, he quickly pulled up around him some tall plywood panels that locked in place to create a full-surround bathroom. Once enclosed, he amusingly waved his hands above the plywood panels and proceeded to tell us about the six women he welcomed aboard the previous evening, and the number of bottles of champagne they drank. He even pointed out a mirror hanging on one of the panels for women to fix their makeup.

"Not one used my toilet," he remarked.

His evening cruises took place without kids and were ori-entated towards romance with an enjoyable drink at sunset. We were taking the day cruise and expected to get our feet wet.

Accompanying Debbie and me on this trip was Debbie's brother Dave and his wife Sue, and two friends, Gwyn Nielsen and Shirt. Gwyn was a friend of ours from New Jersey. Shirt, as he preferred to be called, was a close friend of Dave's. Four of us work as teachers, and we realized that everyone still used outdated flip phone technology, which was hilarious. Here we were taking a trip on the water with another educator, Captain Barry.

He started his tour by announcing, "We're going to be pulling stuff up, tasting things, grabbing things. This ain't no ride. It's an adventure! I have twenty-five years of learning to unload in two hours, so let's get moving."

I could tell our trip was going to be quite an experience when we left his dock with the theme music to *Hook* playing through his onboard stereo speakers. The weather couldn't have been better. It was a bright sunny morning with temperatures in the high seventies and a fresh breeze blowing.

Our first stop was the notorious laughing gull colony across the bay. I was all too familiar with the raucous calls of this colony from evenings on our front porch, but I didn't realize exactly how many birds nested out there hidden amongst the grasses. Motoring slowly into a secluded channel, we could see the fledgling gray fur-ball chicks, born around Father's Day, were almost fully grown; they huddled in their broods with their parents close by. As we got closer, the chicks hunched down in fear, always eyeing the sky for a marauding gull or hawk that could take them any minute. I thought they looked so cute in their fluffy down. It's a shame they grow up to be such annoying adults.

The gull families—always wary of each other, skittish and untrusting—jostled to secure their places, squawking, "keep off my patch!" Out on the beach, we only got an inkling of how these gulls behaved, but here, up close to their colony, we realized their behavior magnified on their home turf.

The shallow water depths prevented us from proceeding too far into the colony, but we moved in close enough to make the gulls nervous and edgy.

Captain Barry then took us to a recently exposed mini sandbar further along the drum-flat surface of the bay.

"This feels good. It's my air-conditioning," he shouted, roaring off at speed he laughingly claimed to be a hundred miles per hour.

"We're going to do some exploring," he announced when we reached the sandbar.

We stepped off the boat onto a solid, rippled sandy surface. It looked beautifully crafted, as if by some unique artist with a special brush that created equally spaced curving lines and striations in the sand. Here and there, small pools of water collected, filled with plant life and miniature crablike creatures that crawled around.

Captain Barry told us that the direction of the rippled surface varied each day, depending on which way the tide was running. He then picked up a clear sticky comb jelly to show us and told us it was harmless.

"Its sticky skin allows food to get stuck on it," he explained.

Next, he showed us some agar seaweed with its lanky, stringy appearance, and another seaweed, nori, which looked like wet lettuce. We were amazed to learn that nori is edible and often used in salads.

Captain Barry asked us to help assemble a seine net he retrieved from his boat. A seine net has weights on the bottom, floats on the top, and poles on either end. One of us held one pole while he held the other to drag the net through the water and scoop up a ton of miniature fishes, including mainly silversides.

"You scarcely know what you are going to find," he said. "I often find baby flounder, bass, and even cute seahorses in the net." After pointing out the various species, Captain Barry quickly released our catch into the bay.

Standing on the lunar-like surface of the sandbar, we noticed some foam in the puddles below our feet. I always assumed this was some form of pollution. When we asked Captain Barry, he replied, "It is known as zooplankton, and it just foams up that way." Zooplankton are microscopic sea critters that swim or drift in water.

I asked if he ever witnessed anything unusual out on the sandbar.

"One time," Captain Barry said, "A huge seal was lying on the bar staring directly at me. I have no idea what type it was, but it's something I don't see every day."

Captain Barry pointed out a floating plant rising upright in the shallow water. It looked more like a root covered in algae with the odd pieces of shell stuck to its green tentacles. He told us that a tube worm created this disguise to use as a hunting blind, similar to the duck hunter's blinds built in the marsh. As small fish seek shelter in the plant, the worm sticks its head out to capture them.

Captain Barry encouraged us to pick up the diminutive brown snails from the pools and hold them in our palms. He then asked us to count whose snails emerged first from their shells and turned themselves over. We chuckled as Captain Barry explained how the snails live.

The marsh periwinkle is the most commonly found snail in the bayside marsh, and it has two tongues. It moves up and down the plant stalks as the tide rises and falls to feed on detritus, algae, and fungus, trying to avoid predators. As the snail moves up and down the plant, it uses its radula (tongue) to scrape food off the plant stems. As it does, it purposely tears the plant and then puts a fecal pellet into the wounded tissue. The fungus grows in and around the wound on the pellet, which provides additional food for the snail to eat. Eventually, the marsh periwinkle returns to the same blade of grass and repeats this process. This activity may be enough to kill any plants already stressed from factors such as changes in salinity or drought. In areas with high concentrations of marsh periwinkles, their grazing activity results in vast areas of dead marsh grass.

This answered my question about why I saw so many brown areas in the marsh grass that year. Given that periwinkle populations can reach as high as sixty-six individuals per square meter, it was not unusual for this to happen.

By now, the tide was fully out and away from the sandbar. Close to the grasses, something moved. Captain Barry got our attention. "Did you see them over there?" he whispered in a hushed voice, pointing at small creatures scurrying and scouring rapidly in the mud. "Those are fiddler crabs. We only see them at a distance because they have great eyesight and will dive into their burrows quickly."

We cautiously ambled over to their burrows where Captain Barry dug two up for us, a female without the claw, and an impressive purple-backed male with his white side claw.

"Male fiddler crabs use their huge claw to perform a waving display as a form of female courtship, rather like us humans if we grew a larger arm," Barry explained. "The crabs also create minuscule spitballs around their burrows, which they display in certain ways to attract a mate. Females choose their mate based on claw size, the spitball display, and quality of the waving display."

Shirt commented, "Rather like when the crowd does the wave in a sports stadium then." We all laughed.

Captain Barry informed us that in many fiddler crab species, the female occupies the burrow of her mate and lays her clutch of eggs. Fiddler crabs are colonial, often living together in sizable clusters. Territorial fighting occurs between the males, and they will go to great extremes to defend their burrows. They also time their burrowing activity to coincide with the tides. They plug their entrances when the tide rises and emerge to feed after it recedes.

We picked up clumps of what Captain Barry referred to as dead man's fingers, a creepy-looking seaweed with clumps of elongated stringy green fingers. Its tentacles hung like those of the character Davy Jones in the movie *Pirates of the Caribbean*.

It was time to head off to another mouth-watering encounter. As Dave helped place the anchor back on board the boat, Captain Barry commented that he earned a promotion to deckhand for his assistance. Captain Barry explained he did this a lot with kids, to whom he gave titles when they helped him on the trip. He also told us he pretended the boat was stuck and then asked kids to help him push it off the mud. Captain Barry makes the kids think they have pushed the boat off by themselves when he really has complete control of the motor. "They feel so empowered," he said. It is all part of the excitement to involve kids in the experience.

As the boat picked up speed in the heavenly summer breeze, Captain Barry cranked up the music from what he referred to as the Captain Barry soundtrack. This time we heard the opening music from the film *Star Wars*. He took us over to Jersey Jim's

Clam Farm, whereupon he pulled up an undersized clam and told us how much time the clams took to grow.

"The watermen call these small clams 'little nicks,'" he said. "It takes three years for a clam to grow to a decent size for eating, so now you can appreciate how much time it takes to bring these guys to your table."

We wanted to know why Captain Barry came to Chincoteague and when he started his pontoon tours.

"In the past, my knowledge about birds only extended to the pigeons in New York City.," he told us. "I came down here and learned about the birds of the marsh, their habitat and movements."

He often takes out birders and is comfortable helping them experience the birdlife.

At each stopping point, Captain Barry shouted to us, "Well, folks, there is more to show you and more to do, so let's get going." And off we motored to the subsequent activity.

We could have lingered for some time in many of the secluded places he showed us, as they remain pristine habitats with no noticeable human disturbance. The water was crystal-clear, and the electric green grasses swayed gracefully, rustling together in the breeze. The warm afternoon sun bathed our skins with just the right heat.

We came across the oyster beds later into the journey.

"Let's eat some oysters!" he shouted. "Those white sticks sticking out of the water are a sign that someone leases this spot. You can't harvest from this area."

He motored to another spot, stopping the boat as it began to drag on the bottom. Then he carefully stepped off the front onto the oozing, dark brown, crusty oysters that lay fastened to the bottom of the channel.

"These oyster beds are very sharp," he said, "so everybody needs proper footwear and to take great care doing this job."

Captain Barry pulled on his sturdy gloves and whipped out a sharp knife to cut a clump of oysters away from their well-secured bases.

"These are the world-famous Chincoteague oysters," he proclaimed. "They're fresh, clean, and amazing."

As he lifted the clump to show us, they glinted in the mid-day sun, the dark brown mud trickling off them, dribbling back into the water. He then stepped back on board and quickly shucked the oysters right in front of us.

"These go for four dollars apiece in fancy restaurants in New York," Captain Barry said. "They aren't as attractive as the ones served in restaurants though, but they taste the same. Who wants one?"

Debbie's brother, Dave, proceeded to chow down one of the raw oysters happily. He gave Captain Barry his approval with a lick of his lips, a thumbs up, and firm nod.

Captain Barry described the condition of oysters at various times of the year. "They are milkier in the spring and much thicker in October near the end of the season."

No rivers feed into the Chincoteague Bay, and there are no factories nearby, so it is ecologically pristine with no pollution. Consequently, the oysters are much saltier down this way.

Leaving the oyster beds, we acknowledged the great respect we had gained for what watermen endured every day—up to their knees in mud, hunched over with their baskets and culling tools to harvest these prized treasures of the bay.

Next, we came across a rather beaten up, dilapidated, wind-blown duck blind. Its former winter skin of evergreen branches had turned a rusty brown, leaving gaps in the walls and allowing us to peek into its dark, damp interior.

"Anyone can build these blinds on the marsh, provided they are safe" Captain Barry remarked.

He then demonstrated with his rudimentary duck decoy how the hunters threw their decoys out onto the water to attract passing ducks. Captain Barry's decoy floated exactly like a duck. He pulled the line in to retrieve it.

"Some decoys now go for thousands of dollars and are very collectible," he said. "You can see them at the island decoy shows that occur here throughout the year."

Coming up close to the grasses on the side of the channel, Captain Barry grasped a fistful of coarse marsh grass, called *Spartina Alterniflora*. He handed a few strands to each of us and asked us to taste the salt on the leaves.

"You may not know this," he said, "but the plant pushes the salt out onto its leaves to deal with the harsh environment. It's their survival mechanism."

He then asked an interesting question, "Why do you think the ponies have bloated bellies? Anybody know? Because they eat a lot of this grass and the salt swells up in their bellies. It's not unlike pictures of kids with swollen bellies in Africa who suffer from malnutrition. Imagine if we ate white bread every day without any nutrition."

No sooner had the salt left our tongues than we were at our next spot. Captain Barry stopped his pontoon boat on a shallow beach covered with sun-bleached shells. He engaged us in a five-minute scavenger hunt, providing us with Ziploc bags to find cool scallop shells or anything else we found interesting on the beach. While we were lost in concentration, roaming and enjoying the experience, a strange trumpet noise sounded from the direction of the boat. Captain Barry was blowing into a large conch shell and waving his arms furiously to summon us back. We could have stayed there for ages on our deserted beach, but his words told us there was much more to see. "More to do and more to see folks, so let's get going."

After we motored for some time to the northern end of the bay, Captain Barry reached over the side and hauled up a wire cage to show us some blue crabs. As he prepared to empty the dripping, black crab trap onto the deck, we saw it contained two huge crabs clinging aggressively to the wire sides. Captain Barry handed us long plastic tongs, much more serious-looking than the ones we used at home in the kitchen. He then twisted one cage door open and using his tongs, attempted to pry a reluctant crab from the wall of its cage. It wouldn't have any of it, so Captain Barry shook the cage violently and tipped it upside down. Immediately the crab fell with a clatter onto the deck and scurried around frantically, its claws held up high in a defensive manner. We quickly scooted back, tucked our legs tightly under our plastic chairs, and froze in our seats, as none of us had ever seen this behavior.

"Anyone want to catch it?" Barry asked. The loose crab was slightly intimidating, and none of us attempted to use our tongs. Since no one seemed willing, Captain Barry got into position and showed us how to pick it up. He was used to handling them. He knelt down and gently picked it up from behind using both hands, grabbing it tightly at the base of its swimming fins where they connected to the main body.

Assuming his educational role, he explained, "Notice that I am holding it so that my thumbs are on top of the joint, and my index fingers are curled underneath. Once you have practiced this a few times, it gets easier. They can't get you if you hold them this way."

Captain Barry said that crabs can draw blood with a nip, but some Eastern Shore folk carry old-time medicines that can help. Many of these remedies, listed in the *Eastern Shore Wordbook* written by Arthur King Fisher, are a little bizarre, such as applying a spider web or soot to the wound, treating a scratch with a poultice of peach tree leaves, and tying an eel skin around the hand if one suffers a cramp while handling the crabs.

Captain Barry explained, "Crabbers can instantly tell the difference between males and females, as the females have red nail polish on their claws."

One of the two crabs he dumped on the deck carried a distinctive massive orange sponge containing eggs, maybe a few thousand of them. "Most people have not seen this orange sponge and don't know that it's a female with eggs," Captain Barry remarked. "They need to throw these back," which is precisely what he did.

After teaching us so much, Captain Barry announced it was finally time to head home. While we floated idly out in the bay, the sun had become quite strong, but we didn't complain.

Captain Barry turned up the thrust on his twin outboard engines, and we took off. The swift breeze instantly cooled our faces. In keeping with his adventure music theme, Captain Barry shouted, "Full speed ahead, Scotty!"

Each time we hit a slight chop, a refreshing splash of spray flew up over the bow. It was a relaxing sensation to watch the beautiful scenery fly past us as we headed back into the channel. We passed under the main bridge leading onto the island—a bridge that could raise should sailboats wish to pass through.

"Before they raise this bridge," Captain Barry noted, "there has to be an EMT on the island. Because we are an hour away from the nearest hospital, the EMTs have to have more equipment on their trucks to keep people alive. In the event the bridge gets stuck, and someone needs serious medical attention, there must be emergency services available. I bet none of you knew that!"

We returned reluctantly to Captain Barry's dock adjacent to the Jackspot restaurant. As we neared, Captain Barry waived and exclaimed a few "Ahoy there's" to people out on boats and others walking along the shoreline. He was a familiar sight to everyone along the waterfront, and many people expecting his raucous, enthusiastic greetings hollered back to him in return.

He used his conch shell once again to sound his return. Once safely tied up, we all agreed we'd had a fantastic experience out with Captain Barry. It was everything we had heard about and more, and we learned so much in the process. We were amazed when he told us that some days during the summer months he takes five of these two-hour trips out, weather permitting. While disembarking off the boat, one of us asked, "How do you have the energy to do this day in day out"? His parting words made it quite clear.

"You have to love what you do."

17

PONY PENNING WEEK

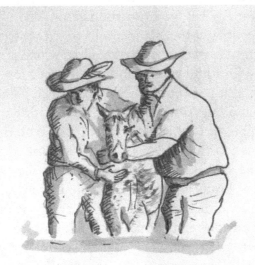

Two Cowboys Rounding up a Stray Foal

David Yeadon, in his book *Seasons on Harris*, quoted:

Islands do indeed possess strange and intriguing qualities. They lure you in with their uniqueness, captivating you with their history, people, and folklore. And while lulling you with the pleasures of enticing isolation, they also spur the very spirit that brought you to them in the first place. They succor the lust for more searchings – more explorations – of island places even further out.

Many visitors to Chincoteague are lured and then captivated by the most popular event of the year, Pony Penning. Held on the last Wednesday before the last Thursday of every July, riders herd wild ponies from Assateague Island across the Assateague Channel to Chincoteague Island.

Debbie and I experienced Pony Penning the first time after we moved to the island. The week before, the traffic built up heavily on the bridge onto the island. The Chamber of Commerce estimates the island swells to over thirty thousand visitors during the week of Pony Penning, which is a considerable increase from the year-round residents of roughly 3,500.

We took a drive around the Wildlife Loop and saw that the refuge put on its own show to coincide with Pony Penning week. The hibiscus bushes alongside the road on the Wildlife Loop bloomed with generous flowers of pink and white. A plant from the orchid family, known as lady's tresses, delicately stretched a celebratory spiral of white flowers up its tall stems.

The island hummed with activity as everyone prepared for the biggest showpiece of the year. We felt an air of expectancy as we drove around town. This would be the eighty-ninth time the island held Pony Penning, to the delight of visitors here and from around the world. Many visitors came because the experience was on their bucket list, and it was something they always wanted to see, especially the pony fanatics. For others, it was the opportunity to revisit family, and the week became a homecoming event. Whatever the reason, the main takeaway for us was the delight we witnessed at every event we attended. It was a time when everyone celebrated life on the island with the wild ponies around us.

It started with an amazing but unexpected encounter at AJ's On The Creek restaurant. On Saturday evening after the roundup of the southern herd, some of the "Saltwater Cowboys" rode into the parking lot at AJ's and tied their horses up for a welcome drink. During the day, the temperature had hit the nineties, and the Cowboys certainly earned some liquid refreshment. (Our server Zebie, who was always attentive to us, told us this happened most years, but like many in the restaurant at the time, we were not aware of it.)

The locals were already outside to greet the cowboys with cheers and claps as they rode in. Customers streamed out of the restaurant with their excited children. Subsequently, a few Saltwater Cowboys hoisted the children onto their saddles for a photo. It was a foretaste of what great times would occur in the days ahead.

The Cowboys' Horses Tied Up Outside AJ's Restaurant

The highlight of the week is the swim itself in the middle of the week. At slack tide on the last Wednesday of every July, Chincoteague's Saltwater Cowboys herd the wild Chincoteague ponies across the Assateague Channel to move them from Assateague Island to neighboring Chincoteague Island. After the swim, the ponies parade to the carnival grounds where the fire company auctions the foals the following day. On Friday, the adult ponies then make the return swim to Assateague Island where they live in the wild for another year.

On Monday, Debbie and I drove over to Assateague beach at six o'clock in the morning to witness the first of the week's events—the early morning beach walk. The Saltwater Cowboys escorted the northern herd along Assateague Beach to join the southern herd in the Wilgus Corral. An endless line of cars followed us. Sensing a tremendous joy in the air was easy. I gazed to my left and saw a mother with her excited children cycling over to the refuge. She had an infant strapped to her back. She towed another daughter in a buggy fixed to her bike. Yet another daughter, around eight years old, cycled furiously behind the buggy, peddling as fast as she could to keep up, a miniature pony doll facing out of her front basket. I wished I had my camera, as it summed up what the week was going to be about—families and kids enjoying the ponies.

We joined an enormous crowd along the beach and waited a considerable time to see the ponies come past. I could tell they were close, as kids started to jump up and down, and people pointed down the beach. The final moment was well worth the wait, as it was a fantastic sight.

The early morning mist hung low, and advancing through it in the distance a wide column of mounted riders slowly approached. I didn't see the ponies at first. The sun edged its way up through the clouds on the horizon amidst a blaze of oranges and purples. A WBOC news helicopter hovered in place above the beach. As the cowboys came closer, the first thing I spotted was a riderless horse, leading them from the front. I later learned that this commemorated the death of Drizzle Wilgus, a Saltwater Cowboy who worked for decades with Pony Penning. A dust cloud with spray rose from the surf as the cowboys and ponies came closer, the cowboys hemming the ponies in tightly against the ocean. One boisterous colt suddenly broke loose, at which point two Saltwater Cowboys immediately broke off to bring him back in line.

Some years the ponies and cowboys advance down the beach shrouded in mist, which makes for an even more dramatic appearance as they emerge from a thick gray cloud. The ponies walked nose to tail, bunched up in bands. The cowboys occasionally struggled as strays struck out across the beach or into the crowds. The spindly legs of the new foals trotted double time, trying to keep up with the rest and their moms. They must have wondered what was happening and been somewhat fearful.

Watercolor of the Beach Walk

The following day we took our houseguests, Hilary Thomas Dorer and Ward Dorer, to the Wilgus Corral to see the northern and southern herds up close in separate corrals. It was an excellent opportunity to study their markings and colors. The newborn foals for sale that year numbered between fifty and sixty. The stallions nostrils flared as they sparred with each other for dominance, their mares quietly moving in small bands around the corral with their foals. Every so often, well-known stallions with names like Riptide reared up and challenged a fellow stallion to keep his mares in line.

Those who had experienced Pony Penning told us how many foals might sell at the auction that year. The youngest purchased ones, called "fall pickups," stayed with their moms behind the carnival to be collected later on. Onlookers at the corral discussed which foals they thought might fetch the most money at the auction, depending on who sired them or if they bore distinctive markings like freckles. The sale took place the day after the Wednesday swim. A sign in front of each pen answered frequently asked questions for the public. I took some photos and later created a pastel painting of the corral looking out toward Wallops Island in the distance.

Gathering at the Wilgus Corral

There are four ways to view the Pony Swim: You can visit the marsh area at the end of Pony Swim Lane and get stuck in the mud. You can go down to Memorial Park, where you will stay clean and dry, but the trade-off is a view of the ponies from two hundred yards away. You can go out on a boat, which is one of the best things to do, but it costs a lot of money, and the tours are booked way in advance. Or lastly, you can stay home and watch the thirty-second clip on WBOC.

On the morning of the swim, the first sounds of activity came from yellow school buses turning down Bunting Road at five thirty. Their white flashing lights on their roofs woke us up. I peered out the window to notice each bus packed with tourists traveling to see the swim.

After the swim, the cowboys and ponies would parade along Main Street directly in front of our house. We took the opportunity to offer parking for watchers. If we carefully organized the cars, we estimated we could fit eight to ten cars on the grass in the back of our property. I made two signs that read "$10 parking or free if you buy a piece of art." It was an idea that Debbie thought of to bring people into our makeshift gallery.

Our houseguests at the time, Hilary and Ward, offered to park cars in the backyard, and in return, we took them out for dinner using the proceeds from the parking.

A swarm of dragonflies danced gracefully around our back porch that morning as great excitement filled the air. At six thirty, the first car pulled into our driveway. We filled our yard quickly, so the signs had worked.

The parade of ponies was also an opportunity to show some pride. Six young men rode around in the back of a pickup truck flying an American flag. I thought to myself that no one flies their national flag as Americans do. It appeared everywhere, even on the loneliest trailers out in the woods.

Hilary sat with Debbie at our kitchen table looking at the satellite images of the road systems on the island to pick a perfect place to watch the swim. After much debate, she decided that rather than battle the crowds, it might be best to view the ponies as they passed directly in front of our house.

At seven thirty, our neighbors at Anne's house laid out oblong tables covered with red and white striped tablecloths for their brunch. Afterward, the guys enjoyed morning cigarettes in their plastic chairs, discussing the price of the food they had purchased. There was a fresh breeze, and the sky was blue as a robin's egg, with not a cloud in sight.

Every so often more yellow school buses passed by with steamed up windows full of excited people going to the swim. The die-hards would stand in knee-deep mud to watch the ponies come ashore from Assateague, and consequently, we noticed them later in the crowds.

Our neighbors placed a dripping hose in their birdbath on the side of the house for those who needed to wash off the mud from the marsh. We, too, left a spray hose out for those who came up from the marsh covered in mud after watching the event.

On Main Street, the crowds appeared thin at first, with people placing a few lawn chairs here and there, including on our front yard. I was impressed by how polite everyone was. People asked if they could sit on our front lawn. Visitors loved telling us their stories, and once they heard my accent, their connections to the UK. Debbie played her bagpipes to the waiting crowd, after which they clapped, having enjoyed the unplanned experience. Many whipped out their phones to record the unexpected musical event.

The same WBOC news helicopter that covered the beach walk a few days earlier hovered above the swim to record the event. We could hear constant chatter coming from the police radios on the street. Suddenly a loud noise sounded in the distance. A canon signaled the start of the swim. The fire company timed this to occur at slack tide when there was minimum movement of the water.

Twenty minutes later, people started to pour up the nearby streets and along Bunting Road to spill onto Main Street. The crowds grew quickly—everyone chatting and laughing, enjoying the euphoria of the day. Young girls clutched their pony dolls. Folks lined the parade route four rows deep, standing on our front lawn. We encouraged small girls to collect shells from our driveway, while older folks placed their chairs and took some welcome shade under our trees. Anne's family next door put a table on the sidewalk and sold waters along with their leftover breakfast food to passers-by.

The crowd began pointing down the road as a lone pony named Spirit trudged at a steady and methodical pace behind a police motorcycle. They let Spirit go on his own before the main show started, as he needed no assistance, knowing exactly where to go. After twenty-three years, he knew how to do it and merely moseyed along, hardly noticing the crowds on either side.

More police motorcycles traveled down Main Street and began to circle in front of the crowds to keep them back on the sidewalk. Huge numbers of people packed both sides of the street, and the police yelled for everyone to stand back. The noise from the crowd grew louder as the cowboys and ponies approached. People jumped up and down, shouting with excitement, as a line of Saltwater Cowboys dressed in their handsome blue shirts headed up the cavalcade of ponies. As they passed, everyone waved, cheered, and held out their smartphones to take photos and videos. More cowboys lined the sides of the herd, boxing the ponies in and preventing escapees. Occasionally a cowboy yelled to keep the ponies in line and moving along.

It was a wonderful family occasion, as the street echoed with the clitter-clatter of hooves. One young girl who stood on our lawn wore her favorite dress with ponies on it. She was so excited as her dad lifted her on his shoulders to see the ponies.

I thought how relaxed this parade was compared to the formal military ceremonies I watched back in London. There, the parades were dressed up, without a person out of place, and the crowd was held at a distance. Here there was a warm, casual setting where everyone immersed themselves up close in the action.

I quickly took the stairs to the top floor of our house to get some better pictures. The stretched-out pony parade lumbered jubilantly past our house. Some ponies were caked in dark brown marsh mud up to their bellies—their small foals were hardly visible amongst them. The foals had no choice but to keep moving and stay close to mama.

As the last Saltwater Cowboys passed, everyone spilled into the street and followed the parade down to the carnival grounds where they could view the ponies close up. After the parade, we invited people into our home to see the art in our makeshift dining room gallery, where I sold prints and note cards. One woman who popped in was so excited about the parade—she said it was her thirty-year bucket list dream to come and see the ponies.

We got to know some fascinating people from around the country after the parade. While in the gallery, we heard their stories—some told me they hadn't painted for years and missed it. We are part of the visitors' experience when they visit the island, so we enjoy promoting it. We see ourselves as ambassadors and discuss how wonderful it is to live here.

In the evening Debbie and I erected a pop-up tent on our front lawn. We added some outdoor lights and hung a display of paintings on some lattice fence panels. The decorative lights acted as a teaser. Many people parked their cars along our street before they walked up to the carnival, so we hoped they might venture off the sidewalk to see my art. It required a conversation to encourage people to come into the tent, but some did, as they were curious about what we offered. A retired United Airlines pilot bought four prints.

The day after the swim, the auction of the foals took place behind the carnival grounds in an intimate arena.

The auction serves three purposes; first, to keep both herds within the mandated limit by the Chincoteague National Wildlife Refuge, second, by removing excess ponies from Assateague Island to prevent over-grazing, and third, to make money for the Chincoteague Volunteer Fire Company. The contract with the US Fish and Wildlife Service allows the fire company to keep no more than one hundred fifty ponies on Assateague. If they didn't sell them off, the ponies would eat themselves out of house and home.

At a set time the evening before auction day, those who wanted a great view of the event from the bleachers were allowed to reserve a seat by taping a towel or piece of cardboard with their names on it to a section of the bleachers. The ensuing day there was standing room only, assuming you could find a vantage point. Luckily for me, being six foot five meant I was able to see over most people's heads. It was a heart-warming social gathering—a wonderful family event with cries of happiness and laughter echoing around the arena. Teenage girls and fully-grown women alike realized their dreams of owning their own ponies.

The Fire Department keeps some of the foals, called "buybacks," as they are returned to the herd on Assateague. They are the most expensive ponies, usually purchased by groups such as the Chincoteague Legacy Group who raise money throughout the year. The purchaser had the right to name their pony when they win it. The Fire Department decides which foals to sell based on a number of factors, such as genetics of the herd and how many stallions exist currently in the herd.

If a foal is born too close to Pony Penning week and auctioned off, it stays with the mother until October, at which point the buyer can pick it up. They refer to these ponies as "fall pickups." Buyers must have approved transport for picking up their pony, as it is no longer acceptable to put the pony in the bed of a truck.

First thing in the morning of the auction, I heard the sound of the auctioneer in the distance asking for bids on the foals. I remembered hearing the sounds of the first night of the carnival a few weeks back. The bidding proceeded quickly. He called, "I see twenty-four hundred... twenty-five hundred...," his voice getting quicker and quicker as the tension mounted. Then he said, "I have twenty-six hundred on Randy..., now twenty-seven hundred on Arthur..., ok all in (with a short pause)..... Sold! For twenty-seven hundred!"

I walked up to the arena to watch the proceedings, where I saw a true mix of people—Amish in their distinctive clothing and a fair sprinkling of wealthy out-of-towners that we didn't see at any other time of year.

It was also a time of great charity. One group, the Feather Fund, helps girls buy a pony. I witnessed a special moment seeing this group in action bringing such delight to others. In 2015, four hundred people from the Chincoteague Legacy Group banded together to buy one of the Surfer Dude progenies for a record buyback of twenty-five thousand dollars. They subsequently named the filly "Surfer's Blue Moon," as she had her father Surfer Dude's blaze down her forehead. The group, prominently dressed in light blue T-shirts, sat together in the stand. I took a photo of Surfer's Blue Moon auction that day and later painted this watercolor capturing the unique atmosphere.

Watercolor of the auction of Surfer's Blue Moon

The light fell on the center of the arena, lighting up the foal's electric blue eyes. Well-known Teaguers, many of whom I had met before, ran the show. They included Denise Bowden, Roe Terry, and Arthur Leonard. The Amish watched in the third row, and the art donations were neatly stacked against the auctioneer's stand, waiting for auction.

Both amusing and anxious moments occurred during the auction. The auctioneer wrongly announced one pony's sex until they looked under her and made sure. Then there was the yearling that needed ten cowboys to hold him down. The bids lowered after the crowd noticed what a handful he was. After a previous buyer backed out of the sale, the poor pony sold for only five hundred dollars. The auctioneer said to the winner, "It's your summer project to break him in."

It was interesting to listen to the way the auctioneer described the ponies, depending on their markings. He referred to them as pintos, palominos, dark bay, black, buckskin, or a chestnut like Riptide. Two cowboys held the fall pickups before the crowd, which always shows a soft spot for the weakest ones. Girls jumped with glee, clapping their hands when they won a pony, and it was marvelous to see everyone sharing so much revelry on the day. It was a wonderful exhibition of humanity at its best. Later in the auction, when a woman in her sixties won a pony, the auctioneer announced, "Even older girls realized their dream of owning one."

Pony Penning week required of us some planning and preparation, but our work paled into insignificance compared to the work put in by the Teaguers and the fire company. It was a great showcase of the spirit of generosity and shared fellowship with others on the island.

After the swim and auction, the island noise levels rose again. A number of trucks made their deliveries since they couldn't make them earlier in the week.

By chance, early one morning a few days later, we watched the southern herd swim back. We didn't know the fire company paraded the ponies back again along Main Street. This was only the southern herd, as the northern herd had already left in horseboxes. After the ponies passed our house, we followed them down to the place where they swam across a few days earlier. Given the reduced crowd, we were able to get a great viewing spot on the bank of the channel. I took some great photos for a painting I later created called "The Swim Back."

18

UNEXPECTED VISITORS

Having an art gallery in our house is an interesting experiment. Because we are inviting the public into our private domain, visitors sometimes stop by after hours or when we least expect them. A few months after I listed the gallery on TripAdvisor, a man banged on our front door at eight thirty one morning. He stated that he noticed we had good ratings and that according to TripAdvisor, we should be open. I had to be careful posting our hours to avoid this going forward.

We are a considered stop for many visitors since we are a residential property that is not in the center of town. We, therefore, don't get a ton of visitors, as not everyone is into art, and some might feel odd stopping at someone's house. However, those that do stop generally have interest, and so tend to buy something. On occasion when it is a slow day, I have fallen asleep on our couch only to be awakened by the doorbell. I have to appear alert and welcoming when I greet visitors, which isn't always easy.

To attract visitors to the gallery soon after we opened, we participated in a local event to celebrate Valentine's Day called "Death by Chocolate." Islanders and visitors visited various merchants along Main Street to get game cards stamped and be eligible for prizes. We asked participants to tell us which of my paintings were their favorites. I then used this to decide which paintings to make into prints.

We had all kinds of unexpected guests. Some dressed up in Valentine red. We enjoyed the boat captains most—they provided the best entertainment, as they knew the history of many of the boats in my paintings.

They told me about Boss Lady that sunk off North Carolina, and how Relentless, owned by Kenny Wayne Rhodes, returned from fishing down in Georgia only to deteriorate. She was then towed from Merritt Harbor and moored at a dock off South Main Street where she remains abandoned, rotting, and subject to the battering of the tides.

One captain discussed the history behind the rusty eyesore remains of the Seahawk near the main bridge to the island. The Seahawk was an old clam boat owned by Russell Everett, an entrepreneur who owned the Landmark Plaza. A person wanted to buy the boat from Everett, so he put some money down and took her out for a sea trial to see if he liked her. He then changed his mind and wanted his money back. Apparently, Everett and the prospective buyer got into an argument. As a consequence, to prevent the buyer from taking the boat, Everett filled the Seahawk with concrete and sank it. To pull it out today would cost a lot of money.

Throughout the Death by Chocolate event, boat captains came into the gallery and shared more information about the boats on my walls. I was told tales about the Gambler that caught fire in the channel. Its remains can be seen today on the far side of the channel. Another boat called the Frieda Marie missed the channel coming in one day and was beached on Assateague.

While most surprises occurred inside the gallery, one day we had a scary accident outside. I was in the back of our property attending to some yard work when I heard a screech of brakes followed by a loud scream and the sound of splitting wood. I immediately ran around to the front of the house. Lying on the lawn, on its side, was a motor scooter, the wheels spinning in the air, with a woman squirming underneath it. I immediately reached down to lift the bike off her. At the same time, I asked her if she was okay.

"I'm okay! I'm okay," she shouted. "I am so sorry. I am not used to this bike. When I took the corner, I turned the handle the wrong way and accidentally gassed it."

Just then, her husband pulled up on his bike, jumped off, and ran over to help. I looked over at my newly installed gallery sign. She had crashed directly into it. That was the source of the sound of splintered wood. The pieces of my sign lay scattered across the lawn.

Once the woman composed herself, I asked her for her vehicle insurance, but she told me the rental shop had not asked them to buy any insurance. I was dumbfounded. Fortunately, they were nice people and offered to pay for a new sign and requested a quote for how much it would cost.

I called the police department and asked them to send an officer to record the accident. I also asked the scooter rental company to send someone out.

At that moment, the woman broke into tears, and her husband comforted her. She was no doubt in some shock after experiencing the trauma.

Once the police arrived, they quickly completed the accident paperwork and provided copies to all. A week later, I mailed the couple an estimate, which they promptly paid so that I could install a new sign.

With my new gallery sign in place, later in March, I participated in the Second Saturday Art Stroll, an evening event sponsored by the Chincoteague Cultural Alliance. Folks visit various retail locations on the island, enjoying arts and crafts, demonstrations, book signings and readings, art exhibits, tastings, music, and more.

Wouldn't you know it; I had another surprise in store for me. Debbie was out enjoying the event while I manned the gallery. When the doorbell rang, I expected to greet the usual tourists or locals. As I approached the door, I checked myself when I saw two tall, tanned, young ladies waiting to enter. Their style was markedly different. I knew from the moment I saw them that they were Europeans. They announced they were visiting the island from Norway. Given that their homeland is covered in snow for four months of the year, they were dressed to stay warm but with a hint of glamor. I found it hard to remain unflustered and immediately fluffed my usual welcome speech. I somehow regained my composure, and after reminiscing about Europe for way too long, I sold them some notecards and wished them a great time on the island. As they left, I had a funny image of them striding into Chattie's Lounge and everyone's mouths dropping. What planet had they come from? They looked very out of place here on the island.

One day a car pulled up in front of the house and out popped a boisterous Welshman from Wales wearing a red Welsh rugby jersey, as if he were just off the boat. He claimed he had stopped because he saw the Welsh flag hanging on the front porch. The Welsh flag is quite a draw for us. He said he was on business and traveling along the Eastern Shore to see it. I could detect his valley accent from the moment he spoke, so we immediately talked about Wales, the rugby, and what I missed most. He asked why I was here and did I enjoy it. For a moment I felt transported back to a small village in Wales meeting the locals.

More surprises continued on July Fourth. I was in my studio early in the morning, preparing for a watercolor class, but

I was not yet dressed for the day. As I glanced out the front window, I noticed four young women walking up our pathway to the front door. I heard one of them say, "I am sure they are open. Do you think it is too early?" When the doorbell rang, I panicked and ran to get dressed as quickly as I could. As I came down the stairs, I noticed five more young women walking up the pathway to join the others. What was going on? It was like I was a tour bus stop. Why would nine young women seek me out first thing in the morning? Every man's dream, right?

I opened the front door and greeted them.

"You are on our list of places we wanted to visit on the island," one of them announced. "We are art majors studying watercolor and would like to see your work. Are you open?"

I replied we weren't, but I would make an exception. I opened the door, and they filed into the gallery.

We discussed watercolor techniques as they moved from painting to painting, taking an interest in how I had created each piece. It was such a joy to discuss my work with other artists and share in the joy of painting. I learned a lot from the discussions; however, I couldn't imagine being in their eyes when looking at my paintings, as art speaks to people in distinctive ways. Putting out my best work doesn't always work, as I was aghast when one of them loved a piece I hated. Most of them subsequently purchased some prints and notecards. I asked about their studies, which they shared enthusiastically, and their desire to visit the art capitals of Europe. It was a very unusual visit, but one that ranks right up there as most enjoyable. It was nice to be amongst smart, educated, well-traveled ladies who loved art.

I reluctantly bade them farewell and wished them a fun-filled evening on their last night on the island.

The day of the Pony Swim, people visited my gallery from all over the US. It was great to hear all the accents and try to work out where everyone was from. For many, visiting Chincoteague for Pony Penning was a bucket list event. Some had wanted to come since they were a child.

A few hours after the ponies had paraded past our house, I noticed a few Saltwater Cowboys standing outside with their whips, spurs, and hats on. A short lady with red hair joined them, and then they filed up our steps in a very orderly way. I had an inkling that it could be Bryce Hurry's mom. Bryce had sadly died in a car accident. Maybe she had come to see the watercolor painting I had created of her son in the Pony Swim Back. I opened the door to welcome them in. They seemed somber, and entered very quietly, not saying much, until one of the cowboys announced, "We came to see the painting of Bryce."

At that moment I realized the red-haired woman was indeed Bryce's mom. What a special moment. Even I was choked up. When she found the painting, his mom let out a great gasp, covering her mouth. She saw her son in the swim back watercolor on the far wall, doing what he loved most, with his girlfriend sitting behind him on his horse. One of the cowboys put his arm around her shoulders to console her as she broke down in tears. I walked over with one of the prints I had made of the painting and said, "This is for you, no charge. I am so sorry about what happened." Some of the cowboys subsequently purchased the rest of the prints for the family.

As someone reminded me later, you are never sure when someone will recognize something or someone in one of my paintings. The paintings preserve a moment in time, and on this occasion, it honored the memory of a special person.

19

A DAY WITH CRABS

The Restaurant Sign at the Crusty Crab

In August, we decided to venture off the island to find a local restaurant, the Crusty Crab Seafood Shack. We had heard great reviews. It is located on the waterfront on the other side of Chincoteague Bay in a village named Greenbackville. The village got its name, supposedly, when people in past times could buy land there for merely a dollar or a greenback.

After driving over the causeway, we took a right turn and followed a road that hugged the bay proceeding north. It suggested it would go on for ages, through open farmland with thick woodland on either side. We eventually saw a sign off to the right for Greenbackville and made our way down to find Harbor Street, where the restaurant was located.

The village didn't appear to have a village center, as there was no main street with stores; instead, we passed many houses in a dilapidated state. This didn't bode well. We wondered just what shape the restaurant was in. We passed one house with its side missing. Others stood neglected, needing serious repairs. Oddly enough, mixed in amongst the decaying homes were some traditional, well-kept Victorian homes, which the owners maintained with pride and kept up-to-date.

We soon found Harbor Street, since it was not a large village. The road supposedly led down to the restaurant. Off to our left, we passed a small harbor with the usual wooden docks strung out along the bulkhead—a few workboats and sailboats moored at their slips. An enormous stack of yellow crab cages at least five feet deep were spaced out along the dock. The tarmac road became much rougher and turned into more of a dirt road with a few potholes and puddles. We began to wonder where this was leading us.

To our right loomed rusty, unused, steel storage containers that looked like they had just fallen straight off an eighteen-wheeler. A wonderful old wooden boat was jacked up on blocks with a blue tarp partially covering it. Then in the distance, we spotted the entrance to the protected Greenbackville harbor. Positioned at the ends of a narrow bulkhead that stretched out into the bay were the familiar green and red channel markers. A space opened up to our right, revealing a dirt parking lot full of cars.

Beyond the parking lot and adjacent to the waterfront sat an unremarkable wooden building that needed a serious coat of paint. Divided into two parts, The Crusty Crab squatted on a piece of grass. We decided not to judge it by our first impressions. The restaurant may not look like much, but we heard the food, fresh off the boat, was great, and that is what we wanted.

The restaurant was a nondescript modern building with a shabby addition on its side facing the bay. The addition was clearly the crusty shack part—nothing fancy, just rustic with generous square windows pushed out to let the breeze in. The Crusty Crab restaurant logo was a crab dressed as a pirate with an eye patch holding up a banner with the title of the restaurant. Painted onto a wooden turquoise panel and framed in wood, it hung to the left of the front door. A giant hand-carved, weather-beaten wooden flounder hung between two windows on the outside wall of the restaurant.

When we opened our car doors, the unmistakable sulfurous odors from the marsh engulfed us.

Customers waited outside the restaurant on some colored plastic chairs. We entered and asked if we could put our names down for a table. Carol, the owner, declined to take our names, saying she would remember our faces. She told us to wait outside. There didn't appear to be any system in place for who sat next, which was confusing. The staff seemed to know some customers and served them first. They naturally favored the locals over unknown visitors like us, I suppose. It was a long wait, but we had the beautiful views of the bay to look at in the meantime. Eventually, our server invited us inside.

We walked through the air-conditioned section in the modern part of the building where a group of locals had their noses buried in various seafood baskets, sandwiches, and salads. They sat rather unceremoniously on white plastic chairs around a heavily scratched rectangular plastic table. Our server led us to the semi-outdoors section and seated us by the window at a table constructed from a seasoned wooden ship's door, with grooved handholds and deep carvings cut into the wood. Above our table, ceiling fans with wooden paddles whirled around to keep the breeze moving. An upturned wooden crab basket serving as a lampshade covered a light above our heads. A forlorn roll of white paper towels sat, curled up on a wooden dowel in the center of the table, and our cutlery housed itself in a simple white paper bag. There were no frills here, but that was okay, as a gentle warm breeze wafting in off the bay created the perfect ambiance. Looking out through the large windows, we took in the vast expanse beyond. Dining at sea level, we watched waves lapping up on the shoreline and crashing against some rocks. Given the exposed location of the restaurant with no protection from the bay, I was sure it wouldn't be such a pleasant place to be when the weather turned foul.

Far away in the distance to the north, slivers of greyish green shimmered on the horizon. These small islands further up the bay reflected into the water. Then I noticed some men standing up to their waists out in the bay. Occasionally they reached down under the surface to bring something up which they deposited into a bag floating on the surface. When our server arrived at our table, she told us they were clamming.

The view was spectacular. Over on the east side of the bay, we could almost make out the bridge onto Chincoteague. Our friends, Jane and Wolfgang, said they occasionally sailed their prized Norse boat, a traditional seventeen-footer with a shallow draft, over from Chincoteague to dine at the Crusty Crab. Since the water levels varied considerably in the bay, they would time their sail with the tides so as not to be stuck. They relied on people power if they ran aground, as they didn't use an engine.

Before we placed our food order, I paid a visit to (what I thought was) the men's room whose name at the Crusty Crab was the "Poop Deck." A single toilet for both sexes, it yielded some quirky features, including male and female symbols on the outside door. Centered above those was a creatively rendered all-gender symbol and the word "whatever." When I entered, a sign above the toilet read, "If you sprinkle when you tinkle be a sweetie and wipe the seatie." Others read, "Take a leekie," and, "Even pirates wash their booty." The bathroom was full of scary pirate heads, some of which were motion-activated and sprang into hearty pirate voices as I washed my hands. It was the sort of place to leave an annoying child to be amused while one ate dinner.

I returned to our table and noticed knick-knacks from the *SpongeBob SquarePants* TV show. It was a weird mash-up of nautical-meets-Sponge Bob, Easter Bunny, and scary décor.

Each server wore a waist apron covered with Sponge Bob motifs, and one wore a T-shirt with skulls covering it.

The menu offered the expected fish and seafood selections. You could even order a "Crabby Patty" hamburger topped with crab dip and melted cheddar cheese. I saw that our meals could be prepared a number of ways. I am allergic to shellfish, so it meant my choices were limited to fish served grilled, fried, or blackened, but thankfully not bludgeoned. I opted for the grilled flounder, avoiding anything deep-fried.

A statement at the end of the menu read, "We are a small Family owned business, on the Eastern Shore and we're trying to make the best homemade food we can for our customers so we can support our little Family." I thought it was a nice line that showed they cared.

The BIG Glass of Wine, written in capital letters on the menu, intrigued us, so we ordered it. They weren't kidding. They should have called it COLOSSAL, as it looked like the glass held a half-gallon. It made up for the extended wait for a seat. Maybe that's what calmed everyone down quickly after they were seated. One glass lasted quite a while and was great value for money at five dollars, even though it was out of a box.

Our meals arrived, and they fulfilled everything we hoped for, tasty and fresh.

Once we finished our entrées, and we asked the server if the desserts were homemade, she replied, "He made it his self."

Once again, we learned the distinctive way that people spoke. When we asked about the size of the desserts, our server simply replied, "We don't do anything puny here."

Before we left the restaurant, I asked our server if I could thank the kitchen staff on our way out for the great fish. The cooks briefly gathered and appreciated my comments, including a woman from the UK who was shocked to meet another Brit. We joked about the Gordon Ramsay kitchen show and enjoyed a few laughs. These kitchen hands worked very hard and wore a smile for us, even though, on some days, I am sure it is hard.

When more company visits, we planned to introduce them to the one and only, unique Crusty Crab Seafood Shack.

Later that evening when we returned to the island, we joined some close friends, Caroline and Howard Lubert, at Assateague Beach to share what we call "Sippee Sauvignon" (concealed wine in plastic cups) and recline in our beach chairs to watch the Perseid meteor shower. The Chincoteague National Wildlife Refuge holds some of the last remaining harbors of darkness on the East Coast for such stargazing. The Delmarva Space Sciences Foundation and the NASA Wallops Flight Facility Visitor Center encouraged the public to discover the starry night sky over the Virginia end of Assateague Island National Seashore at the Chincoteague National Wildlife Refuge.

Caroline is a math professor at James Madison University. Contrary to my view of most math teachers, she is the most fun math teacher I have met. She is also Welsh like me, so we have a lot in common. Howard is also a professor at JMU and teaches political science. Caroline has converted Howard, so he understands and appreciates our crazy British sense of humor and is great fun to be with as well. They are both world travelers and very educated—exactly the kind of friends we like to spend time with because they have an appreciation for life beyond the island.

As the sun began to sink below the horizon, we sat in our beach chairs with our concealed wine and debated where in the sky we might see the meteors.

"Now it's time for the ghost crabs!" Caroline announced excitedly as the last light disappeared off the beach. "Have you seen them before?"

I saw ghost crabs in New Jersey, but they rarely came out of their burrows during the day.

Then we noticed two girls holding a flashlight and poking at something near the water's edge. They used a stick to prod a sizable sand-colored creature, while it scurried skittishly across the sand.

"I think they have one over there!" Caroline shouted, "Let's go and take a look."

When we reached the girls, I saw they did indeed have a ghost crab. My first impression of this pocket-sized, camouflaged critter was its weird eyes perched on the ends of two stalks above its head, which could be rotated a full three hundred sixty degrees. They looked like two periscopes from a submarine looking up at us.

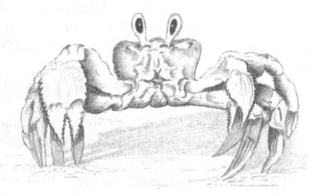

The Ghost Crab

The ghost crab's name derives from its pale, sandy color, which makes it nearly invisible against the shoreline until it starts moving. These regional specialists call the ocean wash to the high tide line their home. When the majority of the daily beach visitors disappear at dusk, the ghost crabs can enjoy the shoreline to themselves. They come out in droves, combing the beaches for a late dinner and foraging on clams, mole or sand crabs, or any other recently deceased sea critter that may have washed ashore. This is also when they seek a mate.

We meandered back to our beach chairs and turned on our flashlights to watch the local ghost crab population scatter. They are a well-loved local attraction that every vacationer has the opportunity to meet and greet when down on the beach.

Ghost crabs live directly on the beach, burrowing deep into the sand for protection from the blazing sun as well as passing predators. The entrances to the burrows will be only a couple inches wide on the surface—beachgoers may notice only half-dollar sized holes in the sand—but underneath the surface, their intricate tracks can run up to four feet deep, not including any outlying branches, allowing a network of protection from the elements. Ghost crabs are not huge fans of the sunshine, and they spend most of their beach days tucked well inside their lairs. They like to do a bit of cleaning by popping out on occasion to remove any excess sand or debris. They breathe through narrow, slit-like openings between their third and fourth legs and can live for extended periods out of the water as long as their gills are kept moist to function.

Ghost crabs are notoriously shy, and with their ability to see three hundred sixty degrees, they are sensitive and aware of any action that occurs around them. Daytime beachgoers, unless they remain perfectly still by either taking a beachside nap or becoming lost in an absorbing book, seldom encounter the crabs. In these cases, a ghost crab may break out of an otherwise-unnoticeable hole in the sand to deposit some of the remnants of their cleaning efforts.

We turned our attention from the terrestrial beach activities to the astronomical world above—what we came to see. It was the perfect night with the temperature a comfortable seventy-five degrees, hardly any humidity, no wind, no moon visible, and—unbelievably—no bugs, which was very unusual for mid-August.

The NASA Wallops Visitor Center provided special perks to enjoy the stargazing events. They issued maps to inform stargazers what they would see that night. The Park Service closed off parking lot 1 at the beach for the disabled, with no lights allowed. Numerous high-powered viewing scopes were set up at the far end of the parking lot by the various astronomy organizations along the Eastern Shore. The plan was for everyone to form orderly lines, and as the various planets and constellations appeared after dark, to view them through the scopes, as well as keeping an eye out for the meteors.

As darkness fell, the stars showed themselves first, increasing minute by minute. Because the island is so many miles off the mainland and away from any major cities, the sky was amazingly bright and clear. Occasionally an annoying car headlight lit up the area, but officials quickly warned the driver to turn them off. The peak time for seeing the meteors was around two in the morning. If people entered the park by ten thirty, the Park Service allowed them to stay the entire night with their blankets, so there was a stream of last-minute cars flowing in.

Everyone waited patiently with eyes trained upward. Every so often a section of the crowd, without warning, let out a sighing *wow* and pointed up to an area in the sky where a meteor had just fallen. It was impossible to get any advanced warning, so we simply craned our necks upward and hoped to see one. We sat in our beach chairs and agreed that each would watch a different part of the sky in hopes that we could share the experience, but that didn't work. Some of us saw meteors, while others didn't.

It became frustrating as the meteors appeared in multiple places in the sky and were not consistent. I finally observed a bright streak, what seemed a fast scratch across my eye from up high, after missing so many that the others saw. Some annoying kids with no interest in looking up loitered about, chatting with their flashlights turned on.

Some people used smartphone apps and pointed their phones skyward to pick out the various constellations. Someone in our group asked if the constellation Cancer was viewable. Cancer, which is Latin for crab, is the dimmest of the thirteen constellations of the zodiac. It lies between Leo, the lion, and Gemini, the twins, and is virtually impossible to see with the naked eye or even binoculars. We had spent the whole day with crabs. They were on the menu at the Crusty Crab, we viewed them on the beach, and now we searched for their constellation in the sky.

One inevitably considers how insignificant we humans are here on Planet Earth. A beautiful sky illuminated like this, I thought, is the very same sky the explorers viewed, unchanged, and yet we are so changed down here. I was moved to realize all I needed to do was to look up and connect with where we sit in this incredible universe.

Debbie and I returned home to enjoy the same incredible view all to ourselves with a glass of wine on our side porch and marveled at the occasional bright slash from above. We saw stars everywhere with extra stars in Cassiopeia and Perseus. Stars leaped and bounced to crowd themselves in. Eventually, the moon rose and shone so brightly that the stars receded as if by day. A broad sweep of arcing light from the lighthouse in the distance lit up the scrubby stand of pines at the end of our yard for just a second. We retired inside, happy that our day of crabs in all its forms was memorable.

20

A WALK TO THE COAST GUARD STATION

After the busy week of Pony Penning, I craved time to explore more of Assateague. I looked forward to wandering alone along the beach.

When I lived in New Jersey, I enjoyed walking along the beach at Island Beach State Park carrying a single fishing rod and spinning with a bucktail lure for flounder. If I caught a keeper, it was a bonus, as it was the journey and enjoyment of being outside that mattered the most.

In late August, I planned to try the same thing here on Assateague Beach while walking down to see the abandoned Coast Guard Station at the end of Tom's Cove. Here the beach is mostly flat with limited dunes for protection on the landward side and a much shallower pitch compared to the steeper slope at Island Beach State Park. South of the parking lot, small dunes on the right with clumps of beach grass dotted here and there, could not offer much of a barrier, subject as they were to constant battering from the numerous Atlantic storms. Beyond these was an extensive wash-over area where the ocean breached many times to wash completely over into Tom's Cove, behind. Further down, closer to the Coast Guard Station, the dunes appeared again. The entire stretch I was about to walk along resembled the outstretched bow of a violin, a shrinking sliver of land gently curving down to the end where the Coast Guard buildings stood defiantly, a hundred and fifty yards from the surf. The vista before me was so wide I could practically see the weather in the next state.

Because this stretch of public beach washes over frequently, it costs the Park Service a lot of money every year to rebuild it and is the subject of much controversy. The Park Service wants to move the beach further north, where it would be subject to less erosion. This is a landscape in constant motion, migrating west every year, with storms the omnipresent threat to Assateague's beach and parking lot.

For part of the year, the park closes the beach to the south to over-sand vehicles to protect endangered species like the piping plover when they are nesting. Once they open the OSV zone again in September, drivers head south to fish from the backs of their trucks along the beach.

I wanted to take some reference photos of the Coast Guard buildings for a watercolor I might paint later on. I expected to walk for several hours, but the fishing would be enjoyable along the way, and I prepared a picnic lunch of my favorite foods. Typically I travel light, one rod in my hand with a bank stick to rest it on, a backpack that contains a tackle box, lunch box, pliers, camera, sunscreen, my wide-brim Aussie-style hat, and a giant brown towel to cover up from the hot mid-day sun. I strap another towel to the backpack to wipe my hands after applying bait or handling a fish. For this trip, I made some homemade rigs to catch croaker and brought my usual two-ounce Chartreuse bucktail lures tipped with scented gulp for the flounder.

When I arrived at the beach parking lot, I could taste the saltiness in the air, as if a vial had been slowly uncorked, releasing a tangy scent. The richness tantalized my nostrils—the ocean breeze, with its mixture of sea salt and familiar air, is like no other. For me, it conjures up a sense of welcoming. Many of us are conditioned to link the beach with relaxation, thanks to the pounding surf, which releases vast amounts of negative ions in the air for an increased sense of calm and mood enhancement.

The beach was ablaze with umbrellas in an array of crazy, gaudy colors, every shade the mall sold, each one plunked down randomly with no thought to coordination. The OSV area lay cordoned off for the birds, so I ventured out on foot, a journey that not many walked, due to the distance and the heat of the day. I looked forward to having no vehicles to contend with and a vast open beach to myself. As I strolled along the surf, the never-ending chatter of sunbathers filled the air. Their coconut suntan lotion wafted up my nose every so often as the air dispersed the annoying vapors from the spray cans, applicants hastily discharging the chemicals with no consideration of others or the environment. At last, I passed the last of those with beach chairs and parasols.

As I stepped along in solitude, I wondered how many ever walked the beach alone to discover its secrets. The receding tide gently lapped against a gradually sloping tidal wrack, the slight shelf above the moist sand that sloped down towards the water. The wrack line comprised a repository of wreckage from other places. Some objects were natural—shells, mermaid's purses, and the impressive tossed up brown shells from horseshoe crabs that look like World War II army helmets. I was annoyed to see the wrack line littered with human-made items such as cigarette butts, food wrappers, and various plastics. The wrack line reminded me of the lines of age on our own faces—lines that give a full face character and tell of its life, just as the wrack line told of the life of the items along it. The rewards of my walk would not be measured by what

I knew I would see, but in what lay ahead on the wrack line. The unknown became an attraction for me.

Above the line where the waves stopped, the footmarks of many shorebirds marked the damp sand. Taking a route higher up on the beach, I noticed the paw prints of a fox wandering off into the shallow dunes, no doubt patrolling for chicks or eggs.

One cannot walk on this vast beach without feeling humbled and no larger than a speck of sand. How insignificant we are. Our tracks merge with those of other animals and birds, so we all share a kinship, a map of where we all stand.

After a while, I came across a husband and wife fishing. We greeted each other, and they remarked, "The fishing is better in the fall. There's nothing doing today." Despite this news, I ventured on with high hopes.

The sea was a thin sliver of calm Prussian blue velvet, the kind of blue that conveys a sense of peace and serenity. The ocean was as still as a millpond, like a slumbering giant, its powers untapped, muscles unflexed, quietly dozing and dreaming, as the waves gently washed ashore. The waves kissed the sand with saline lips of bluish green. A gentle breeze playfully filled the sails on a sailboat at sea, fluttered beach flags, and gently nudged along the clouds. Since the waves took their cue from the wind, it was a reminder that this breeze was a mere hint of the wind's power, that when roused could toss whole ships like toys onto the beach. However, this breeze told only of sweetness and delight as I strolled along the beach content, whole, and at peace.

I asked myself why so many people revere the sea. Maybe it's because of the mysteries that lie beneath its surface. Unlike the land, where thanks to apps like Google maps we know every corner, the ocean hides its secrets, some places still undiscovered, and there is a constant fear of the unknown.

Gavin Maxwell in his book *Ring of Bright Water*, suggests some answers:

There is enduring mystery and excitement in living on the sea-shore, which is in part a return to childhood and in part because for all of us the sea's edge remains the edge of the unknown.

I continued my walk down to the Coast Guard Station, but I didn't see any signs of fish, and no birds chased schools of baitfish. I stopped every twenty or thirty yards, cast out my bait, and then set my rod into my homemade rig, which allowed me to watch the rod tip for a bite. My rod rested on a forked bank stick with the butt secured into the sand between my large toe and the adjacent toe. In this position, the rod stood upright at a forty-five-degree angle, and this enabled me to sense from my toes the slightest movements from a fish. I even laid back against my backpack and didn't have to hold the rod for sustained periods, which would have been tiresome.

Resting and fishing with my rod set up

While I relaxed and fished at the same time, the sand gently soothed and swept over my toes. Its silky-soft touch was warm or cool depending on how deep my feet dug in, and it felt like tiny gritty granules of sugar pressed against my skin. It cradled my body and conformed to hold me when laying down so I could take in a peaceful time.

I positioned my wide-brimmed Aussie hat slightly forward to shade my eyes, and my considerable brown towel covered my shoulders. As I lay back, I entered a kind of meditative state and gazed up, fully relaxed. The clouds above were full but non-threatening, floating along in the cobalt sky.

In this contemplative state, childhood memories of British beaches came back to me. What a difference Assateague beach looks compared to those I remembered from the UK. Back there, they felt colder, and even on a rare hot day, finding sand to lie on was a rarity, as most beaches I was familiar with in North Wales lay covered with pebbles and slimy green seaweed. I did, though, remember the fascinating marine life in the rock pools that collected at low tide, which I hadn't seen in this part of America.

As I pictured the clear rock pools from my youth, I drifted off. Memories of a poignant day in my childhood drifted into my mind like a mist. I was seven years old and camping with my family by a lake. Steve, my brother, and I darted off as we often did to explore the area. I remember running along a dock that stuck out into the lake to join Steve, who was at the far end looking at something.

"Hurry, Dan, or it will be gone!" he shouted.

I was excited and sprinted as fast as I could until my feet began to slip and slide on the dark green slime that covered the entire deck. Before I knew it, I tripped, caught my foot on a nail, and skidded sideways off the dock into the dark waters below. Steve hadn't seen a thing, as he was busy looking at something down the far end. I made a feeble attempt to catch the edge as I slid over, scraping my knee while trying to stop my fall. I plopped straight down into the water and sank below its cold surface. I was terrified—I couldn't swim.

As I descended, I opened my eyes and glimpsed a swirling hazy murk of light green, which began to darken and slip away from me as I made out the large black pillars that descended from the pier above. I feverishly clutched at a barnacle-infested post, but it was slimy and coated my hands in a jellied substance. I slid off it immediately, not able to hold on. I looked up again and spotted the dappled sunlight that seemed miles away. I panicked and gasped, swallowing a ton of water. It filled my lungs as I spluttered, unheard, well below the surface. I had no idea how to float up. Suddenly I felt helpless. I panicked, swirling both arms furiously like a dog.

It was then for a moment that I felt a weird sense of peace. I saw a bright light and shimmering figures above me. I could hear muffled shouting and felt the sinister black dock posts tremble around me.

I felt a sudden jolt around my neck as a clenched hand grabbed my shirt collar and two beaming eyes greeted my rise from below. A stranger yanked me up onto the pier, where I laid on my side coughing up what surely was half the lake. As I lay there, I heard Steve yell, "Where have you been? You missed it! A huge fish was swimming at the end of the pier!"

A splash of ocean spray woke me from my dream, and I immediately felt the sun's heat burning my face. My dream brought me back to the day I nearly drowned, but here I was beside an ocean and not that slippery deck that nearly cost me my life. If that man had not been walking his dog and seen me go over the side, I wouldn't be here.

Luckily, I woke in time; otherwise, I would have sunburned. And that is precisely how it is in August on the beach. It was time to stand up, dust myself down and continue my walk. As I did, the honey-gold grains of sand, gleaming in the sunlight, fell to the ground around me like nature's confectioner's sugar. It felt exhilarating to be alive.

Ahead of me, from the wrack line I heard a high-pitched assertive peep coming from a stocky, petite bird protected due to its endangered status. It whistled so loudly for such a tiny pale piper. As I approached, the piping plover drew my attention by taking short, slight runs and then stopping in tiny depressions in the sand. Trying to lead me away from the high tide area where its nest probably was located, it piped with a high note each time it stopped and then scurried out towards the incoming waves along the shoreline. Once I passed, it flew back above the high tide line, presumably to check on its nest.

As I approached the Coast Guard buildings, the area above the high tide mark appeared littered with tree stumps, driftwood, and gnarled branches. Scattered along the shoreline lay chunks of peat the size of car seat cushions. They were from an ancient beach that had eroded away some time ago, I later learned. I enjoyed this personal time alone, with the beach entirely to myself like it was mine. It was one of the few places on the island I felt I could shout out... a place to find solace, my own meditative silence in the wild.

Henry David Thoreau once recalled of his time at Walden Pond.

"I find it wholesome to be alone the greater part of the time. I never found a companion that was so companionable as solitude."

The great Yorkshire writer Alfred Wainwright detested conversation when he was out on his hikes in the Lake District fells in England. He once said,

"Walking alone is poetry: walking in a group is only prose."

I thought that to be funny, but I can relate to what he means. It was poetry for me that day.

Next to the Coast Guard Station a gigantic steel lookout tower stood out, topped with what appeared to be a generous sized osprey's nest. Like many such structures along the shore, the ospreys favored these commanding sites for nesting.

The Assateague Beach Coast Guard Station house, garage, and boathouse are part of the Assateague Island National Seashore. The station house and the garage (the original boathouse) were built in 1922 when they created U.S. Coast Guard Station 150 at the southern end of Assateague Island. During World War II, the station had additional responsibilities of surveillance for enemy ships and saboteurs. Looking at it now with its masts and antennae missing, one would not guess it performed that role.

The Coast Guard Station was decommissioned in 1967, having served for nearly fifty years, supporting the brave men who did what they could to make the waters around Assateague and Chincoteague islands safer, rescuing imperiled boaters.

When not assisting boats, the U.S. Coast Guard battled high winds and the ever-present mosquitoes. The shifting barrier island and the shallowness of water access was the station's eventual undoing; in spite of this, the government has worked to preserve the station, which is a designated Virginia Historic Landmark.

In the boathouse on the Maryland end of Assateague above a drawing of a beach rescue are these poignant words, attributed to the U.S. Life Saving Service: *"You have to go out but you don't have to come back."*

"The Blue Book states we have to go, but it doesn't say a damn thing about having to come back," Keeper Patrick Etheridge once stated after being warned his lifeboat may not make it back after a rescue. The Blue Book mentioned the regulations of the Life-Saving Service of 1899. In Article VI "Action at Wrecks" section 252, page 58, it states:

In attempting a rescue the keeper will select either the boat, breeches buoy, or life car, as in his judgment is best suited to effectively cope with the existing conditions. If the device first selected fails after such trial as satisfies him that no further attempt with it is feasible, he will resort to one of the others, and if that fails, then to the remaining one, and he will not desist from his efforts until by actual trial the impossibility of effecting a rescue is demonstrated. The statement of the keeper that he did not try to use the boat because the sea or surf was too heavy will not be accepted unless attempts to launch it were actually made and failed.

Regardless of how you felt, you battled the storm, even though your own life was in danger. You might not come back, but history will tell the story of your heroism.

The same heroism is evident in the UK. The Royal National Lifeboat Institute is the charity that saves lives at sea. The RNLI motto is "Let not the deep swallow me up." The family motto of the RNLI's founder, Sir William Hillary, is, "With courage, nothing is impossible."

I turned back toward the beach, and after trying my croaker rig with no success, I tried my lures tipped with gulp, but had no luck with that either. Maybe flounder only frequented the bay and not along the shore. *Surely they frequented the surf as well, similar to New Jersey,* I thought. I tried numerous spots along the entire beach but to no avail. I reminded myself that the sport is called fishing and not catching.

I met interesting folks along the way. On the way back I ran into a couple of lads using shark rigs, who amused me with their stories about giant sharks. They were excited about the sharks they caught, but disappointed they measured under the size limit to keep them.

I passed the spot I rested in earlier, my body shape still visible as an outline in the sand, evidence that I formed my own tracks and presence on the beach. It made me think of the paths and tracks we take on this planet. As Ralph Waldo Emerson wrote in 1850,

> *All things are engaged in writing their history...Not a foot steps into the snow, or along the ground, but prints in characters more or less lasting, a map of its march.*

Walking back from the Coast Guard buildings, the wind started to blow, and the tide advanced rapidly. The ocean unleashed its power, whipping up tempestuous waves that crashed, growling, against the shore, coating my eyelashes with salt. The roars were so loud no other sound could penetrate. Lengthy wisps of fine spray tore loose from their menacing crests. I sensed the current was moving parallel to the beach, moving huge volumes of sand that it scoured from south to north.

I felt in awe of the scene, maybe similar to the way William Wordsworth once wrote about the view of Tintern Abbey when he first viewed it from the banks of the river Wye.

And I have felt
A presence that disturbs me with the joy
Of elevated thoughts; a sense sublime
Of something far more deeply interfused,
Whose dwelling is the light of setting suns,
And the round ocean and the living air,
And the blue sky, and in the mind of man.

As I hiked back, I noticed rolling action further offshore. A pod of bottlenose dolphin coordinated their attack on the bluefish (known as snappers), which arrive to feed at this time of year. The brown pelicans above gave away their presence by plunging in with folded wings to harvest the fish. The pelicans flew in family groups as the lead bird caught the air and the others followed exactly behind in the slipstream to catch the backdraft. Everyone was catching fish but me, but that didn't matter. I also spotted ruddy turnstones, oystercatchers, and sanderlings above the tide line where they dibbled and pattered in the sand. It was a welcome change to see these waders as opposed to the omnipresent laughing gulls back at the house.

I cast one last time for the croaker, but none were present. It would have been rewarding to take home a fish or two, but I savored the long walk as well as the birds, the colorful scenery, and the interesting people along the way.

I once again came upon the crowded bathing beaches. The waves rose up the beach, leaving behind a swash that rushed back again to meet the roaring turbulence below. The sonorous heave of cresting waves crashed like the sound of falling stones, or the breaking of a grand chandelier, leaving lacy foam behind as trails. The waves that broke nearer the shoreline fizzed and bubbled as if someone dropped a giant Alka-Seltzer tablet into the surf.

The tide charged in. The waves now gouged undulating cuts the entire way down the shoreline. Some hissed, washed, polished, and lashed the pebbles before sloshing back down again. The immense waves looked like Chincoteague Ponies, rearing up before crashing down onto the beach, pounding the sand with their white foam hooves.

My day began with the ocean gently caressing the beach as a mother to her newborn, but now these waves showed me their raw power, creating troughs in the sand as they tore away at the beach and washed the mole crabs out for waiting fish. I trudged heavily up and down the cuts and tried to avoid the wind-torn peaks crashing on the beach with indomitable fury. Walking off the beach toward my car, I looked back one last time to see my footprints washed away by the waves as if I never visited. The well-known British Poet John Masefield wrote a poem titled *Sea Fever*. I indeed encountered it that day. Here is an excerpt from his poem:

> *I must down to the seas again, for the call of the running tide*
> *is a wild call and a clear call that may not be denied;*
> *And all I ask is a windy day with the white clouds flying,*
> *And the flung spray and the blown spume,*
> *and the sea gulls crying.*

I felt not only the wind and spray, but powerful forces from the sun's heat and the power of the ocean. The sun proclaimed itself master over me as it blazed down relentlessly, offering me no adequate shade other than my wide-brim hat and spacious towel. I couldn't imagine how travelers made it across scorching deserts. The sea transformed herself from a sleeping giant at the beginning of my day into a churning rage by the time I reached my car. The power of the ocean excites us, scares us, and provides for us.

The sea and sun reminded me of the forces of nature to which everyone is subject.

As Charlotte Bronte once wrote,

The idea of seeing the sea - of being near it - watching its changes by sunrise, sunset, moonlight, and noonday - in calm, perhaps in storm - fills and satisfies my mind.

The hike that day wasn't merely a physical walk; it allowed me to discern, to conjure up a dream from childhood, but more importantly, to contemplate my existence on this planet.

The beach walk provided me with the illusion of seclusion for a few hours in a place that was almost pristine. It yielded surprises and allowed me to discover, as if I were in the wilderness.

21

VAST SKIES

Pastel of a Marsh Sunset

People watch the sea and its ever-changing moods. Why do we also watch sunsets?

If it's been a clear day on the island, a sunset is a guaranteed show at the end of the day. We have the good fortune to experience the wonder of these natural events often. The island is four-and-a-half miles off the mainland; Assateague beach is even farther out. This provides a full unobstructed view of the horizon as far as one can see, where the warm colors of the setting sun take us into a magical world. Debbie and I joke that some days we can see the weather in the adjoining state.

Often people simply sit in their cars down by the beach, totally mesmerized by the view in front of them, as if time has stood still. The Assateague beach provides the best unobstructed views of sunrise and sunset. Should the Park Service proceed with moving the beach, it will take away an exceptional experience as well as the memories for many.

Some days we have no idea we will enjoy a pretty sunset until the very last minute when a curtain lifts on the horizon and stops us in our tracks for the parting show, as the white light from the setting sun trims the edges of the clouds. The sudden appearance of the sun at the end of a rainy day often signals the arrival of the following day's weather front.

As an artist, I view the sky like one massive sketchpad with sunshine acting as the colors and the wind, with its brush strokes, the painter. Together the sunshine and wind paint beautiful paintings one after another and at no time stop, as every day presents a pristine canvas to work on. Brooding moody clouds coming from the horizon suddenly brush aside a beautiful day, as if an artist spilled a dark gray color onto the canvas. It's a constantly changing sky and one that many people seldom notice as they go about their day.

The Victorian art critic and essayist John Ruskin aptly stated that we hardly notice half of the world we live in above the horizon every day. As he once said,

> It is a strange thing how little in general people know about the sky. It is the part of all creation in which nature has done more for the sake of pleasing man, more, for the sole and evident purpose of talking to him and teaching him, than in any other of her works, and it is just the part in which we least attend to her.

> There is not a moment of any day of our lives when nature is not producing scene after scene, picture after picture, glory after glory, and working still upon such exquisite and constant principles of the most perfect beauty, that it is quite certain it is all done for us, and intended for our perpetual pleasure.

> Sometimes gentle, sometimes capricious, sometimes awful, never the same for two moments together; almost human in its

passions, almost spiritual in its tenderness, almost divine in its infinity, it is surely meant for the chief teacher of what is immortal in us, as it is the chief minister of chastisement or of blessing to what is mortal. And yet we never attend to it, we never make it a subject of thought.

Perhaps we have our eyes too focused on the material possessions around us and don't look up. This is especially true today—so many people live an indoor life built around technology, and their eyes continuously look down at their phones.

In an article published in the British magazine *Country Life*, Jay Griffiths wrote,

Both immense in size and ephemeral in time, part of the appeal of sunrise or sunset is its very transience – the work of artists is to trace its vanishing resplendence as it races across a fugitive sky. In Old English, sunset is sunnansetlgong, suggesting the going down of the sun that settles itself into evening.

Griffiths shared examples of how the great masters tried to capture the essence of a sunset.

In Monet's work, this fleetingness hints of loss, a sadness for a world always on the point of disappearing. In his painting Le Soleil Levant, *he tried to paint the rising orange sun, but his eyes were drawn inevitably to the blues. The crimson and yellow sunset of* San Giorgio Maggiore at Dusk *accorded Monet one gasp of rapture.*

Monet stated, "Color was his day-long obsession, joy, and torment—that could never last: the possibility of light is barred by the fact of dark."

Van Gogh painted as if he were the yellow and the gold; in *Sower with the Setting Sun*, the huge sun cradles the hand of the sower in its generous arc.

The Old Master with perhaps the most complex representation of sunsets was J. M. W. Turner. He used light to stream like liquid thought, each color lustrous and backlit by an intensity of gold.

In his painting, *Sun Setting over a Lake*, gold is more than a paint – it seems to become the precious metal. In *The Lake, Petworth: Sunset, a Stag Drinking*, its world of sky, lake, trees, and swans can become once more–for just one gilded moment–the Age of Gold. Turner produced these amazing sunsets.

In the sunset of his own life, Turner's last words were, reputedly: "The Sun is God."

Walt Whitman wrote of a sunset as:

Corroborating forever the triumph of things. Sunset can elicit a depth-charge of soul-values, the cadence of evening harmonies, a softening decrescendo – a quieted credo of tranquillity.

Why do we celebrate sunsets? Each of us rushes to capture, document, and save sunsets from vacations and special occasions as if hoarding photos of their splendor will help us remember that wonderful atmosphere when we took the photo. We can then point to an album or shuffle our thumbs on a smartphone through twenty versions of the same scene later and say, "This was my vacation on the island." A phone or camera viewfinder becomes a cramped window into which the amazing sunset must fit to become valid. In the interest of finding the best angle we twist and turn to capture the best shot instead of simply absorbing the experience in front of us.

Taking a picture is an attempt to sum up an experience using only a fifth of the senses available to us. So much more occurred at the time to make that scene more memorable, be it as the salty sea air, the flock of snow geese, the calls from gulls nearby, or the sulfurous smell of the marsh.

Many of us who experience sunsets regularly on Chincoteague are no longer compelled to see them through a digital device. Rather we absorb and enjoy them with our own eyes. Maybe so many great ones spoil us. Ruskin, who in 1876 didn't own a camera, of course, aptly described a memorable sunset,

An entirely glorious sunset, unmatched in beauty...deep scarlet, and purest rose, on purple grey, in bars; and stationary, plumy, sweeping filaments above in upper sky...remaining in glory, every moment best, changing from one good into another for half an hour full, and the clouds afterwards fading into the grey against amber twilight.

Some of the sunsets we experience on the island rival the description that Ruskin provides. Occasionally the elements conspire to create an exceptional one. I pause to savor the light and the wonder of the whole spectacle. It gives me a sense of peace and rest, the wonder of what lies beyond this life we live, the softness of the changing colors. It's no wonder so many of us enjoy fires when the colors of yellow and red burn so brightly.

There is a reason sunsets are timeless and the constant standbys of poets, writers, and romantics—because they are inspiring. Mahatma Gandhi observed their power when he stated,

When I admire the wonders of a sunset or the beauty of the moon, my soul expands in the worship of the creator.

Maybe the real reason why we celebrate these instances of natural beauty is that they are simply that, a sense of romance at the end of our day. Sunsets enable us to be prone to romance similar to when we first fall in love and the experience overwhelms us, taking our breath away and leaving us speechless.

Sometimes from our front porch, I am lucky enough to catch the sun hovering above the horizon. At this time, it is possible to see it actually moving, ever so slowly downward. I stop to watch its final descent into the far trees, expecting it to set them alight as it plunges into their dark forms. It is a very personal experience, as I marvel at the world we live in.

The amazing colors of Mother Nature and her wonder never disappoints us; she has the power to astonish us every day. A sunset also heralds the contemplation of another day, for, as the sun's dying rays pierce the horizon, we look forward to another day with its endless opportunities. Everyone knows it doesn't last, yet we enjoy the last remaining embers of the day.

Here are some quotes that I believe capture the essence of a sunset.

Everyone can identify with a fragrant garden, with beauty of sunset, with the quiet of nature, with a warm and cozy cottage. – Thomas Kinkade

My sun sets to rise again. – Robert Browning

It is a beauteous evening, calm and free, – Wordsworth

Every sunset brings the promise of a new dawn. – Ralph Waldo Emerson

Every sunset gives us one day less to live, but every sunrise gives us one day more to hope. – Ritu Ghatourey

The last taste of sweets is sweetest last. – William Shakespeare

Here on the island, we tend to see better sunsets in the late fall and winter. Maybe there is a reason for that? In the fall, the days grow shorter as the earth is in transition. During this time of year, weather patterns allow dry clean Canadian air to sweep across the country and down to Chincoteague. This cleaner air allows more colors of the spectrum to make it through to our eyes without getting scattered by interfering particles. The skies at sunset glow with the most spectacular hues, blooming with reds, yellows, and orange variations with the pink tinting of clouds as they move across the horizon.

Summer isn't ideal, because air circulation is more sluggish, and the photochemical reactions, which result in the formation of smog and haze, proceed most rapidly. Several conditions have to be in place for a colorful sunset: low humidity, some cloud cover, clean air, and calm winds. The amount of moisture in the atmosphere affects the colors of our sunsets. Lower humidity will produce tones that are more vibrant, whereas higher humidity mutes the colors because of the water content in the atmosphere. The seasons of autumn and winter typically produce lower humidity than in the warmer seasons.

If the weatherman is speaking about such clouds as cirrus or stratocumulus, we had better have our camera batteries charged, as the chance for a super sunset is at its best! Even gray days can give great sunsets with beautiful red stripes on the horizon, but they only last a few minutes. When there are no clouds in the sky, but one can see some thin clouds at the horizon, there is a chance of a magnificent sunset as the sun filters through these clouds to create exciting color variations.

Clouds are a crucial factor in predicting dramatic sunsets, for without clouds there is not much to see. But clouds don't create the colors; clouds serve as the canvas to display the colors the light is painting. High- to mid-level clouds are the most effective canvases, as they will reflect the colors of the setting sun. That is why we see those gorgeous after-sunset colors of pinks and purples reflected into the clouds. On the other hand, if the clouds on the horizon are low and thick, the sun will not be able to shine through them. Puffy clouds or dark rain-filled clouds won't reflect much light.

Clean air helps us see the colors in a sunset. Since the lower atmosphere is exceptionally clean here in Chincoteague, more vivid colors pass through.

Wind is a factor, too, that can either enhance or destroy a beautiful sunset. A change in wind direction can cause the clouds to develop ripples or billows, which can create a stunning effect as the setting sun reflects a red glow onto the ripples.

Conversely, the wind can cause clouds to close up and obscure what could have been a great sunset.

Scientists claim that the best conditions for amazing sunsets are mid- to high-level clouds, thirty to seventy percent cloud coverage, clean air, low humidity, and calm winds. If each element is in place, then we should see a spectacular show.

People connected with nature report greater happiness and have more positive emotions than those who do not share this connection. Studies have shown that watching sunsets causes psychological effects in those who watch them, including health benefits and long-lasting satisfaction in life. Visitors to Chincoteague often choose to come here permanently for a better quality of life, and I am sure part of that reason is not only the proximity to the ocean but the ever-present vast skies and sunsets.

Extensive research exists on how sunsets affect our moods. A study at the University of California, Berkeley found that positive emotions aroused by natural beauty led to increased prosociality and behaviors characterized by concern for others. In one experiment, volunteers first looked at pictures of nature scenes and then played a game, which allowed them to be generous or stingy about giving away points to other players. People ranked nature images in order of beauty. Volunteers who viewed the most beautiful nature images gave away more points, compared to those who viewed less attractive pictures.

The appreciation of natural beauty can boost well-being, but the key is to engage with the experience actively. Not everyone does this. To reap the rewards of a sunset, one needs to stop whatever one is doing and really notice and appreciate the show in the sky. In John Macfarlane's book, *The Old Ways*, he writes,

> *Landscape and nature are not there simply to be gazed at; no, they press hard upon and into our bodies and minds, complexly affect our moods, our sensibilities. They riddle us in two ways – both perplexing and perforating us.*

I create pastels and watercolors of the beautiful sunsets on the island; whenever visitors come to my in-house gallery, these are the paintings they enjoy the most. Consequently, I have painted many more as time has gone by. I often venture out to collect reference photos. One trip was particularly memorable.

I hoped not to be disappointed, as the conditions appeared ideal for an exceptional sunset. By mid-afternoon, scattered clouds floated by with clear conditions and no wind. I drove out Beach Road to a place where three key elements existed—two in the foreground and one in the background—that were important for my painting. The two in the foreground consisted of a hastily constructed hunter's duck blind and some Oyster Castles placed in Tom's Cove the previous year. In the background were the uniquely shaped buildings of the Wallops Rocket Facility that set this painting in Chincoteague.

The timing for my photograph coincided perfectly with a low tide. At around five o'clock, the sun started to set, and the tide was at its lowest point, providing me with the perfect scene.

My Pastel Sunset

I parked my car in my favored spot alongside the road to make sure each important element lined up perfectly. I noticed on a previous visit that when the tide was out, the grasses and channels formed silvery sinews that led one's eye directly out to the main features, that of the duck blind and then on to Wallops.

On this particular day, however, one unplanned occurrence added the perfect addition to my sunset painting. Coincidentally, on an oyster bed that emerged at low tide, were two watermen using their culling hammers to cut away at the oysters, their Carolina skiff pulled up on the bar near them. The watermen could not have been more perfectly positioned in my photo and added the missing ingredient, that of men working the water, and a sense of scale for the painting. The watermen and their skiff looked naturally part of this landscape as if they were there for decades. The sun began its slow descent to the horizon, melting into a backdrop of mauves and dark gray finger clouds the breeze shooed away.

The sun fell slowly enough for me to see it move through each layer of cloud and as it did, it was free to pick out its colors and began to burn like a furnace seen from the open door of a steam engines firebox, a blend of hot oranges and yellows. The dark angular-shaped rocket buildings and towers stood solemn and black against the orange glow. With the cove partitioned by seams of grass and mud and the water in the foreground so still, the colors of the sky reflected two skies, one on top of the other. The effect was doubly amazing. The two watermen formed mere silhouettes—hunched over, working feverishly, hammering away—taking not a moment's pause to view this incredible show, for they worked with a purpose and pursued it diligently. It was as if they knew only so much time remained to harvest their prize and leave.

I took numerous photographs, and even though the pomp and ceremony of the sunset were gone, the afterglow was equally as spectacular as the fallen rays then tilted upward and caught the lower edges of the upper clouds, tingeing them with pink fringes like the edges to a soft cushion. I walked back to the car and slowly drove away. The watermen were still working away, nearly in pitch dark. I had enjoyed a unique moment, for the elements conspired to conjure up the perfect view, one that alters every day, with every sunset.

Peter Davidson wrote in his book, *The Last of the Light*:

> *This is the time of the summer night loved by the Romantic poets and painters of the early nineteenth century, this peaceful evening offering its glimpse of other worlds, the physical land-scape of twilight opening out into territories of the imagination whose 'spiritual music' sounds most clearly at nightfall.*

This is the ephemeral beauty of Chincoteague Island, for it offers a vast horizon that allows us a glimpse of other worlds. I remember one afternoon when I left the YMCA, a flock of fifteen great white egrets flew overhead, gliding effortlessly and majestically over to the marsh. *How many gyms can people walk out of and see that,* I thought. If visitors took time to slow down, they might appreciate some of these sights.

Some of us have a natural tendency to stop and stare at a breathtaking sunset or a flock of birds. When we do, we are likely caught up in the moment. Our minds get a break from fretting over the past or worrying about the future. Afterward, we are refreshed, and life becomes better.

Apparently, greater engagement with beauty is associ-ated with higher levels of life satisfaction, gratitude, and a spiritual outlook. The link is strongest for engagement with natural beauty, compared to artistic beauty such as a painting, symphony, or poem, or moral beauty such as an act of charity, loyalty, or kindness.

There is something inherently powerful and spiritual about sunsets, and we can benefit from incorporating such experiences into a regular ritual.

Some people say sunsets provide an easy way to combine meditation, a sense of peace, and the wonder of who is the creator of everything.

According to Peter Davidson,

Ruskin sought refuge in the skies of evening as if their unstable glories could somehow instruct or console him. Ruskin tested his own abilities to paint verbal Turners.

Here is what Ruskin said:

The whole sky from the zenith to the horizon becomes one molten mantling sea of colour and fire; every black bar turns into massy gold, every ripple and wave into unsullied shadowless crimson, and purple, and scarlet, and colours for which there are no words in language...the upper sky...modulated by the filmy, formless body of the transparent vapour, till it is lost imperceptibly in its crimson and gold.

The great poet Henry Wadsworth Longfellow summed up the setting sun with these words,

After a day of cloud, wind and rain sometimes the setting sun breaks out again, and touching all the darksome woods with light, smiles on the fields until they laugh and sing, then like a ruby from the horizon's ring, drops down into the night.

It was as if he visited Chincoteague, for his description echoes what we experience regularly.

22

STORMS

A Giant Shelf Cloud Rolls Over Marsh Island

We all remember beautiful sunsets but dislike the occasional bad weather. After Debbie and I bought our house, we came down from New Jersey to decorate and experienced our first significant storm. Due to the wide-open expanse of the bay in front of us, the very cold, high winds flew in and introduced themselves. It reminded us of the awful gale we endured during Hurricane Sandy in 2012.

Our neighbor, Joe, told us people living on the bayside know that three days of northeast winds, followed by a shift to the northwest, will cause extremely high tides. If there is a full moon as well, an island storm becomes worse, as the water in the bay comes up over the shoreline, flooding areas where bulkheads don't exist.

During the storm, the wind forced its way into the tops of our front windows and came in through the corners, despite the tight-fitting double insulation. We tuned into its presence on the island, more so than in our former lives on the mainland, as the changes in the wind speed made us listen to its timing and its relative strength. This storm was a force with its own ways and could not be seen or controlled. It was simply there, like a large, real being. Its alternate moaning and lulling were unsettling and menacing.

Our house exhibited a form of yielding to the wind, essentially bending to its power in the time-aged way it was used to. The house had experienced many weather events since its construction in 1889, but it still seemed ephemeral. With every strong gust, we felt our house shudder slightly, maybe due to its balloon frame construction, with the timbers forming one continuous stud, extending from crawlspace to roof.

Lying in bed in the dark, we felt the house breathing with every wind gust, like a giant stirring. The fact that our four-poster bed was two-and-a-half feet off the floor probably accentuated the sensation every time the gusts came. We felt tremors, like the small bumps one gets when experiencing turbulence on a transatlantic flight, or a mini-earthquake every twenty seconds.

Sleeping on our moving bed of Jell-O was impossible. As the gusts hit, the bedroom sounded like someone was peeling tiny pieces of Velcro apart, and at any moment the walls would tear away and us too. Due to the tremendous force exerted on them, the window frames squeaked and creaked; I simply hoped the glass was strong enough to withstand the sixty-five mile-per-hour gusts. A breeze also came flying up through the cracks in our floorboards, so we placed a rug over them. We loved that our house breathed, but didn't want it breathing too much.

At one point during the night, our front doorbell sounded, and for a moment, I wondered who would be out in this awful weather. I guessed it was the force of the wind, but I still checked. When I pulled the front door open of course, there was no one there. I tried to open the outer storm door; it was practically immovable, as the extreme force of the wind bore down on it. I marveled at the power of nature and how helpless we are. Thankfully, the front doorbell was, battery operated, so I removed the batteries to solve the problem.

When I returned upstairs to use the bathroom, I noticed white caps in the toilet bowl, which rocked from side to side when each heavy gust hit the house.

Somehow, we blocked out the giant washing machine with its whistling and tearing sounds and slept through the rest of the night. The next morning we awoke in a foreign land, with not a cloud in the sky and bright sunshine. A weird silence hung in the air—no sound ran through my ears, and the wind was but a whimper of its former self, like the occasional exhales every so often from a runner. Main Street temporarily flooded at the next high tide. We laughed at identifying various objects that floated down Main Street, including a cooler, garbage can lids, an ornate light fixture, and multiple planks of wood.

We lived through our first nasty storm and knew what to expect the next time. The experience taught us just how vulnerable and how subject to the raw power of nature we are—how storms can suddenly creep on us without warning, like the one in the summer while we watched the movie *Roan Innish* in the park.

At least if I were sailing in the bay, it would be daylight, and I could see indications of squalls coming from the horizon. In those circumstances, the sky shows a rapid sign of curdling and changes its demeanor quickly, bringing rain showers that march over the bay with force.

There have been some notable storms on the island, but the Nor'easters can be the worst. They create more issues than hurricanes because they can sit over us for days and dump a ton of water and wind, whereas hurricanes tend to pass through. One of the worst Nor'easters hit Chincoteague in March 1962, and it was comparable in strength to the most intense hurricanes of the historical record. This powerful storm was a slow-moving winter event fueled by the combination of several low-pressure systems. What made the storm so destructive, and responsible for such widespread coastal change, was its duration and timing. The storm lasted for several days that included as many as five high spring tides at some locations. Flooding became a significant issue as the tides rose. Today we tend to worry about every high tide, so I can only imagine what it must have been like to witness the enormous tidal surges that took place in 1962.

When a Nor'easter drives a ton of water into the bay, the water rises almost to the causeway. On those stormy days, the island appears marooned, barely above sea level, and water stretches as far as the eye sees, punctuated by clumps of bushes and the tops of grasses that used to define marsh areas and channels. The high winds and rising tides cause the waves to breach parts of the causeway, forcing the town to close it for periods. It is times like these that we realize that a foot or two more, and flooding is a reality. Islanders pay attention to the tides to gauge what might happen and when it might be safe to travel again.

We also experience impressive fronts approaching from a distance, inch by inch, as if a giant gray blanket were slowly pulled up over our eyes. A front can come through at any time, but this far from the mainland, their approach is more dramatic as there is time to see them coming. They herald change, whether rain or fine weather the following day.

Once during the summer, we witnessed a rare cloud formation, a giant shelf cloud rolling across the bay. It was an ominous sight, like a spooky end-of-the-world, "close-encounters-of-the-third-kind" experience. A shelf cloud attached itself to the base of the parent cloud, which was usually a thunderstorm. The underside appeared turbulent and wind-torn as it rolled towards us. These cloud formations curled up and filled the entire sky like a vast carpet silently unfurling itself until it was directly over us, then the wind and rain rushed in behind it.

We live on an island with an ever-changing sky and numerous weather conditions in a single day. We might start the day with cool mist on the beach that burns off to a blazing hot day. Later in the evening from our front porch, we might watch the cool mist descend on the bay. A beautiful sunset is no prediction of the followings day's weather, for a complete change often occurs. One thing is for sure, we don't need a widescreen TV, because we already have one outside our front door, with a vast selection of channels to watch for free.

FALL

23

THE GOLDEN DAYS

The Mobile Duck Blind

Fall heralded the start of school, a much quieter time on the island, and many changes occurred in the marsh. The type of visitor who came to the island also changed, as the partygoers left and the more welcome birders returned.

The players on the wildlife stage were about to be replaced as well. The summer act ended, and everyone transitioned into a slower, more settled season. Before this changeover occurred, agitation and jitteriness were apparent in the marsh as the days grew shorter. The position of the sun in the sky changed to a shallow ark. A longer slanted light bathed us, instead of the full-on beams that beat down during summer. This altered how we perceived color and light. The contrasting shades of green that dominated the summer landscape gave way to an earthier tawny gold palette. New colors in my watercolor palette came into play—burnt sienna, raw umber, and raw sienna.

An excerpt from Emily Pauline Johnson's poem, *Marshlands*, captures how the light changed.

A thin wet sky, that yellows at the rim,
And meets with sun-lost lip the marsh's brim.
The pools low lying, dank with moss and mould,
Glint through their mildews like large cups of gold.

Our fall skies started to change from unruffled, clear bright blue to more troubled weather systems bringing showers and wind. The clouds took on darker underbellies as cumulonimbus clouds appeared on the horizons and brown hues started to rise up the Spartina Alterniflora grasses. The migrants focused on fattening up, ready for their southward flight.

The nights became slightly cooler as the island slipped into fall. In late September, when I drove to my job as a teacher at the high school, the whole marsh appeared to be restless and on the move. A considerable flock of tree swallows flew low, gorging themselves on the insects over the grasses in the bay on their way south. A modest pod of dolphin rose out of the water in the channel near Marsh Island, and I knew it was probably the last time they fed here until the following year. Every morning the egrets and terns gathered into ever-tighter flocks as everyone prepared to move on to their winter habitats. The summer season was over, and the curtain dropped on the vibrant colors, ready for a much-needed rest.

One evening the great blue herons, mostly absent since spring, appeared in the bay to stake out their winter locations. They competed over the same length of channel or creek, which each bird defended rigorously. Given their rasping call and gruff, stern demeanor, locals refer to them as "crankies," which I thought was an appropriate name. Few were seen during the summer, as they bred somewhere else in their colony. As they glided past, they looked wonderfully primeval, the very image of days gone by.

September began with increased wind and billowing clouds. The sky was a churning mixture of cobalt blue and cobalt violet with a touch of raw sienna on the horizon. The lower angle of the sun's rays cast a blinding light onto the marsh pools. The air shimmered with dancing sunbeams in the late afternoon. The diving ducks arrived and gathered in higher numbers as the season progressed, and the mosquitos came out in full force once again as their last hurrah before it got colder. We were relieved when the constant chirping from crickets around the house died down. We hadn't forgotten our summer invasion.

One morning on my drive to work, I noticed how empty the laughing gull colony looked alongside the causeway. Back in May, it teamed with a whirling myriad of gulls flying continually in the hot breeze. Now the only evidence the gulls bred here were the numerous dead bodies that lay battered and bruised against the guardrail from their first flights into oncoming traffic.

The temperature on the island dropped to sixty-one degrees with fifty-seven degrees reported on the mainland. This differential increased as the colder weather came in because the warm water around the island insulated it and kept it warm in the fall. The reverse effect took place in the spring.

The dainty, elegant black-necked stilts no longer fed in the pools on the right of the causeway, as they had departed a while back. The considerable flocks of white and glossy ibis no longer flew over our house to roost. Every evening in the summer, we had enjoyed them, but now the skies were empty. The juvenile hummingbird that was at our feeder the entire summer left on September fourth to cross the Gulf of Mexico and head on to South America. I wondered if he made it.

In September, the annual herb salicornia growing in the marsh started to turn an intoxicating rich burgundy color. This stringy branched plant has stems that resemble slender swollen fingers. Occasionally sold in grocery stores, or served in restaurants, some people refer to it as sea beans, samphire greens, or sea asparagus. After cooking, the flesh on the plant resembles seaweed in color, and the flavor tastes like tender spinach stems or asparagus. In two weeks, it was drizzled across the marsh like a string of rubies, and formed a luscious deep red carpet, adding a patchwork quilt of contrasting golds and reds to our landscape. As Ralph Waldo Emerson wrote,

> To the attentive eye, each moment of the year has its own beauty, and in the same field, it beholds, every hour, a picture which was never seen before, and which shall never be seen again.

Lining part of the causeway were pokeberry bushes that put forth branches full of tempting dark blue berries. Their red stems added to the autumn colors, together with Debbie's late-blooming nasturtiums in our garden.

On my drive to work, as I turned the corner by the Wallops airbase, I could see pink muhly grass—or purple lovegrass, I am not sure which—growing behind the fence, bathed in the early morning sun. The grass glistened with frost and resembled cotton candy. The early morning light caught the soft, billowy pink grasses and blurred the landscape like an Impressionist painting. The bulbous heads of goldenrod appeared coated in quadricone gold with tints of Indian yellow from my paint box. As the sun rose, the whole marsh looked ablaze in a fiery cloak of fugitive colors, from the rusty auburn reds of salicornia to the lightning gold tips of the spartina grasses, and the yellow heads of the goldenrod.

The goldenrod swarmed with monarchs, red admirals, and painted lady butterflies, having rested and fed themselves for their onward migration south. The mottled colors of the painted lady and orange and blacks of the monarchs fitted in perfectly with the autumn palette. The blaze of color was nature's final fireworks before it rested, but it also pointed to the future, too, a rebirth that happened every year.

I noticed a few great blue herons sitting on the edges of the channels guarding their stretches. Over the ensuing days the egrets, ibis, and various herons, except for the great blues, fed tightly together in their families, forming an ever-growing flock. Joining them were this year's juvenile ibis sporting their light brown and pinkish colors. Soon the whole flock would fly south together. Some days there were so many white egrets that they looked like a patch of fresh snow. When I visited the beach, I saw a few laughing gulls lingered; their winter plumage gave them the appearance of granddads due to their receding hairline. They didn't look half as menacing as they had in the summer with their bold brown robber-like hoods.

When I returned home at the end of the day, there was a chill in the air as late afternoon temperatures fell quickly. For the first time, I wore a sweatshirt to sit on our front porch. It was more peaceful, with no laughing gulls with their caustic shrieks or tourists on their noisy scooters. There were no bugs, either, so I sat out for much longer enjoying the ripples in the bay and fall colors melting away on the horizon.

In the mornings, a hefty black dredging boat, The Murden, slowly made turns in the channel opposite as it sucked up the sand from the bottom of the bay. The U.S. Army Corp of Engineers brought it back every year to maintain the channel depths. As it performed its dredging maneuvers, its hull gradually sank lower in the water as it filled up with sand. Then it motored down the channel to a dumping spot and came back a full three feet higher in the water.

I was reminded one day how close we live to sea level. On my drive to the mainland, I crossed over Queens Sound Bridge where a ferocious northeasterly wind drove the waves from Chincoteague Bay up against the rocks, which cast a great shower of spray onto the causeway. At high tide, one wrong wheel maneuver could take me off into the bay. Drivers frequently disobeyed the speed limit and passed me on the double yellow lines. It was easy to get upset with them, but this is sometimes how it is down here despite it being a more relaxed place to live.

When I returned later in the day, I could see hunters busily repairing their duck blinds for the upcoming season. They used evergreen branches taken from the loblolly pines to camouflage their blinds, which stood precariously on wooden supports out in the marsh. Duck decoys filled their pickup trucks.

According to Cork McGee, the hunters didn't use duck blinds much back in his day. Instead, they simply stalked their prey by crawling. Most people hunted, and the sons learned from their fathers. Cork learned hunting from Charlie Clark, the stepfather of his future wife.

Cork described what it was like to hunt at an early age.

"At aged eleven, I went off and shot a white egret that I stuck down my boots to hide him. I was always off shooting something. I used to shoot and eat shorebirds at aged fifteen. I'd even eat the sanderlings and blue herons. Black duck or pintail was the best tasting though."

This shocked me, as I couldn't fathom how someone could kill, let alone eat, a little sanderling.

Cork made his own decoys for hunting at first; then the plastic ones came in. In 1957, he started taking hunters out for ducks and geese.

"I learned to carve and am self-taught just like Cigar Daisy," he said. "We used to hang out with each other."

Cork's final remarks were rather telling of current times.

"The new youth are not carving these days, so it's sadly dying off."

One morning when I looked out of our living room window, I was surprised to see what appeared to be a mobile wall of marsh reeds traveling past our house. I followed the reeds around the corner to see what it was and realized it was a boat, camouflaged as a duck blind, towed on a trailer to be launched down at the dock. I wondered how successful the mobile blind was, compared to the stand-alone ones.

In October, the marsh was ready for the hunters. It wore its old man's clothes. Earthen hues of various browns and yellows mixed across the landscape, now bathed in much longer shadows beneath soft cerulean skies. Some days the marsh looked like a vast camel hair coat laid flat on the ground, other times the grasses stood straight up or trodden down like the wet fur on a fox's coat. It was a time for dormancy to set in and the return of ice, should we have a harsh winter.

After a few days of rain, we knew the pools on the refuge filled up and brought in more ducks, so it was the perfect time to take a drive around the Wildlife Loop. Hooded and common mergansers (known locally as hairy heads) came in to feed, displaying their familiar head-pumping displays. The common mergansers sported striking white-crowned heads and soft Belgian chocolate sides, with the females showing off their 1980s mullet hair-dos and cocky attitudes. It was now easy to spot the distinct white heads of buffleheads (known locally as dippers) sparkling in the sun as they bobbed up and down in the pools. The name "bufflehead" derives from "buffalo-head," for the male's odd puffy head shape. The first tundra swans of the season provided even bigger splashes of white. The last flocks of tree swallows twittered, stooped, and skimmed above the tops of the grasses like tuna in a feeding frenzy, to scoop up the remaining insects on their way south.

Since there were fewer distractions from the traffic and tourists, we noticed the smallest changes in our backyard. I heard the familiar whistling song from white-throated sparrows that migrated south and fed below our feeders primarily at first and last light when they probably felt safer from hawks and nearby cats. At dusk, they were the janitors of the birdfeeder, cleaning up after everyone else left. The ordinary house sparrows fed earlier in the day.

For my birthday, Debbie gave me a unique bird feeder that came with a motion-activated digital camera. I mounted the camera in a position directly opposite the feed tray, so it aligned with the height of a bird's head. Depending on the height of the bird, I guessed we might get photos of backs, rumps, and all kinds of weird angles. After finally figuring how it worked, I charged the camera, loaded the SD card and hoped for the best. A few days passed and eventually, the birds deemed the feeder safe enough to land on and began feeding. I didn't pay much attention to it for the rest of the week.

On the weekend I unclipped the camera, hooked it up to my computer with the particular card reader I purchased and opened the various folders that popped up. There was nothing there until I opened the last folder. It held 122 pictures. The first few were disappointing, blurred fog-like images, like those fast-forward pictures you see of car headlights going down a highway. I then selected the "show entire images" mode to make it easier, and as I looked across the captures, I noticed a few images with birds' heads or at least partial ones. It was hilarious viewing the half-captured angles. They were not of my favorite birds but portraits of the annoying grackles that frequented our yard. In a few snaps, the camera caught the wonderful iridescent blue-green colors of the grackle's feathers. From a distance, this bird appears black, but when viewed close up, the plumage is actually quite beautiful. The grackle poses were like those I remembered when six of us tried to fit into a photo booth in the train station; everyone crammed in displaying crazy poses.

In my photos, each bird perched awkwardly with a shocked look in their eyes. It was as if the birds actually had expressions on their faces and mastered the selfie. None were remarkable, but it was a fun experiment. I replaced the camera into its holder again and hoped for something more exotic than grackles and sparrows the succeeding time.

A Grackle Selfie

On our frequent birding excursions, we became familiar with where certain species consistently fed around the island. A few Forster's terns, already in their winter plumage, lingered where they perched the entire summer, chattering together, evenly spaced in a line on the bridge over to the refuge. From there they could swoop down on a fish below or hover first and then plunge into the cooler waters. We always chuckled when we observed their lazy man's fishing technique. Terns are agile flyers that few shorebirds can copy, as they tilt from side to side to display their acrobatic skills.

On occasion, egrets and glossy ibis fed in the gut in our backyard. The laughing gulls re-establish their colony every year in the same place close to the causeway. Oystercatchers (known by locals as sea crows) feed on the clam beds out by the Queens Sound Bridge where they wade in the incoming or outgoing tides. When the oysters open their valves underwater, the birds use a unique stabbing motion to thrust their knife-like beaks into the bivalve and prize the shell open.

The watermen also come out to the same place at low tide to harvest the oysters. They work hard, hunched over, up to their knees in dark mud, using their culling hammers, chipping away and dropping oysters into their plastic baskets. It looks like a cold, backbreaking job.

In mid-October I was happily back outside again sitting on our front porch, probably for the last time until spring. I wore long pants and a heavy sweatshirt as opposed to the T-shirt and shorts I wore the entire summer. It was teatime, as the British say, so I enjoyed some homemade blackcurrant jam on whole wheat bread with four British digestive biscuits.

The sky was a robin's egg blue, with not a cloud in sight. A slight breeze wafted over me as I breathed in the fresh, crisp, autumn air. The sun bathed me in its raw sienna light, warm and comfortable, not the full-on baking heat from summer. The slight chop in the bay settled down, as there was no boat traffic. A vastness of rippling water extended out to the marsh, behind which lay the mainland trees in the distance. A lone bald eagle with his stark white head soared high above the bay, his flat wings making wider and wider circles as he meandered south. A rising tide sent a flock of Yellow Legs away from their disappearing sandbar, uttering their distinctive "tew" calls. The annoying homeless summer crickets were still hanging around, blaring away in duets, enjoying their last few weeks of life.

The traffic still passed, but no infernal dying-weasel noises were coming from the rented scooters. People occasionally strolled by, but they were mostly Teaguers now. When the cars didn't pass, the shorebirds and crickets competed for my attention, until the harsh snarl from the exhaust of an annoying truck wiped them both out. A black squirrel made his umpteenth trip along the telephone wires above the house, carrying another precious pecan nut to his hidden winter larder. Suddenly the sun slipped behind J & B's Deli, taking with it the brief warmth it conveyed. The chill took hold, so I headed inside, once again wondering if this were the last time I would sit out.

Activity on the island in November slowed down even more. The only obstacle that prevented me from getting to work was the overweight ducks that crossed Main Street in their droves. They formed one outstretched single-file line and struggled to make it to the other side. Sometimes it took a full three minutes for the duck train to make its way across the street. The timing for getting through the ducks was quite tricky. If I were running late for work, it could be the difference between being on time or five minutes late. Usually, one lead duck stepped off the curb and strode boldly into the street before the others knew he was off. Other ducks watched, dipping and bowing their heads. There was then a split second before another duck followed suit. If they followed quickly, the gap closed for me to pass. Once the flow started, it was an orderly line, like customers queuing for an English bus as they waddled across. They weren't quick, as they had gorged themselves on free Don's Seafood handouts. Many times I waited patiently for the ducks to pass. Some days were worse than others.

It was also the start of the hunting season, when ducks were hunted from around November 12 to 25, and then again from December 13 to January 28. The hunters targeted deer from November 15 to January 3. The sound of gunfire woke us in the early mornings and reoccurred in the evenings. Out in the marsh, it sounded like a popped champagne cork or someone repeatedly slapping a heavy rug against a brick wall.

One day, I noticed two hunters with a truckload of bufflehead ducks. I was curious to learn how to cook them—and if buffleheads even tasted nice. I found out they are the worst tasting type of duck, like most divers who feed on mollusks off the bottom. Some people described them as flying rats that tasted like rubber Wellington boots, not that anyone admitted to actually eating a boot.

"Not many of the ducks taste good unless you like liver," Roe Terry told me. "If you like liver, then you'll like ducks. Even a black duck or a pintail, they are all going to be pretty strong. These puddle ducks eat kelp, minnows, and silversides."

Roe provided advice on how to prepare them.

"The best you can do is fillet the breast off them, cut it in half, stand it up, and cut it again. You want to expose the inside of the blood vessels. I soak them for two days in ice-cold salt water with a tablespoon of vinegar. This pulls out all the blood. Rinse them off, season them with flour, and fry them. They are pretty good, but you have got to get the blood out."

He told me that in Maryland, if you hunt in the fields, the geese and the ducks ate corn and soybeans, so they taste like a farmyard chicken.

We have yet to eat any ducks from the area, so I cannot make any judgments. I was perturbed when I learned that some hunters only cut out the breast meat from the buffleheads, wasting the majority of the duck. It would, therefore, take a large number of buffleheads to make a meal.

I also learned how to tell the difference from a distance between a dabbler duck such as a mallard and a diver like a bufflehead. The position of the legs on dabbler ducks, such as the mallards, is in the center of their bodies, so they fly upward when they take flight. Divers' legs, on the other hand, are positioned further back on their bodies, and therefore they have to skirt along the surface to take flight.

Early in the morning, the duck blinds were now occupied by hunters, some only a hundred yards or so away from the causeway, their heads clearly visible, popped up over the tops of their blinds. If I were a duck, I would see them immediately and fly away. Driving to work, I would think how close my car was to the guns and that one casual swing in the wrong direction could be fatal for one caught in the crossfire. Admittedly, it was an unlikely occurrence, but, having guns so close was very unnerving.

A hunter told me that in the colder months when the weather was freezing, the duck hunting was better. The ducks congregated in the few non-frozen pools around the island and were easier to hunt. When it warmed up, they became harder to hunt, as they spread out again and visited nearby ponds and rivers.

Every evening at around five thirty, we noticed a huge tractor-trailer come past our house and turn down Bunting Road. Two hours later it came back the same way and so became slightly bothersome. We didn't know why it was here until we spotted the extensive lettering on its side that read "NAFCO Wholesale Seafood Distributor." We realized it was picking up the oysters from the Chincoteague Shellfish Company on East Side Drive. We learned that the harvesting of oysters traditionally took place during the months containing the letter "R." This timing is debatable these days as the original rule addressed concerns about the taste and health of shellfish in the summer. The rule also allowed shellfish the time to repopulate.

On our way to the refuge, we often stop for breakfast at the Chincoteague Diner, one of the few places that stay open in the winter. It is always a pleasure to receive a warm welcome from Stephanie, always smiling and cheerful, no matter how crazy her day. On one recent fall visit, she immediately asked if it was the usual tea and coffee with an extra round of toast for me. After breakfast, we took a drive on the Wildlife Loop to see what changes occurred.

How refreshing it was to be outside again without any mosquitos, not a hint of them anywhere. We noticed the taller spartina grasses in the channels stood straight up like the hairs on a deer and the late-flowering white groundsel bushes along the road teemed with newly arrived dark-eyed juncos from up North. Generously sized common loons patrolled the channels like mini battlecruisers, their straight, upright necks like ships funnels, occasionally diving alongside the horned and red-necked grebes. It was a delight to see the marsh harriers again. One glided low above the grasses, tilting its straight wings back and forth, ready to drop onto its next meal. The angled sunlight caught the harriers' unmistakable bright white rumps as well as the iridescent speculums (patches on a bird's wing) of the incoming blue and green-winged teals.

A belted kingfisher flew straight along the gut, announcing its harsh rattlesnake-like alarm calls. It perched on a bare branch, staring down at us with its punk-rock hairstyle prominently on display. It didn't look belted to me; its belly had a brown smudge across it rather than a clear belt. The kingfisher was notoriously difficult to photograph as it flitted about in an agitated state.

Out on the pools, the ducks grew in numbers and fed on the duckweed beneath them. On some days, a couple of hundred northern pintails, known by Teaguers as "spigtails," descended on Snow Goose Pool alone. The ducks looked so demure with their tall, elegant necks with thin white stripes extending up to their chocolate-brown heads. Their nickname is "the greyhounds of the air," which I think befits their sleek appearance. The shoveler ducks gathered, too, with their distinct burnt sienna colored bellies that coincidentally mirrored some of the markings on the Chincoteague ponies. Already a few tundra swans had arrived for the winter. Their numbers would grow to a few hundred by early January. When we turned the engine off and rolled down the car windows, we heard their characteristic bugling calls. Toward the end of the Wildlife Loop, we heard a commotion in a thick stand of phragmites close to the road. Inside the reeds, a considerable flock of blackbirds settled in to roost. A mixture of starlings, cowbirds, grackles, and red-winged blackbirds called in a cacophony of squeaks, croaks, and squawks at various pitch levels.

Later when we visited the beach, huge flocks of double-crested cormorants flew offshore, heading south, and a sizable flotilla of newly arrived surf scoters bobbed up and down between the breakers, occasionally diving to feed. When I looked through my spotting scope, I observed something special: northern gannets. They must have been a mile offshore and looked like fast dropping white flares corkscrewing one after another into the shimmering ocean. Among them were a few unusual birds I hadn't seen before, parasitic jaegers. These birds are pelagic—common to the open sea—and are known as avian pirates because of their habit of stealing food from gulls and terns. It was a shame that both birds weren't closer, so I could watch the show with a front row seat. Flocks of herring gulls and ring-billed gulls frequented the dunes, replacing the omnipresent screeching laughing gulls. The comings and goings of each bird species were very evident that day as the season changed.

The conversation I enjoyed back in August with the couple fishing on my walk to the Coast Guard Station came to mind, as red drum were now caught in the surf. I remembered they told me November and May were the best months for catching the migrating striper and drum. As I was busy, I made a promise to myself to venture out next May to try my luck. I'd wanted to catch a striper for ten years.

Driving home, we noticed a white plastic bag caught on an overhanging branch in one of the guts. It had been there since August and bothered me, as this was such a pristine place. I had hoped the rising tides would have removed it or that some environmentally conscious person would have waded out and grabbed it. We pulled into our driveway to see an enormous flock of well-fed American robins stripping the orange berries from our pyracantha bush until a vigilant sharp-shinned hawk swooped in to catch a robin for dessert.

Many times I am reminded why we chose to move to this land of vast skies and beautiful sunsets. When driving to work across the causeway in the early morning, sometimes a rare, glass-like surface stretches out forever in the bay to a vast horizon, with thin low hanging fog. Hunters duck blinds loom out of the gray, like Conning towers on a submarine surfacing from the deep. I turn the dial on my radio. Handel's *Water Music* plays to serenade me across to the mainland. I look through my car's rear view mirror and watch the round orb of the sun creeping up above the horizon. It forms a perfect circle of deep shimmering fluorescent orange, sometimes overlaid with mauve fingerlike fluted clouds that stretch along its base. It rises so quickly that, three minutes later when I take the bend at Wallops Flight Facility, it is already well above the dark outline of the island, its rays beginning to light the landscape. I look again to my left between a clearing of trees at the visitor center. The whole marsh is lit up in golden greens and brassy yellows to greet the day. I notice the blue sky laced with white contrails. Some days I count at least twenty planes that make these marks, a busy world above me, while I drive alone and at peace through the wakening marsh below. Whatever awaits in my teaching day bears no comparison to its sublime beginning.

The stores and restaurants on the island started to close for the season. The very popular Ray's Shanty closed in October; AJ's and the Jackspot would close in January. Our neighborhood became quieter as most houses were either summer rentals or second homes, and we didn't see our neighbors between Christmas and Easter. Their houses became colder and dark, except for the odd security lights left on a timer. It was a peaceful and restful time after such a busy tourist season. It was so quiet that, at night if I am reading my book alone in the house, the only sound I hear comes from a great horned owl hooting outside after dusk and the occasional churning gurgle from the refrigerator in the kitchen.

The first formation of ice and subsequent freezing of the marsh pools triggered the time when the last remaining shorebirds made their journey south. The willets with their pronounced black-and-white wing flashes and the yellowlegs, who were everywhere since late spring, made their final exits. The town ducks stopped crossing the road as frequently and gathered instead into one group on the grass by the bridge and at the gas station for free handouts. I figured these were the ducks' winter haunts. They dispersed in the spring to their favorite nesting places, like our backyard.

The days became darker and shorter as the temperatures dropped and the ice set more frequently into permanent layers. A more pronounced chill was in the air as I ventured out to collect the mail from our mailbox and smelled the enticing aroma of fried onions wafting over from J & B's Deli. The island gently slipped into dormancy as winter beckoned. Everyone's thoughts turned to the holidays and the unique ways that Teaguers celebrated them.

Here is a poem I wrote, to sum up my experiences of fall on the island.

An Ever Changing Stage

A curtain of golden marsh grass rules
against the blue sky of a Robin's egg.
Wild winds whistle more ducks into the pools
as the tattler calls on his bright yellow legs.

Great wide bands of emptiness yet full of life.
Sulfurous smells from the darkest mud of old.
Rasping crooked herons bent over in their familiar pose
The wind, relentless scouring these men of old.

Ponies play the main roles each day
as crowds come from far away to stay.
The unexpected appearance of a Riptide star
on the beach, in the woods, or near your car.

The stage changes its golden cloak
for the dullest, dormant time descends for all.
Then to be reborn from the stems that winter broke
into the fullest greens for another curtain call.

24

ALONE IN THE WOODS

One evening while I was sitting on the porch watching another magnificent sunset, a large, dark, stocky bird flew swiftly between the houses opposite and out to the dock. It was markedly different from what I had seen before, fast and direct, settling on top of a dock post. I noticed a similar shape in the summer but hadn't paid much attention to it, presuming it was just a green heron because of its stocky size. This time I got a better look and knew it wasn't a heron. I rushed back inside to get my binoculars.

Sure enough, the minute I trained my eyes on the dark silhouette, I could see that two ears stood out prominently above its head against the gunmetal backdrop in the bay. It was a great horned owl. We often heard them in the woods behind our house but had never seen one.

At this time of year, the owls become more active as they court in the run-up to their breeding season. During the night, they detect the slightest difference in voice inflections to know each other. The crooning between them stimulates the breeding cycle. Some say their calls help us fall asleep.

In most Native American tribes, owls are a symbol of death. Hearing owls hoot is considered an unlucky omen. Owls are the subjects of numerous "bogeyman" stories told to warn children to stay inside at night or not cry too much; otherwise, the owls may carry them away. They are another sign of change that takes place on the island. To experience the uniqueness of the owls' world, one has to take a walk in the woods, which becomes a totally altered landscape at this time of year compared to spring.

The tourists had left, and there were, thankfully, no bugs to deal with. This presented the perfect opportunity to listen closely to the woods and marsh. I set off wearing a thick sweater to drive the Wildlife Loop. It was late afternoon, clear and crisp, with no wind. The birds were settling down for the evening. A flock of young tricolored herons gracefully flew off to roost in another location. The rewards of my drive became apparent when I turned the car engine off and simply listened through the window.

Breeze.... Honking.... Croaking.... Breeze again.... Ocean waves in the distance.

I looked out over a vast swathe of sunbathed golden grasses and heard the soothing mellow calls of distant tundra swans and yellowlegs, nothing else. Remembering what Jon Young stated in his book, *What the Robin Knows*, I caused no wake. I sat in my car in total silence.

Absorbing the soothing natural sounds around me, I noticed through my rearview mirror another car creeping toward me. It was some way behind, but I heard it eventually, as its mechanical purr pierced my peaceful world. It crawled by, and after a protracted pause, the sounds from Snow Goose Pool once again engulfed me. I filled my lungs with fresh cold air, listened to the soft, wistful echoes from tundra swans, and felt my body sink deeper into my driver's seat in complete relaxation. I hated turning the key to start the engine, as it immediately brought a sharp re-entry into the sound of manufactured machines that drowned out the real world. At that moment, I thought how I missed walking the Wildlife Loop in the spring before cars were allowed to enter at three o'clock in the afternoon.

I then headed over to the Woodland Trail I had visited many times. The parking lot was empty, and I had the place entirely to myself, which made it perfect for listening for owls. A new sign at the entrance to the trail read, "Watch out for falling trees and branches." I was about to understand why they erected the sign.

The Assateague Refuge birding guide lists six species of owl on the island, so I decided to seek them out. A few days before my walk, I did some research. A question puzzled me. Why did I hear owls so clearly from far away on cold nights? I learned that at night, temperature inversions occurred, so dense cold air sank to the ground and the warmer air, close to the Earth's surface, rose. The warm air trapped the colder air and sound waves near the ground, so when the owls hooted at dusk, the sound waves trapped below the warm air were forced to travel horizontally over a much greater distance than usual. This explained why I could always hear people from a distance coming down the trails in the spring.

The Woodland Trail consisted of a tarmac pathway that absorbed most of the sound coming from my feet. It was relatively silent, but I was careful to watch out for bike riders who sometimes came up quickly from behind. I immediately noticed the colors and textures of the dried grasses on the sides of the pathway. The tall dog fennel's soft puffy tops reminded me of the plumes on horses that pulled old-fashioned funeral carriages. Broomsedge stood out with its yellow, straw-like rusted clumps. The delicate miniature white flowers of sweet everlasting grew in patches here and there to provide variety among the grasses. The sky reminded me of the metallic, iridescent, pearlescent shimmer inside a freshly shucked oyster shell.

As I entered the woods, I left the grasses behind, and from nearby bushes, I heard sharp *"chink"* calls coming from white-throated sparrows and juncos as they found suitable branches to sleep on for the night. They communicated with each other: *Hi John! I am over here. Where are you? Are you ok over there?* Their calls interspersed with those from towhees issuing their loud, distinctive, two-parted, rising *"chewink"*, or as some would say *drink-your-tea!* which lasted about one second. Then the brown thrashers chimed in from the low bushes with their grunting *"tschuck"* calls.

Earlier in spring, I hadn't noticed how damaged the woods were by pine bark beetles and storms because an immense amount of greenery had grown up so quickly to conceal the discarded limbs and stripped trunks. Now, I could see many dead pines looming scarily above me. Some had split open, snapped like matches, revealing their growth history. The aging of the trees made me think of my own mortality. Finding full stands of unaffected pines was not easy at first. The remaining trees rested from this year's ravaging, having stored enough water and sugars in their cells ready for the following spring.

The loblolly pine is the second most common species of tree in the United States, after the red maple. Pine is plentiful and useful but considered a cheap timber compared to oak, cedar, and walnut. The very name is scorned as the scent from household cleaners and candles.

I passed among trees standing utterly still, like statues in a living museum where no leaf dared to fall. Their trunks rose high into the sky, with stretched out finger-like silhouettes, dark and imposing. Their irregular gnawed branches spun off in random directions. Some loblolly pines rose over a hundred feet into the air like white marble columns, stripped of every needle and bark, and naked. Their outer armor, fragments of their bark, lay discarded and lodged in young pines and thorn bushes. It was a somber sight, and I wondered how they supported themselves. A moderate wind would surely bring many more down.

I spied what looked like a figure walking further up the pathway, only to realize when I got closer that it was the bleached white trunk of a fallen tree. At one point, I spied a white-tailed deer stick its head out further up the path. A nervous herd followed, one behind the other, cautiously sniffing the cool air and treading softly. They were shocked to see me, a man alone in the woods at this time of day. They bolted and bounded back into the brush, crashing about randomly in the understory as they retreated further into the safety of the woods.

The path cut through a thick growth of phragmites reeds. The sounds of sparrows came from either side of me and reached a crescendo as I moved deeper into the woods and neared their roosting spot. Numerous white-crowned and white-throated sparrows hopped about in front of me as if to lead me away. It was if a thousand sparrows were on the move, calling, twitching, and scraping together in the reeds.

Despite the safety of my walk on the terra firma pathway, I did have one embarrassing mishap. There came from the brush a unique tacking call further up the path. I was inquisitive and wondered what bird or animal was making it. Even though the light was fading, I noticed a fallen tree trunk that offered me convenient access to the brush. Stepping up onto the trunk gave me a better vantage point to investigate the source of the sound. I cautiously placed my right foot onto the trunk and immediately felt it roll, so I hesitated. Placing one foot in front of the other, I slowly edged along it carefully. The sharp tacking sound came again, much closer, so I leaned forward slightly to peer into the brush. As I did, my back foot found some inconvenient slippery fungus. I fell "ass about face," as the saying goes in England, toppling back into a nasty thorn bush.

Well, you can imagine the unmentionable curse words that followed thereafter, when I hollered aloud to myself in the woods. I added my own sounds to the evening air for the wildlife to decipher. Whatever bird or creature called immediately took off, and no doubt giggled its head off. As I grappled with the thorns to free myself, I remembered the well-known phrase, "If a tree falls in a forest, and no one is around to hear it, does it make a sound?" Well, if asked the same question, but I replaced the tree with a man falling into a bush, the answer would be an emphatic yes—and it hurt, too. Having extracted myself from the tangle of the Triffids, I was relieved to get back on the pathway.

As I turned a corner, the arboreal giants on either side of the pathway stretched thin by moonlight. The moon rose above me like a polished broken button glowing in the sky. It was in its waxing phase, so more than half of it showed. The stars came out one by one to greet me. They shone like a million sparkling diamonds everywhere. More and more appeared every time I gazed up. We are so far away from any cities that our view of the night sky is incredible. I felt caught between the vastness of the galaxy above and the history of the island beneath my feet. The moon became more prominent as I made my way further into the woods. I noticed my shadow cast across the path. The air felt cool and crisp on my face, with a slight breeze brushing my cheek. The temperatures plummeted quickly as the cold air sealed in the warmer air radiating from the woods. This created the perfect conditions for owl listening. I sensed how noisy I was, even though I was on the path. When my sneaker caught a dried leaf, the sound ricocheted across the woods. Its awful tearing scrape on the tarmac pierced the silence around me. Even a sizable maple leaf that fell from a nearby tree clattered down like tin foil onto the path. It reminded me of a line from the poet John Clare,

The woods in silence they speak happiness beyond the reach of books.

A satellite or plane—I am not sure which—crossed above me with its flashing light. I heard what sounded like a door shutting in the distance that told me the hunters were still out on the bay.

I was taken aback to hear an occasional spring peeper call faintly from somewhere out in the woods. I read later this does occur in the fall, and amphibian researchers debate the reasons for it. Some say the length of daylight connects to their calls, as fall and spring have similar photoperiods. Others think autumn peeps are merely infant males testing out their calls before freezing up for the winter.

As darkness came, as if they were on a timer, the birdcalls petered out; the forms of bushes and trees became less defined, except for the dark tracery of the bare trees that joined the fading golden sky. There followed a period of rustling and jostling in the undergrowth. I became totally at ease with the remoteness and slowness of my twilight walk that took me away temporarily from a fast world devoid of patience. My senses became acute, my ears wired, and I noticed the tiniest movement around me. I moved from the known visible world to the realm of secretive creatures that moved in shadows.

I spotted what appeared to be a flashlight blinking ahead of me. It blinked twice, and I wondered who else was out in the woods. It came from inside the woods and wasn't someone on the pathway. It bothered me when it blinked twice again, but it stayed at a steady distance. As I turned a corner, space opened up before me on the horizon. Much to my relief, I saw that the blinking light was the lighthouse with its strong refracting light.

I was now deep in the woods. Some eerie sounds came from the weakened remnants of dead trees, creaking at every push the breeze gave them, their boughs rubbing against each other. Occasionally, a great limb squeaked, cracked, and then collapsed with a heavy thud that shook the ground. I considered watching long enough to see a tree fall, but none did. There was a rotting, earthy smell in the chilly air, the tang of decaying leaf mold like wood smoke from a fire or overripe fruit. The woods became still, with only the stir of awakening nighttime animals rooting in the underbrush and a few hostile screeches from afar, as nocturnal animals emerged for their nightly patrols. I stopped when a soft, whirring sound suddenly approached overhead. A flock of ducks flew agonizingly close above the canopy, their wings in unison, like a well-oiled, high-pitched sewing machine. Something moved me, a certain something, an indescribable air about where I stood that spelled enchantment. The tall skeleton-like trees stood silently with me.

The well-known Scottish writer W.H. Murray wrote:

In short withdrawals from the world, there is to be had unfailing refreshment. When his spirit is burdened or lightened, the natural movement of a man's heart is to lift upward, and this is most readily done in the wild, for there it is easy to be still.

Here I was, still and enlightened, and exactly when that silence was pervasive, the first owl hooted from way back in the woods. Each species sounded a unique call, but I wasn't familiar with them yet, except for the only one I recognized, the distinctive classical hooting of the great horned owl, nature's heartbeat in the night. They were the masters of the woods at this time of year because their sight and hearing put them in command of the dark. The owl's senses can detect the slightest movement of a mouse under the leaves. Through their superior eyes, they watched my every move as I stepped into their world.

The subsequent call came from an eastern screech owl, which sounded similar to a horse on helium. The owl trilled from a tree not that far from the path, so I waited for another.

To see the owls, I had modified a flashlight, placing a red filter over the end. Owls react more naturally to red light; it doesn't scare them as much since their eyes are not sensitive to red. To the owls, it appears very dim. Some owl watchers even take tape-recorded owl sounds with them to attract the birds.

The screech owl called again, so I readied my flashlight to illuminate an enormous tree roughly eight yards from the pathway. When I heard the whinnying horse call, I turned on the flashlight, and slowly moved the red beam up the trunk. I paused briefly at a cleft in the tree, where I picked out two yellow eyes peering down at me, surrounded by a stocky ball of rusty feathers. The owl wasn't grand in the slightest, approximately the size of an American robin with chocolate and copper feathers, smooth like the round balls of Lindt truffles. His face was curious, and similar in shape to a concave satellite dish. For some reason, I expected him larger, given his voluminous call. I heard other owls calling back in the woods, so I switched the flashlight off, left him to his nightly business, and moved on.

There are three other species resident in the woods, but I didn't hear them that night—the long-eared owl, the short-eared owl, and the barn owl. Snowy owls occasionally visited the beach areas during the winter, but seldom visited the woodland. I read that saw-whet owls overwintered on Assateague, but I didn't hear them that evening.

Immersing myself into the silent nighttime world of owls was exhilarating. My hearing gradually grew sharper and more tuned in acutely, so any slight rustle in the understory or a remote branch snap was magnified. I found it exhilarating and rejuvenating to be out alone at this time of year, with no one around to bother me. In fact, I was the noisiest life out that evening. The landscape was calm and gentle. The woods had emptied themselves of songbirds, warblers, and people, and one could see further at this time of year. The thick green foliage from spring's growth was long gone, leaving the bare skeletal outlines of bushes and trees exposed to the bitter wind. The human onslaught dissipated, and the silence was total except for the nocturnal creatures.

As I returned to my car, a gigantic snap drew my attention further in the woods. The wind picked up, and a weakened tree fell, having succumbed at last. A comforting sound came from Swan Cove Pool beyond the woods. *Were they back?* I wondered. The call was familiar. I had heard it before—a voluminous call like thousands of barking hounds that echoed across the sky.

The snow geese flew south as they did every year. They would remain with us for winter and provide a fantastic spectacle in their large flock near the beach. Over the years their numbers have fallen, caused by the increase in temperatures. They now winter further north of us. We used to sometimes see nearly ten thousand birds when we visited in the early 2000s.

Above the geese calls, the scary, high-pitched bugle of a rutting Sitka deer in the distance abruptly punctuated the air. It was haunting and sounded like a woman screaming in pain, which sent a chill through me. I knew what this call was, but anyone else hearing it might be concerned about what occurred out there.

I drove home relaxed and calmed from my nighttime excursion and familiar with the unique sounds of the woods. Those who only go out in the day see only half the picture. They are untested on their ability to withstand a walk at dusk, which offers a remarkably different experience. I later came across a German word that described my experience accurately. *Waldeinsamkeit* means a sense of solitude, being alone in the woods, and a connectedness to nature.

WINTER

25

CHRISTMAS BY THE SEA

Christmas Decorations in Robert Reed Park

The town decorated for Christmas around November 12 by attaching festive lanterns to the utility poles along the streets. Each major street on the island had themed lighting. Maddox Boulevard displayed the standard Christmas symbols such as bells, boxed gifts, snowmen, Christmas trees, and stockings. Religious icons such as praying angels, prayer hands, a harp, and candles decorated Church Street. Willow Street presented the favorite beach icons—shells, seahorses, starfish, and two animated mermaids that jiggled amusingly when we passed them. A garland of greenery wrapped every utility pole in the central part of town, with traditional white lanterns attached to each that swayed in the breeze.

Christmas by the Sea is a series of holiday events beginning just after Thanksgiving and running through New Year's Day. The island welcomes visitors with the words "Merry Christmas from Chincoteague" written on two giant red Christmas balls placed on either side of the main bridge.

Debbie and I find it interesting that the town uses the word Christmas because, in New Jersey where we both lived before, people commonly say, "Happy Holidays." When talking to Christians, most people say, "Merry Christmas," but if you are speaking to those who are not Christian, then "Happy Holidays" is appropriate. Both greetings work for me. In a mixed group, people tend to say "Happy Holidays," to include everyone. We live in an interfaith nation, a country where we respect a full range of religious faiths, as well as those who in increasing numbers profess no religious affiliation to any organized religion.

Tall rectangular red banners with the Christmas by the Sea logo hung on straight horizontal arms attached to each utility pole. Garlands neatly twirled around black wrought iron street lamps, with a tidy red bow at the top. Town employees spent a lot of time decorating the downtown, imparting a nostalgic mood to the island, with a slight hint of Dickens in the décor.

Above its building, the popular Bill's Seafood, one of the best-known restaurants, featured a large lighted display of Santa raising a martini cocktail in his left hand. Instead of reindeer pulling his sleigh, two animated lobsters drove it, and their antennas flipped up and down. Given the town's conservative religious views, it surprised me that Bill's got away with Santa holding a cocktail glass, but the restaurant has been here for some time, and the owners do a lot for the community. Bill's Seafood offered a prize of a one-hundred-dollar gift certificate to the person who could guess the number of light bulbs in their Christmas display.

The island Christmas festivities started with the tree lighting ceremony and the arrival of Santa at Robert Reed Park at five in the evening on the Saturday after Thanksgiving. It was a joyous opportunity for visitors and locals to partake in a very Chincoteague hometown experience.

Four giant white Adirondack chairs, known as the Love Chairs, stood on a raised platform on the lawn at the far end of the park. Each chair is ten feet tall, weighs more than five hundred pounds, and displays a single letter to spell out the word LOVE. On this night, a green holiday wreath circled the letter O, and a heart symbol replaced the letter V.

Given that Chincoteague is supposedly the happiest island in Virginia, and Virginia has declared itself the state for lovers, these chairs are very popular. Everyone takes photographs of friends or loved ones sitting on them. To get a picture of empty chairs, with no one on them, one must be there early morning or mid-day when everyone enjoys other island activities. At the tree lighting ceremony, the Adirondack chairs rarely emptied. Children and families soaked up the Christmas atmosphere and mobbed them.

We bundled up for the tree lighting ceremony against the cold winds whisking off the bay. The evening began with a performance by the Chincoteague Pony Drill Team. Five teenage girls dressed in their attractive white puffer jackets with red scarves and black riding hats mounted their Chincoteague ponies, ready to trot into the park to entertain the crowd. A red blanket with a snowflake design decked each pony. Around the ponies' necks and legs were festive, red and white Christmas lights. The drill team trotted into a makeshift arena roped off around the gigantic Christmas tree in the center of the park. The lead rider carried the American flag, while a woman sang the national anthem from the steps of the library. The crowd fell silent and listened to her beautiful booming voice as the ponies circled the Christmas tree. After she finished, the drill team performed their routine, which comprised various interweaving maneuvers around the tree. At the end of the performance, each pony placed its front legs up on a short podium in front of the crowd; an impressive display met by huge applause.

The master of ceremonies told the crowd the proceeds from the hot chocolate sales would go to Operation We Care – a Delmarva group that sent six hundred care packages to deployed US soldiers around the world.

After the announcements, the crowd stepped over the temporary roping, cordoned off for the pony drill team, and filled the space around the tree in the center. Someone amusingly remarked they felt like the Whos from *"How The Grinch Stole Christmas"* being told to come into "Who Square" to sing a Merry Christmas song. We listened to a few carols from the Chincoteague Elementary School Chorus after which the crowd was encouraged to sing a carol that isn't one of my favorites, "Santa Claus is Coming to Town." The atmosphere was fun and lighthearted as overexcited children rushed around enjoying the occasion.

Suddenly, the wail from a fire engine reverberated down the street. The islanders knew exactly what that meant—Santa was coming! Children raced to find a vantage point on the library steps. Multicolored lights bounced off the buildings along Main Street, heralding the arrival of jolly old St. Nick. Santa appeared on the Chincoteague fire engine with his lead elf, Miss Chincoteague. The crowd cheered and clapped as he stepped down from the engine and made his way through a path of high fives to the library steps. There, he addressed the crowd and promised to bring snow. As he announced the words, "I promise to bring snow," two giant snow machines positioned on the sides of the audience burst into action, catapulting fake biodegradable snowflakes high into the air and over the crowd. At the same time, the tree lights switched on, and people jumped in the air, cheering and taking photos. It was just as Dr. Seuss's Whos would have loved it—a jubilant and fun time.

Once the crowd thinned out, a group of us made our way over to the Island Theatre, to watch a free showing of the iconic *It's a Wonderful Life*. Every year this movie opens the Christmas By the Sea season to get everyone in the mood for the holidays. This is a popular film, especially when shown on a widescreen. The audience packed inside the theater, where Santa made a second appearance, strolling down the aisle and wishing everyone a Merry Christmas. For the children who hadn't seen him on the library steps earlier, it was a pleasant surprise.

The movie not only amplified the visuals, but the enormous screen drove the touching, emotional plot forward, leaving everyone with the impression they actually experienced it firsthand. We noticed objects and scenery we had not seen before on a TV screen. We felt we were there in the movie with great acting, and none of the modern CGI (computer graphics) we have these days. While the movie played, sensing the responses of others comforted us, especially when they reacted the same way we did.

A weekend later, the pre-Christmas events presented the Homes for the Holidays tour, which offered an opportunity to check out the history and charm of homes on the island. Debbie and I picked up our tickets, a map of the home locations, and a program at the first property. Then we looked for the red numbered stars located on posts outside each property. The first place we visited was not a home in the least, but the recently built Marina Bay Hotel, which looked like any massive chain hotel, so we were skeptical at first. Stepping inside, we were pleasantly amazed at the tasteful decoration that fitted in with the Chincoteague landscape. The foyer was decorated in a nautical theme with hanging ropes and two weathered wooden oars retrieved from a ship's lifeboat, tastefully positioned. The turquoise ocean color walls and sand-colored curtains kept with the island beach theme. Custom carpeting depicting a rough map of the Eastern Shore ran throughout the hallways.

Our second stop was a cute and cozy waterman's home on Main Street. The miniature rooms, sloped ceilings, and generous wood trim took us back in time.

Afterward, we drove to view a ranch style home on one of the back streets north of town. The exterior gave us a hint of what we were about to experience. Its covered outside porch was festooned with gaudy Christmas decorations. When we entered, the owners proudly proclaimed that they started decorating back in October. I can only describe the décor as one of Christmas overload or Christmas on steroids, for every square inch of the home displayed what I call kitschy "Made in China" Christmas decorations. Even the walls behind the ornaments were painted green and red, so after the tour when they removed everything, they still lived with the insipid Christmas colors. It was the kind of place kids love, but if I woke up there every day, I'd be driven mad begging for plain walls. The owners were very welcoming, however, and very hospitable, having made such an enormous effort to decorate their house invitingly for everyone. It simply wasn't our taste.

After recovering from seeing every color in the rainbow, we visited a wonderfully restored Victorian home tucked away down a gravel back road. One of my art students, Robin, owned the house. She was a decorator and showed off her eclectic taste using soft beach colors in a classy and well-coordinated way. Robin greeted us with homemade starfish-shaped cookies and led us into a cozy living room that featured a warm, glowing gas fire. Before we left, she gave us some sand dollars she gathered from the beach at Wallops Island. Her husband remarked, "The beach at Wallops has a much gentler slope than here on Chincoteague Island, so the sand dollars are mostly washed ashore intact."

At every home we visited, the hosts were overly generous, serving hot apple cider and cookies. We were so full after the first two visits that we couldn't consume anymore. After Robin's home, we visited another restored Victorian home at the end of yet another lane off the beaten track, this time looking out into Oyster Bay. This charming residence immediately offered up its history and character. An unusual brass entrance knocker in the shape of a salmon hung on the door. We had to lift the salmon's tail and slap it down to announce our presence. To the side of the property stood a historic shed, recently donated to the island museum, that was once used by Miles Hancock, a famous Chincoteague decoy carver. When we entered the home, we immediately felt the warmth generated by a log-burning stove that kicked out a lot of heat. The gorgeous, tilted, heart pine floors, steep and narrow stairs, and lower ceilings typical of the Victorian period enthralled us.

After lingering too long, reluctant to leave the warm coziness from the stove, we moved on to experience a stark contrast. Nothing could have prepared us for the change we encountered in a modern multi-level home raised on stilts. When we pressed the doorbell, a tall, scary man answering the door startled us with his Slavic accent. He reminded me of Jaws, the character with the steel teeth in the James Bond movie *The Spy Who Loved Me*. We entered a room very metallic in nature, passing a black drum set and an electric guitar standing in the corner. Shiny gold-colored cushions were strewn across a sofa, and jet-black drapes covered the windows. I felt transported backstage to a Metallica concert or a Bond movie set—I wasn't sure which. We took the stairs up to where the black theme continued with a black bathroom and a jet-black shower and hot tub. Then we entered the master bedroom where, in the middle stood what appeared to be the Tardis from Dr. Who, but in fact was a strange looking tanning machine. Someone behind us made our small group laugh by announcing it was an orgasmatron.

Exploring the house further, we saw coin-infested Christmas trees dotted everywhere. Someone quietly remarked that the home was like a lavish Barbie world and somewhat plastic. Attached to the ceiling in every room hung the spookiest single bladed heavy-duty ceiling fans I have ever seen. The one-armed choppers looked like airborne guillotines to me—just plain dangerous.

When we stepped outside, not quite sure which film set we had just exited, the weirdness continued outside the house. Instead of seeing lit up reindeer on the lawn, hideous-faced Huskie dogs loomed at us, pulling some sleighs. We weren't quite sure what to make of the home except to walk away, and once safely back in our car, we burst out laughing.

The last tour stop was off the island to see, coincidentally, a friend's home. Bill and Joe spent weeks decorating their four thousand square foot home at Corbin Hall, a private gated community. A "Warm Hands and Warm Hearts Giving Tree" for needy children greeted us at the front of the property. Bill and Joe had asked visitors to donate mittens, gloves, or hats and hang them on the tree. The house was so massive that Bill and Joe had enlisted the help of friends to guide tours throughout the many themed rooms. First, we saw the Seattle Seahawks room decorated in the team's colors, then an Asian room, a country room, and lastly a giant scary Santa located around a corner. Of course, Bill and Joe served wonderful snacks and appetizers for everyone to enjoy. We told Bill about some of the homes we visited and the weird interpretations of festive décor we experienced.

The holiday home tour was far from traditional and made for an interesting day getting to know the unrelated hidden places on the island.

That evening, we visited our friends, Lin and Sam, at Miss Molly's Bed and Breakfast in town to watch the Old-Fashioned Chincoteague Christmas Parade from the inn's front porch at seven o'clock. Marguerite Henry stayed at Miss Molly's Inn to write her book *Misty of Chincoteague*, which made the island famous. The Marguerite Henry room can be seen in the inn.

The weather was damp and chilly, but fortunately, it was a dry night for the annual holiday parade. Like the carnival in July, it brought out most of the locals and drew many visitors from off island. A band named the Saltmarsh Ramblers kicked off the pre-parade celebrations at six o'clock.

It was great to see Lin and Sam, as they had been very generous and supportive to us over the years. We talked and joked in their kitchen, where Lin was busily preparing a range of tasty appetizers and drinks. We filled our glasses with wine and went out on their front porch, where we sat in white wooden rocking chairs, ready for the parade. The damp air made the chairs feel slippery and slightly wet with dew. We rocked them back and forth to stay warm.

The cold penetrated our bones, and the parade hadn't started yet. On the opposite side of the street, a woman sat motionless in a beach chair enveloped in dull-colored blankets that formed a rippling mass of folds reaching down to the sidewalk. Every so often, the pile of blankets moved, and her small head appeared out of the top with an arm extended from the side clutching a soda. She wore so many layers around her that she looked like Jabba the Hutt from *Star Wars*.

Fishing boats unloaded on the town dock behind Miss Molly's Inn. The air was heavy with the smell of fish, which the breeze brought directly over to us. Combined with the occasional waft of cigarette smoke coming from those watching below us on the street, it made for an unusual olfactory treat.

We ventured back into the cozy rear kitchen of the inn to refill our wine glasses. Lin and Sam write down the names of their guests on a chalkboard in the kitchen, so they remember who stays in each room. Lin was chatting, and I was looking over the board when I burst out laughing.

"Hey," I said to Lin, "I don't see Top Gear written on your board!"

When Debbie and I used to stay at the inn, they always scribbled me down as "Top Gear." Sam thought I looked like Jeremy Clarkson, who hosted the well-known British TV series called *Top Gear*. Sam often called me "Top Gear" in his joking way. It was a fun memory of some wonderful stays with them.

This was our first Christmas parade on the island, and we didn't know what to expect. The crowd was similar to those at the carnival grounds in the summer, but with more clothes on and definitely a lot more camo. What followed was very hometown and true to the island's nature, a somewhat slower parade than I saw elsewhere.

A siren on a fire truck signaled the start. Two police cars drove slowly side by side down the street. From their car trunks, police officers threw candy into the crowd. A color guard followed, marching solemnly.

Next, a stream of Chincoteague fire trucks blasted their horns and flashed their lights, which got everyone's attention. In fact, just about every fire company on the Eastern Shore participated, so heaven forbid if there was a fire elsewhere while it was in progress. At one point when the parade halted, exhaust fumes and smog filled the air from all the fire engines, sports cars, and motorbikes.

One of the only high school marching bands to participate was from the school where I teach, so I was able to recognize and wave to some of my students. A few uniquely decorated boats passed by, which one wouldn't see in the mainland parades. There was a contest for the best floats in various categories, such as the best pony drill team. I was told no one really tried to compete, as Lowe's Home Improvement store always won. Apparently, they gained an unfair advantage because they sold the decorations. Lowe's used one of their enormous flatbed delivery trucks to create a magnificent Christmas scene with Santa and his reindeer. The theme for the parade was "old fashioned," but to me, the huge flatbed truck didn't quite fit that.

The parade participants threw so much candy into the crowds from their floats that the kid in front of me was able to fill an entire plastic grocery bag. Candy showered up onto Miss Molly's porch, so I reached down and picked up a few pieces of Tootsie Roll for the kids. When I bent down, I noticed a drain cover on the street with the letters "Made in India" stamped on it. *How farcical was that given where we are located*, I thought.

The parade continued with an eclectic mix of Chincoteague businesses, including the cleanest yellow cement truck ever, and three equestrian drill teams, which were a welcome change from all the vehicles. Everyone constantly shouted "Merry Christmas!" as more candy hit the road like a rain shower. The organizers told parade participants to throw it downward, or it became a projectile for the eyes, but I guess some didn't listen.

Each town from the mainland showed off its beauty queen, proudly perched atop a colorful snazzy sports car. Miss Chincoteague and Little Miss Chincoteague drove by, giving vigorous waves with gleaming smiles. Unfortunately, Miss Bloxham's sports car broke down, so they pushed her to the side of the road where she sat looking rather unimpressed.

It was like many American hometown parades, with plenty of locals who knew each other and families strung out along the parade route. In the end, Santa appeared with his elves on top of a fire engine, energetically waving to everyone.

After it was over, Debbie and I left the inn and sauntered back through town to our parked car. We were horrified to see the sidewalks littered with trash, especially around Don's Seafood. We found it disgusting to see such behavior in such a beautiful place. Did the spectators really expect the town to clean everything up? People had dropped their fast food containers, drink cartons, and candy wrappers from the parade onto the pavement and throughout the downtown area.

To take our minds off the appalling litter, we stopped in to talk with Jane and Jon at Sundial Books, as they stayed open late. They always extended a warm welcome, and their store was a cozy place for an entertaining chat that inevitably revealed the recent news on the island. Jon and Jane told us they enjoyed a profitable evening with plenty of buyers in the store. They saw many types of people come and go and always maintained a pleasant and positive disposition, even if some customers bothered them on occasion.

I discussed the littering with Jon, and we somehow got onto the subject of recycling pick up. Many people would be willing to pay for recycling pick up on the island, something we routinely did in our former lives in New Jersey. On an island as beautiful as Chincoteague, this is important, especially in populated places such as the hotels and businesses along Maddox Boulevard. Many of the visitors certainly are used to recycling in their communities.

During the Christmas period, more stores and restaurants closed and their varied hours made it impossible to predict which would be open. The tourist T-shirt shops were the first to shorten their hours.

At the Chincoteague Cultural Alliance Christmas Party, we were fortunate to get to know more of the Teaguers. We met Terry Howard and his wife Judy, both of whom grew up on the island. They joined our table, and an enthralling conversation ensued. They treated us to their experience of what it was like to live on the island many years ago. Somehow, we got onto the subject of holiday gift giving, and they told us many years back people bought a "Spider" as a gift. I was immediately confused, thinking this was literally an insect, but a Spider was a rustic and weathered cast iron pan that fitted onto a cradle, whose legs spread out over a fire.

"The spider was originally only the legs part," Terry told us, "but it became known as the pan that fits on top as well."

"We used to live in a converted chicken house that was very rough and yet we seldom complained about it," Judy explained.

When I asked Terry about the Teaguer dialect, he replied, "The building of the causeway has led to the erosion of the original language of the island as it brought new people here, and with them unfamiliar ideas as well."

I told them about a visit I made many years ago to Smith Island and how I understood the islanders' accent. It was close to the Cornwall dialect that I knew from the UK, or pirate talk as some might jokingly say. Consequently, I could understand the Teaguers way of speaking.

Terry gave us a snippet of his own history

"I was born at my home on the island in 1938 at a cost of $35, which was charged by the doctor for me and my twin brother. The midwives were known as 'grannie women' back in those days."

He told us he worked hard and had to be resourceful to make ends meet by selling clams and blackberries. He also told us he didn't like the term Come'ere.

"People make a choice to come here and shouldn't be labeled as such," he firmly stated,

I am not sure everyone shares his view though, as there is still quite a bit of distrust of the Come'eres. I witnessed the same thing back in Wales when English people started to buy homes in Wales because they had more money. Some of the locals didn't care for them back there either.

It was a pleasure to meet genuine, laid back, plain folk who undoubtedly lived through a rough upbringing, and yet they knew how to get on with life and didn't complain. Their life was simple and yet abundant in so many ways that some people can't understand today. Terry and Judy don't focus on or feel distracted by material possessions.

The following day Debbie and I put up our simple plain white Christmas lights on the outside gutters and bought one of the last Douglas fir trees at Lowe's for eighteen dollars. It smelled heavenly when we brought it inside the house. We used traditional red bows with garlands for the front steps and placed a floodlight on the front lawn to illuminate the front of the house. We then took a drive to see the Christmas lights around the island. Friends recommended we visit the home of

Steve Potts, the owner of Bill's Seafood Restaurant. His home was located on East Side drive and referred to as "Christmas Manor." When we arrived, we were not disappointed. An impressive nativity scene laid out on the lawn, and numerous illuminated elves climbed up the balconies outside. The lights shone like a landing strip for miles. The house down from us on Bunting Road also decorated every holiday and had an outstanding display that took forever to arrange.

Debbie and I drove off the island to get our last minute supplies and gifts so we could stay at the house over Christmas and not have to go anywhere. It was a much-needed quiet break. I prepared a large log fire in our front living room, ready to enjoy during the peace of the holiday.

One evening close to Christmas, a Chincoteague fire truck drove around the southern end of the island with Santa and his elves illuminated on the top. You knew it was the Santa engine as it approached our street. It gave a drawn-out wistful blast of its horn, very different from the usual emergency sound. The fire engine slowly cruised by with lights blaring. Santa waved to the excited kids who dashed out to see him. He later made a special trip to the island YMCA to say hello to Barbara Walker. That's just how it is on the island.

There were virtually no neighbors around us at this time of year. We had not even seen Joe, who lived two doors up. Our house, with its numerous lights and decorations, stood out on the corner. Debbie baked two of my favorite foods, hazelnut bread and blueberry crisp. I made a batch of homemade Glühwein, a German mulled wine, which turned out well, considering it was my first attempt.

On Christmas Eve, it was so quiet it felt like there was no one living on the island. Cars didn't pass our house regularly as they used to, and we felt a strange aloneness like we were marooned on a distant, isolated planet. The fact that we didn't have a TV accentuated the sensation of being out of touch, but that was what we preferred.

That evening, we drove off the island to attend service at Emmanuel Episcopal Church, the whitewashed wooden country church in the middle of nowhere. When we reached the mainland, the country road leading to the church appeared swaddled in a veil of poltergeist-white fog, clinging to and enrobing everything it could. The fog drifted and ghosted, glided and dangled in pockets around our car, snagging and snaring every ditch and tree without mercy. Although it looked ethereal, delicate and fragile, it packed a punch far above its weightlessness. It writhed and coiled in the delight of the holiday, its ghostly scarves wrapping the plowed fields either side of us in a maze of mist. The fog was so dense that we couldn't see what lay ahead, even though we knew the road, so we took it very slowly until we arrived at the church.

Christmas magic was in the air. It was a cozy, simple Christmas service, mostly local families with visitors from out of town. The church had been tastefully decorated with a huge Christmas tree set up in one corner, adorned with tasteful simple white ornaments. Sprigs of holly with bright red berries hung from the rustic wrought iron chandeliers. Looping green garlands with white candlelights decorated the sidewalls. Poinsettias adorned the altar, adding a crimson splash of color up front. During communion, we drank from the hugest chalice I can ever recall, a historical cup connected to Queen Anne that apparently told an interesting history. The woman behind us sang every hymn loudly, a line in front of everyone else, which was rather amusing. At the end of the service, we proceeded by candlelight out of the church singing Silent Night, and then everyone gathered outside for a final blessing. It was a pleasure to see two of my students from school, Becky and Jackie.

After the festive service, we headed home in the dense fog once again. Leaving the mainland, we turned to head along the causeway toward the island. We observed nothing except the road ahead, barely fifteen yards visible, with nothing either side of us. It felt like we were driving into a wall of fog and could drive off into the bay at any moment. During the four minutes it took to cross the causeway, we could see no lights until we arrived at the island.

Out of the fog, the traffic lights appeared first on the bridge, followed by the red logo of the Island Resort. Driving through downtown moments later, we found it totally deserted, like a scene from a science fiction movie or a deserted western town. I expected to see tumbleweeds rolling down the street. The familiar everyday stores looked mysterious, hiding, looming out at us in their whitened haze at the last minute, like images from some half-forgotten dream. We felt entombed and locked in a heavy gray blanket. It was as if we lived in central Siberia surrounded by our own stars and moon all to ourselves on the island.

Once home, we were in a festive mood, so we watched *The Christmas Story* on our DIY big screen TV via our computer and projector. It felt odd that no cars passed our house, nothing but total silence and peace, as the fog swirled around the street lamp.

The fog comes in
on little cat feet.
It sits looking
over harbor and city
on silent haunches
and then moves on.
- Carl Sandburg, 1916

We awoke on Christmas day to bright and sunny conditions with no wind and forty-six degrees, so we agreed to embark on a picnic out at the beach, a tradition we have enjoyed every year since. After a leisurely morning hanging around the house and opening our gifts to each other, we headed out.

A few days back, one of the rangers at the refuge posted some photos of a snowy owl that recently arrived on the beach. This was an exciting occurrence at Chincoteague since snowy owls didn't visit often. When their principal food, lemmings ran low, snowy owls migrated south along the northeast coast for the winter, returning north again in March. I had never seen one, but I read they were the largest of the owls, looked very ghostlike, with a face like a cat with bright yellow eyes. They are diurnal, unlike most other owls, meaning they feed both in the day and at night.

Snowy owl on the Beach

A refuge officer sighted the owl between the ocean and Tom's Cove, below the south parking lot, heading toward the Coast Guard Station on the wash-over section of the beach. We set off, half hoping to see Hedwig (the owl from Harry Potter), on our walk. We parked at the far end of the south parking lot and then set off toward the wash-over section. Many people were out on the beach, so I doubted whether the owl would show itself, given the number of disturbances. After a few hundred yards, we asked another couple who were heading back if they had seen it. They immediately responded yes, but it was way down the beach near the Coast Guard Station. They told us a truck and an enthusiastic crowd followed it, which did not bode well. My heart sank, as this was quite a distance to walk, nonetheless, we continued, and while we did, peered down at the sand looking for intact and interesting shells.

Suddenly out of the corner of my eye, off to my right, I saw a huge, heavyset white bird flying with deliberate wing beats out above the Tom's Cove shoreline. It was larger than a gull. My many years of instinctive birding recognition kicked in, and the owl's distinctive shape immediately informed me it was indeed the snowy owl. I pointed at it and shouted, "There it is, Deb!" We both stopped in our tracks.

After flying for a short distance, it glided down and perched on a sand dune near the shoreline. It had probably been disturbed further south where the crowds were and flew up our way where it was quieter. Its bright white silhouette stood out starkly against the dull brown colors of the grasses and sand. No wildlife documentary can kindle the feeling and pleasure of seeing such a wild bird in its natural surroundings. Words and photos can't capture the emotion.

A flock of mobbing seagulls persisted in bothering the owl, so it took to the air again and disappeared, flying northbound over the parking lot. Excited about seeing it, we decided to head back to the car and told another couple about the owl. They introduced themselves as Ray and Robin, and after a ten-minute chat, they felt like best friends. Both had traveled to Europe, and each spoke of Celtic backgrounds like mine.

After an interesting discussion, we bid farewell and left Ray and Robin to search for the owl. Five minutes later, we were surprised to see the owl fly over our heads again and head south. It came to rest near some discarded washed-up netting lying on the beach. This time we got much closer to it, and I could take some photos. Ray and Robin saw it fly by, too and came over to join us. Other birders and wildlife photographers noticed it as well, so we formed quite a crowd, while maintaining a safe distance so as not to frighten it off again. The poor owl spent its time harassed by either the gulls or us humans traipsing up and down the beach the entire day.

Even though it was a warmish, sunny Christmas Day, we enjoyed a "White Christmas" ultimately, seeing the snowy owl.

26

RINGING IN THE NEW YEAR CHINCOTEAGUE STYLE

The Homemade Horseshoe

On New Year's Eve, we attended the annual Horseshoe Drop in Robert Reed Park. Equivalent to the ball drop in Times Square, we were excited to experience the horseshoe version in which a giant homemade horseshoe dropped down a flagpole at midnight. This was an early prototype horseshoe that has been much improved in recent years. When I looked at the so-called horseshoe, it appeared to be an inflatable rubber tube divided into separate compartments to give the impression of a horseshoe. It glowed a coppery yellow color, and it was tied to the top of the flagpole with some rope.

As the pivotal midnight moment arrived, everyone began to cheer and clap, while someone approached the bottom of the pole to release the horseshoe. There was a pregnant pause and a collective holding of breath when nothing happened. The man yanking the rope uttered a few choice swear words as the reluctant horseshoe swung back and forth, uncooperative at the top of the pole. The yanking continued—and the swear words, too, just out of earshot of the kids, I think! It clearly would not budge because something was stuck, so the man began to yank it even more violently. I could sense a desperate situation and had the feeling something bad was about to happen. Teaguers are fun people, so seeing the lighter side of the situation, they began to clap as someone behind us remarked simply, "Awkward."

The calamity proceeded from "oops" to worse, as the man tugging the rope gave one last, enormous pull and managed to yank the lights clean out of the horseshoe, so the display was plunged into darkness. The horseshoe remained up the pole while everyone froze with their mouths open. Then all at once, everyone hugged and kissed each other regardless. This is part of the charm and the way of life here. You never know what funny thing will happen next on the island.

On New Year's Day, the annual Polar Pony Plunge took place at the beach on Assateague Island. Participants dressed in themed costumes and ran into the ocean.

Every year the organizers announce a different theme, and participants dress up accordingly. This year it was Disney characters. The participants stood around in the cold checking out each other's costumes. They made last-minute adjustments, as once they entered the surf, their costumes might come off. One of the most hilarious groups of participants was Snow

White and the Seven Dwarfs, but something was very wrong with their appearance. When Snow White turned to face me, I saw that she was a very large man, and to me, that just wasn't right. We couldn't unsee that. The dwarfs were different sizes, thereby altering the idyllic image of the characters in my head.

Participants started to remove their clothing, and then without a lot of warning, everyone responded to instructions to be ready. A short countdown launched a hysterical mass charge toward the surf. Most half-heartedly, gingerly, and timidly shuffled into the shallows, but some brave participants embraced it wholly by diving in completely. Once wet, everyone bolted immediately back into waiting towels and warm clothing, cheered on by their friends and family. It was a brave undertaking amidst a brazen declaration of the brutally cold winter weather that lay ahead.

Later in the day, we drove through the Chincoteague National Wildlife Refuge. Dark green loblolly pines flanked the road. After we turned a bend, the pines ended abruptly, and the green curtain drew back to reveal a vast marsh landscape on either side of the road scattered with ponds. In the distance grazed a few ponies, distinguishable as merely brown and white blobs and appearing to stand still. A shallow gut ran alongside the road where great blue herons stood, cold and motionless, hunched over, guarding their particular feeding stretch. The dark forms of black ducks moved slowly across gunmetal gray, dimly lit ponds in the distance.

At this time of year, the dead trees stood out like withered white skeletons. The wind gnawed at them constantly, weakening them further, so they discarded their limbs randomly into the grasses below. They could barely stand, like old men, and formed lifeless scars scratched into the deep green pines behind them. Bone-white egrets stood out starkly as if an artist scratched away holes in the dull painted landscape to reveal the bright white paper below.

No color distinction existed amid the vast monochromatic carpet of dull grasses that drew the eye out to the horizon. The coarse grasses proclaimed their raw toughness, while the cutting winds and tides constantly tugged and tried to dislodge them. Five months earlier, in a warm breeze, the grasses shimmered and swayed in a multitude of variegated greens and yellows.

When I pulled over to the side of the road to peer into the gut, tiny brown-headed nuthatches scoured the pines above our car, calling to each like rubber ducks with a squeaky voice. They flitted about quickly and in an agitated manner from cone to cone, checking each one for seeds.

We noticed the textures and shapes of plants more at this time of year. We weren't distracted by a myriad of summertime colors and nature's constant activity, so the darks and lights in the land became more noticeable—the drooping jet-black seed clumps of the sumac and the bowed heads of the shriveled-up goldenrod.

When we reached the beach parking lot, we saw the ring-billed gulls gathered in a tight flock, puffed up like plush toy dolls trying to keep warm as they faced their bodies into the ravaging wind. Their heads retracted into their bodies for warmth. They appeared to have no necks and chose to walk rather than fly to conserve energy. We slowly drove past them, and when I lowered the car window, they immediately took to the air but quickly returned, hovered menacingly close, waiting for food. The gulls looked starved and crowded around our car, reminiscent of children scrambling for candy after a piñata is broken open. When we tossed out some leftover scraps, they resembled mad dogs in a meat house, pouncing on every piece, which they devoured in seconds.

Even olives and leftover salad were gulped down until the gulls realized the food wasn't that appealing and nonchalantly picked at it. It was a cruel game I played with them, lowering and raising the car window repeatedly, to see the gulls take flight each time, raising their hopes, waiting for something tasty to be thrown out.

Our world and the gull's behaviors oddly have similar comparisons. Gulls pursue their prey together but also exhibit intense individuality and rivalry. The popular novel *Lord of the Flies* by William Golding focused on the tension between human's group thinking versus individuality, similar to that of the gulls. Gulls have become the great competitors at the beach, focused and driven, practically like us humans having an inner city drive about them as they squabble and fight for scraps. When I hear the yearning, keening cry from a herring gull, it sounds almost human and seems to speak of sorrow and unattainability, a mournful, distant call that haunts the beach.

The beach was an abandoned place, glistening wide open and cold. The tide had erased the thousands of footprints from summer. Deep cuts in the sand resulted from the continuous drawing and erasing of the sea's art that changed daily. The beach had been scoured clean, unwelcoming, with no warmth from the soft sand as before. Now a bitterly cold northerly wind came roaring at me, seeking a weakness in my clothing. The air was laden with moisture from the sea, which drove into my body.

Scandinavians would love this island, for they believe there is no such thing as bad weather, only bad clothing. They have a passion for nature that cuts to the heart of what they call *friluftsliv* (pronounced free-loofts-liv). The expression translates as "open-air living." It was popularized in the 1850s by the Norwegian playwright and poet Henrik Ibsen, who used the term to describe the value of spending time in remote locations for spiritual and physical wellbeing. The island offers its unique remoteness to roam away from the mainland.

The beach was utterly unfamiliar to me now, compared to the walk I took in August to the Coast Guard Station. Aside from the cold muted colors, it bore a grim appearance that spoke of its roaring power. There were no distracting smells from suntan lotion or the scent of ozone coming off the bay. The wind ruled and drove salt onto my face, which acted as a cleanser to wipe away the cobwebs from the past year. There was a spiritual quality about the place; whether this was the solitude or the sound of the wind, I am not sure which. The lack of summer smells and crowds focused my mind on the fundamentals of the beach and its purpose.

The sand was unyielding and solid compared to when I ambled on its soft caresses on those blistering hot days in summer. The recent frosts and cold temperatures froze the ground; it felt nothing like the soft gritty sensation of sand that molded itself around my toes on a sunny day. I missed swooshing it over my feet, digging my toes in hard, its tactility rubbing coarsely against my skin. I came across a pattern on the sand where a flock of gulls had rested in one place. Their webbed feet crisscrossed over each other in a tight grouping creating an interesting overlapping mosaic pattern.

The beach was not as plentiful as summer—it gave up few treasures. The black leathery egg cases from the skates with their distinctive hooks on the ends lay discarded here and there; shells lay broken, embedded in the hard sand like shattered china cups scattered randomly on the gentle gradient of the beach. I was curious how moon snails wove such perfect whorls and circles around their shells, rather like a spiral staircase at the bottom of which was a trap door to protect the snail from predators. In places, the wind sculpted the sand in a herringbone pattern, the ridges perfectly spaced. Resilient, honey-colored beach grass sprung up out of what was left of the dunes. It didn't resist the wind but instead swung back and forth, its tips writing beautiful cursive curves in the sand.

The waves cleaned the shoreline every twelve hours, and the holes, cracks, and eddies filled once again. Sand shifted from place to place in an unending push and pull dictated by the waves. Rewrites about the beach occurred every day, repeatedly, so the story was never finished, but merely rearranged. Every section was different in the perfect harmony of show and tell.

We strolled off the beach and over to the shoreline by Tom's Cove. Scattered along the wrack line were broken parts of a window from a shack out in the bay. The wooden window frames were scoured a dull gray and torn apart, with nails protruding from their sides. I lay the pieces on the sand to reform the window and collected other interesting items from nearby to form a beach collage inside the square frame.

Just as I prepared one of my watercolors, I looked for items that added texture and color. Some rust-colored horseshoe crab shells served as a fence when lined up next to each other, above them, I placed pale cream washed-up reed grass across lengthwise. One giant horseshoe crab shell made a perfect moon in the sky, laid on its side. I scraped a few cloud shapes into the smooth sand around the shell with a stick and inserted a burnt piece of wood with its blackened charcoal surface into the reeds to indicate a black clam bed.

Then I came across a small, mottled, diminutively striking crab shell in a brilliant cobalt blue tinged with salmon pink edges. The color combinations blended well, as they are opposites on the color wheel. It stood out immediately against the dull browns on the beach and begged to be included, so I set it on top of the reeds. An oval piece of wood spoke to me, tangled in the wrack line. Its grain was a unique tiger pattern, molded and smooth on every side from its constant battering in the surf. I placed it on its end to give the impression of the sail on a sailboat out at sea. I arranged my collection of items to depict my coastal scene and took a photo for fun.

I then picked up the colorful crab shell and placed it carefully inside my jacket pocket to take it home. It would join the display on our guest bathroom shelf with other keepsakes and unique treasures we collected from the beach.

My Beach Collection

When I got home, I gave my beautiful crab shell pride of place in the center of our bathroom display shelf. Twenty-four hours later, I noticed that the striking pinks and cobalt blues were beginning to fade. I hastily dipped it in cold water, but the colors never returned. It was like the forlorn specimens of beautiful tropical birds at the Natural History Museum, which when stuffed and displayed, just faded in comparison to how they really looked. I did some research and found that moving a shell from its damp salty environment into a warm dry home, causes the colors to fade. The pigments in the shell react to the warmer temperatures and lose their brilliance. It didn't matter, for whenever I gazed at that shell, I still pictured it on the beach the moment I first eyed it, like a sparkling jewel in the sand on a dull winter's day.

27

SHUTDOWN AND PEACE

Watercolor of the Marsh in Winter

We witnessed a dramatic slowdown of activity on the island. As the marsh became less hospitable, we noticed how wildlife endured a much harsher landscape. We spotted birds we hadn't seen before. The first of these was the American bittern, sometimes referred to as the old man of the marsh, who skulked around the fringes. The bittern is a member of the heron family and returns each year to the Chincoteague Wildlife Refuge in winter, but it doesn't breed here. I always wished to see the elusive bittern, even back in the UK where they were also rare.

I was delighted one bright day in January when our gift of the day was viewing one feeding on the edge of a gut out by

Swan Cove Pool. It was much grander than I thought, having the strangest lime green-colored legs I have ever seen. As I took its photo, it stood still for quite some time, ignoring me as if I weren't there.

The bittern's common nickname is stake driver, after the sound it makes—a wet guttural sound, like a metal stake driven into the wet ground. To produce the sound the bittern contorts its neck horribly, puffing it up like a bullfrog and then swallowing upward, forcing air through the outstretched pipes of its neck and into the frosty silence. Debbie and I didn't hear it on this occasion, but we enjoyed seeing this odd bird numerous times in winter. Each time we observed the bittern, he appeared disillusioned, not showing any sign of interest or emotion in the world around him, merely staring into the water below and sporting his snazzy green legs.

Dan Liberthson captured the bittern's disinterest in the world in his poem *The American Bittern*.

I thought you postured and displayed
to dazzle and entice coquettish hens,
but then I learned you are a hermit,
a taciturn recluse who grumbles in the marshland.

In winter, one of the sights we enjoyed the most was watching skeins of thousands of snow geese strung out in their elongated daisy chains, arriving above Swan Cove Pool. Scientists have determined that the V-shaped formation these geese use when migrating serves two important purposes. First, it conserves their energy as each bird flies slightly above the bird in front of him/her, resulting in a reduction of wind resistance.

The birds take turns being in the front and then falling back when they get tired. In this way, the geese can fly for extended periods before they must stop for rest. The second benefit of the V formation is that it is easy to keep track of every bird in the group. Flying in a formation may assist with the communication and coordination within the group. Fighter pilots often use this formation for the same reason.

The geese descended like an avian blizzard out of nowhere from heaven above, and sometimes the sky was so full of them I thought I might have been temporarily inside a snow globe that someone shook up. Each family gently swirled down together to join the rest of the flock on the water. Their cacophony of honking was a winter treat we enjoyed. Each bird emitted a single syllable honk, and when together as a substantial flock, they sounded like an enormous pack of baying hounds.

Winter's frigid fist was clenching, and the hummingbirds at our feeder were a distant memory. A gentle hush cloaked the marsh ponds, now coated in snow geese, who stood out whalebone white against the cobalt blue sky.

The author John Lewis-Stempel wrote,

It is in the thrill of winter that you can feel the terrible, lovely contradiction of nature best. Beauty and barbarism always go together. Haw and thorn. This Canaletto-blue sky, this stark frost. Yin and yang.

A recent snowfall served as a vast dustsheet, similar to one used to cover furniture. Out on the vast drum-flat surface of the marsh, the snow glistened, painfully bright, forcing us to squint. Underneath its white blanket, the marsh rested before the spring onslaught came again with people in their cars and motorcycles.

The lifeless smell from the monotone marsh invaded the air around us. Cars became less frequent along Main Street, and the Chincoteague residents cocooned themselves in their homes. The stillness of island life in winter – empty beaches, gray skies, and the constant wind – was rendered even more profound by the comparisons to the frenetic summer tourist season when upward of thirty thousand people visited the island. Winter allowed me to appreciate the quality of silence in the marsh, the perpetual peace and solitude of nature resting.

We looked forward to hearty homemade stews, sitting in front of our cozy fireplace, reading enthralling books, and seeing the classic movies that played at the island theater. Every Friday night we could watch a classic movie for only five dollars, with favorites such as *Jaws* and *Lawrence of Arabia* meant for the large wide screen. At the end of a busy teaching week, it was a pleasure to relax and lose oneself in one of these larger-than-life films. We also enjoyed meeting our local Come'ere friends and briefly socializing before the movie played.

I wondered how the Teaguers fared during the dark winter months, as very few places were open, and there wasn't much to do. I didn't see them at the classic movie nights. Maybe they spent time together at one another's homes enjoying the wealth they brought in from the tourist season. We knew they gathered after church for family dinners. Some Teaguers told us a few used the wintertime to work on their decoy carvings, many enjoyed comfort foods, others enjoyed a drink or two or watched sports on their gigantic TVs.

Our evenings were quieter and community orientated. We really didn't miss having a television, as our lives didn't depend on TVs and electronics. Most of what we needed, like the world news, could be gained from our laptops. I would rather paint, write, or read a captivating book in front of our fire.

The only merchants still open were the large chain hotels, like the Comfort Suites and the Hampton Inn, and Bill's restaurant. Before we ventured out, we called to ask whether a place was open and until when. Some stores that were frequently visited—like Steve's Bait & Tackle shop—and Sundial Books, a community meeting place, often stayed open longer.

After the holidays, brutally cold temperatures brought a biting wind that drove its way into the top corners of the windows in the front of the house. Despite the annoying drafts, we felt warm enough with both heat pumps blasting away. I often retired to my studio upstairs with a view of the bay, where I warmed the room like a fine red wine. Comforting warmth radiated from the baseboard heater beneath my feet while I painted. Relaxing classical music took me into my own focused world. Occasionally I looked out at the desolate, windswept gray bay in front, with its rolling white caps furiously riding about, and the muted colors of the marsh. It was such a change from the vibrant electric greens of midsummer.

The View from my Studio

We liked this quiet rejuvenation period and savored the rest and peace it brought. We weren't distracted by the need to do something outside; this encouraged us to make the best of our inside existence for a few months. The island was subdued, at last—the kind of silence that allowed one's mind to wander and simply savor the quiet time. When we needed a break from the isolation, we took a drive on the wildlife refuge; we learned how the wildlife endured these stark and desolate months in a landscape where the wind ruled everything and scoured every channel with its constant battering.

As the temperatures fell further, down into the twenties, the deeper pools started to freeze up. Some birds stuck it out, particularly the great blue herons that we spotted the most. They had returned in more significant numbers in the fall to populate the landscape. Why they chose to come back and endure these freezing conditions baffled me, but they did. In our more temperate climate zone, maybe they figured that the worst days were limited, so they gambled and chose to endure them.

I learned that the great blues have a more variable diet than their relatives and can survive off voles and mice during the winter months when the water is frozen. Most of their heron cousins had flown south, except a few great egrets that remained here until spring. On the harshest days, the great egrets retreated from the open marsh to the less exposed and protected inner-woodland ponds near the Island Nature Trail.

Another bird that stuck around in large numbers was what birders referred to as "butterbutts" or yellow-rumped warblers. Most of their kin were enjoying insects in the tropics, but virtually every time we took a drive, we saw flocks of butter-butts feeding along the roadside. Bryan Pfeiffer, who writes a Vermont birding blog, calls them the winter warblers. Due to the absence of insects, the birds switch their diets in winter to fruits such as juniper, mountain ash, and viburnum. They also consume the fruit from wax myrtles and bayberry, which are common here. To digest these fat-laden waxy fruits, they have an adapted digestion system. The yellow-rumps have elevated levels of gallbladder and intestinal bile salts, which aids the passing of these fruits through their systems as they digest them more slowly. This is why they appear quite comfortable feeding on the wildlife refuge and are able to inhabit a winter range further north than their cousins.

From our house, we noticed a massive flock of Brant geese bobbing up and down in the bay, like stately galleons. Considerable flocks of these geese overwintered with us and then flew north in the spring. Their distinctive bright white rumps glinted in the afternoon sun. A few black-backed gulls perched on the parapet each day on Queens Sound Bridge, viewing the marsh channel below. They always chose the bridge as their vantage point to scan for food.

A limited flock of tree swallows hunkered down close to the road on the Wildlife Loop. *What were they still doing here?* I wondered. At first, I thought they were small piles of pony poop, until the whole flock rose up reluctantly and then fluttered back down to hug the ground for warmth. They should have left earlier with the huge flocks of tree swallows that scoured the grasses.

Winter grew dour, with much of the vitality and color sucked out of the marsh grasses. They were a dirty brown color with a dull slate color in the pools. When the days were oppressive and overcast with a Welsh drizzly rain, the varied browns of the grasses popped against the dark green pines, a phenomenon caused by the refraction of light. The clouds pressed down, wringing the light from the narrow channels.

Despite its dead appearance, the marsh was patient and scarcely slept. It is a place of constancy, waiting each year to wake again in spring.

The animals have three options for surviving the harshness of the weather: migration, hibernation, or resistance. Most birds—the ducks, shorebirds, and other water birds—already left our feeding grounds for warmer climates further south. This made way for the diving ducks, great blue herons, and hardy species like the black ducks that faced winter with resistance. The great blue herons fitted in perfectly with the drab palette of marsh colors, standing perfectly still to blend into the background. Their giant yellow eyes beamed like a ship's lantern in a dark storm. They didn't seem a bit ruffled by the colder temperatures. When the weather becomes unbearably harsh, a slightly lower hunch indicates their only sign of distress. Their appearance grew bedraggled at the end of the day from the daily onslaught of wind and rain that pummeled them, yet they stood in their pools or on the edges of guts like stoic loyal palace guards, keeping watch on the pool beneath them.

In addition to a thick layer of feathers, the great blue herons have one unique factor that helps them survive the cold temperatures. They are able to circulate blood through a countercurrent heat exchange, isolating the blood that flows in their legs rather than circulating it throughout their entire bodies. This helps to keep their body temperatures higher. They also have specialized scales on their feet and legs that help minimize heat loss.

Cavity nesters like nuthatches, flickers, and woodpeckers use tree cavities and nest boxes to stay warm. This provides protection from the weather and helps the birds hide from predators.

The winter flounder hibernate and swim under the ice where the sea meets the tidal water. Upon the onset of our freezing temperatures, worms and minnows bury themselves in the mud at the bottom of the marsh pools. Meadow voles huddle together under a blanket of snow to keep warm, where during the day they enter torpor, a resting state in which their body temperature plummets, and then heats up again for active feeding and foraging in the snow in the evening. Voles build tunnels through the snow and use these to emerge in the spring. They also are wary of the great blue herons that seek them in particular during the harsher winter days.

The animals and birds that stayed in place remained active, resisted, puffing their feathers out to keep warm, scavenging like the gulls on the beach for freebies thrown from our car, or hunting for the few animals around that foraged above ground.

For many, it was a very hungry season when they didn't know where they would find their next meal.

The red-tailed hawk was present on most of our drives around the Wildlife Loop; sometimes several perched along the route. Their excellent vision enabled them to spot prey at great distances. They must have wondered why we humans were out in such lousy conditions. These birds are deep wood nesters but seek open ground for their hunting. In winter, when their prey is scarce, they expand their territory and use up a lot of energy to fly further distances to sustain themselves.

In the summer, the hot season's thermals and rising air buoy them, but now it was much harder to forage. Consequently, the hawks prefer to hunt from perches where they could glide down to catch their prey. Their daily hunt for food in this bleak landscape is challenging. They perch on a branch for hours with their breasts puffed out to trap warm air between their feathers. Like us, they have few defenses against the cold and spend many tortuous hours perched in this defiant state. Sometimes the hawks shelter deep inside a stand of loblolly pines shielded from high winds and rain, patient until it becomes calmer to venture out.

We humans also sought warmth and comfort at this time of year, perhaps sitting by a log fire in our living rooms, wrapped up in a warm blanket or wearing a wool sweater, as the cold winds raged around outside.

In mid-January, we finally caught a break in the weather and enjoyed a day with bright sunshine, reduced wind, and moderate temperatures in the mid-forties. This time we took a walk on the Black Duck Trail to enjoy the quiet, subdued landscape. As Debbie and I strolled away from the road along the narrow tarmac trail, the background noises from cars faded, and a gentle breeze wafted over us. A soft ocean roar filtering through the broccoli-shaped tree crowns of the loblolly pines was the same rushing I heard in the woods back in spring when I ventured out to discover the Bivalve Trail. We immediately noticed the nasal sounds coming from charismatic brown-headed nuthatches, urgently foraging away in the nearby pines. They flitted about in an agitated, obsessive-compulsive manner, scarcely resting, twittering to each other like squeezable rubber duck toys, moving quickly from one tree to the one after. We strolled into a silent dreamy landscape that rested in peace with its structural essence stripped bare to reveal its skeletal forms. It was so quiet that the faintest snap of a twig was audible twenty yards away.

In addition to the breeze, the ever-present music was the gentle scraping of the phragmites reeds, as their Naples yellow bone-dry stalks brushed against each other. The ponds on the sides of the path looked like my steeped morning tea, so dark that I couldn't see the bottom. Moving closer to peer in, I could see ripples suddenly fanning out from a tiny fish or invertebrate beneath the surface. We heard the occasional "tick" from a cardinal and high-pitched sustained whistles from white-throated sparrows as they scratched about at the base of bushes. We commented to each other that it wasn't necessary to see anything, as the silent walk itself was rejuvenating, with the gentle lullaby of the wind caressing our chilly faces.

Hiking back to our car, we heard the distant sound of gunfire coming from hunters, like heavy rugs slapped against walls. In January they awoke us on weekends at seven o'clock, blasting away at the ducks on the marsh.

At least we briefly experienced a period of solitude that day, separate from the busyness of this noisy world.

Later in the day, we enjoyed some unique sounds of the season parked by the visitor center out at the beach. It was now late in the day, and we were alone. No other cars were out, so we turned our car engine off to hear the tundra swans calling on Swan Cove Pool.

Watercolor of the Tundra Swans

They sounded fluty like a young school band trying out for the first time, with the faint roar of the ocean in the background. Some emitted a short bark or mellow bugle. The vast pond broadcasted their haunting calls that drifted over the surface, rolling away into the distance. It was a soothing treat. At no other time of the year would we be able to enjoy this extraordinary natural music.

28

MARKET STREET ANTIQUES

Instead of taking a drive on the refuge, sometimes we took trips onto the mainland. We made an interesting discovery one day when we visited Market Street Antiques in Onancock down the Eastern Shore peninsula. This is a wonderful showroom with over sixteen hundred square feet of antiques, collectibles, signs, vintage kitchen items, gift items, used books, candles, soaps, jams, and teas. You rarely knew what treasures you would find there. In season, they carried fresh produce, but now it was quiet.

We also knew they dedicated as much floor space in the back to architectural salvage, which is what we wanted to explore. We were searching for some reclaimed doors for a brand-new closet we planned to build. We wanted solid wood period doors to fit in with the age and decor of our house.

Entering the store, we met the salvage expert, Jeff Miller, who proceeded to tell us fascinating tales of his trade and the interesting finds he made on his journeys around the Eastern Shore. He was originally from Kentucky, where, he said, "Any older homes or barns found there are snapped up quickly and restored. Here, on the other hand, the state of buildings on the Eastern Shore is depressing. Owners frequently let a property go, so buildings fall into disrepair and then have to be torn down."

This theme was becoming familiar. We had noticed many examples of period homes and restaurants that needed more than a coat of paint. Jeff sought the rights to salvage many period homes, where on one occasion, he said, he found an eighteenth-century grandfather clock buried inside the walls. He also found floorboards longer than nineteen feet in some houses. I asked Jeff about the kind of trees that used to grow on the Eastern Shore that could produce such lengths of a floorboard.

"Giant tall oaks once grew here," he replied, "but as they became harder to find, the lengthy wider floorboards became scarce. In some cases, narrow floorboards could actually be older, not simply the wide boards. Fashion many years ago wasn't that important, so they used whatever materials were in supply and available. Over time, building styles changed again, and the wider floorboards became more fashionable to install."

Touring the showroom, I noticed some termite damage on the wood frames.

"Some of the salvage pieces have considerable insect damage," I commented to Jeff.

"Barns and homes don't survive here because they get ravaged by termites and beetles," he replied. "The humidity in the summer also serves to speed up the process when surfaces are not protected."

I asked Jeff whether he stocked any wooden gingerbread trim for the outside of a traditional Victorian house like ours.

"Sorry, whenever it comes in, it sells immediately," he said.

We looked around the salvage section of the showroom and found two matching pine doors with original features. We also found some matching brass hardware with some elegant ceramic and porcelain doorknobs. For ninety-four dollars we came away pleased, strapped the two doors onto our car roof, and celebrated with a hearty lunch at the local Irish pub, The Blarney Stone.

On our drive back to the island along the causeway, we passed pickup trucks parked on the sides of the road. We could see duck hunters peeking out above their blinds further out in the marsh. Surely the ducks noticed them too. Two days later would be the last day of duck hunting, so the early morning rug slapping and popping sounds would no longer wake us up.

29

WINTER'S WRATH

American Woodcock

As the temperature dropped in the bay, we noticed the channels gradually iced up completely. A number of snowstorms also contributed; a frigid vice grip finally took hold, and the island reached a state of what I called "shutdown." Despite these bitter conditions, it was strangely enjoyable.

When one particularly fierce blizzard blasted through in January, we literally couldn't go anywhere or do anything except to gaze at the all-out feathered-pillow fight occurring outside. The world—well, *our* world—came to a halt. We remained held hostage and restricted to simply gazing out through our snow-encrusted windows. Our family room window faced almost northeast, so we felt the force of any wind or rain on that side.

After dark, from the cozy warmth of our couch, I could observe a tall streetlight shining a soft yellow light onto the electric cables below. I could tell the relative strength of the wind-driven snow or rain depending on how quickly the precipitation dripped from the cables below. The flakes of snow would sweep sideways through the arc of light while the storm relentlessly pounded away. We knew that Mother Nature was in charge, so we waited it out.

Amusingly, during these bitter temperatures, the US Fish and Wildlife Service issued a notice that early January marked the Earth's perihelion. They stated, "This is the time when the Earth is at its closest distance to the sun during orbit." It didn't feel warmer to us.

The familiar landmarks around our house gradually became obscured, everything wrapped up in a white frenzy that swirled densely in every direction. The snow was usually democratic to everything and settled in even layers, but this time the blizzard whipped it up, leaving drifts eighteen inches high behind our cars and the garage. I was astonished to see the hungry little sparrows clinging for dear life to our feeder, trying to grab a few seeds before they retreated into the arborvitaes.

Anne's house next door had its sides and windows slowly blasted by snow, as if by a paint sprayer with a frosted glaze. On the storm-facing northern side of our house, the snowflakes built up on our window screens, entombing the window in a frosted cocoon like that of a caterpillar. The flakes flew in dense clouds, whipping each snowflake into every corner it could find. The snow softened the outlines of our trashcans and woodpiles, transforming them into other shapes. It also distorted the acoustics so we couldn't tell which way an ambulance came from when it finally labored past our house to attend to an emergency. I felt sorry for those who were out in the blizzard conditions. What was, possibly, the only snowplow on the island gave notice with flashing yellow lights that reflected off the windows before it lumbered down Main Street.

We felt cozy, though, eating comfort foods like shepherd's pie and stews. During these frost-bound winter storms, the most eligible place to be was within hailing distance of a wood-burning stove or, in our case, our fireplace. What I remember the most is the lack of noise—the sheer, wonderful silence all around us.

I wondered why the bay took a while to freeze up and learned that salt water froze at a lower temperature—28.4 degrees Fahrenheit—compared to fresh water, but it thawed sooner in the spring. The tide laid up sheets of ice in stratified shelves along the shore. At low tide, the sheets cracked and slid over each other, causing even thicker slabs of ice to form on the banks around the marsh. They looked like discarded thick-plated French door windows. As the temperatures fluctuated, these slabs thawed and broke off from where they anchored and flowed sluggishly down the open pewter-colored channels. When viewed on the online town webcam, the channel looked like a scene from the St. Lawrence Seaway when the icebergs thawed in spring. The huge slabs gathered speed in the currents and then careened up into the grasses, where they sheered them off at their bases.

This formed part of an important process that took place every year, especially when the marsh froze up. The sheered grasses, once captured by the incoming tides, traveled back out and then sank into the bay to decompose. Over time, they broke down and fed a host of minuscule marine life. So the cycle repeated continually out in the marsh.

The hefty ice blocks also destroyed some of the duck blinds on the rise and fall of tides, and many lay disfigured and dislodged, or they floated in several pieces along the bay. The remnants of hunters' blinds littered the marsh, and bushes that couldn't withstand the harsh windswept open environment lay uprooted, stripped bare, and left exposed on top of the spartina grasses like tossed up dark skeletons. The gales blew unrelenting, with a bone-chilling bite, unimpeded across the marsh, and tore away everything in their path.

February brought prolonged icy conditions. Most days only reached a high of nineteen degrees. The vast bay in front of our house was completely frozen and looked like a scene from Antarctica. Ice slabs and notches protruded up out of the surface, just as one sees in a BBC Nature series, or as if someone made a cake and sprinkled white chocolate shavings on top. There was an urge inside me to set off across it with a team of dogs, racing my sleigh between the ice-locked buoys.

We assumed the refuge froze solid too, but when we took a drive, we had a pleasant surprise. On coming across a pond on the Wildlife Loop, an uncommon bird proclaimed its presence from the inky-dyed, rippling surface. The ice-locked tufts of grass parted to reveal a lone canvasback, a handsome duck we had never seen before. It stood out with its stunning deep chestnut head, feeding contently alone. Supposedly, these ducks got their names from the canvas bags in which Chesapeake Bay duck carcasses shipped en masse to restaurants. I cannot fathom why anyone would shoot such a splendid looking duck. The canvasback diving duck doesn't make frequent appearances around the refuge, at least not where the public has access. I have no idea of their numbers these days, but I suspect they are not widespread. If the weather hadn't been so harsh, we wouldn't have seen it, since they tend to spread out and feed elsewhere when the weather is fine.

Another six inches of wet snow fell in mid-February. We weren't sure if the Park Service had plowed the wildlife refuge, but we drove out regardless and were relieved to see the road was clear. We learned that, because the refuge is federal property, it is one of the first places plowed after a storm. The snow had built up in dense, soggy clumps on the tree branches, weighing them down. Many loblolly pines looked at a breaking point. I feared that more would fall if the wind picked up before a rapid thaw. The additional weight of the snow on their crowns and limbs could be disastrous. They had endured the pine bark beetles and now faced these harsh winter snowstorms.

As I gazed at the destruction wrought from the recent winter storms, I thought back to a description given by the celebrated environmentalist John Muir. In his account of a windstorm in the pine forest of Yuba in 1878, Muir ventured into the woods when the storm hit and afterward said,

Colossal spires 200 feet in height waved like supple Goldenrods chanting and bowing low as if in worship. The almost steadfast monarch of them all rocked down to its roots. Their lithe, brushy tops were rocking and swirling in wild ecstasy.

I imagined what it must have been like to be out when the storm hit our tall trees; what it was like to hear them swaying in the wind, creaking from the additional weight of snow. Even the dog fennel and broomsedge grasses lay collapsed under the weight of the season.

Lucky for us, everyone chose to stay home that day, so there were no cars. We took our time, driving around the Wildlife Loop at a slower speed than usual, stopping for a minute or two to search the landscape for any signs of life. Anything alive we easily noticed in the pristine crystal landscape.

On that memorable drive, we sighted the most towhees and cardinals I had ever seen in one location. A sweeping swathe of red cardinals dotted the landscape, like a field of red poppies set on a white carpet, or as if someone sprinkled bright red rose petals everywhere. Many birds "played in the street" as that was the only place to find food.

We had our biggest surprise, however, at the end of our drive. On returning to the parking lot, we noticed the snowplow had uncovered some of the grass verges, exposing various kinds of grubs and worms for the birds. While slowly circling the lot, close to our car we spied a Wilson's snipe, hardly noticeable with its deceptive camouflage. Its blended bars and flecks seamlessly echoed the leaf litter around it.

John Clare paid homage to the Snipe in his poem *To the Snipe* in 1832.

Lover of swamps
The quagmire overgrown
With hassock tufts of sedge—where fear encamps
Around thy home alone

As if the snipe wasn't enough excitement, close by, an American woodcock bobbed up and down, performing its amusing disco dance routine. I learned later it rocks its body back and forth while stepping heavily with the front foot to rustle up worms, making them easier to detect in the soil. It looked like some dance moves I once performed in the seventies.

Only the severe weather had made it possible for us to see these two species, because both were forced from their deep wood habitat to find food. The sightings were serendipitous after such a significant snowstorm.

We drove home over the bridge, noticing a few marbled godwits feeding below on the exposed oyster beds. We tallied up the birds we had seen so far: the American bittern, brown-headed nuthatch, Bonaparte gull, parasitic jaeger, canvasback, snipe, woodcock and the most memorable, a snowy owl on Christmas Day. Not bad for having no expectations for winter.

We made a mental note to drive again after a snowstorm.

COMING
FULL CIRCLE

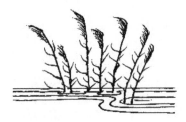

30

VISITING AN OLD FRIEND

Watercolor of the Bivalve Trail

After spending the winter cooped up inside our house for what felt like six months, we couldn't wait to get outside again. The bay appeared to let out a great gasp of release as the salt water melted more quickly than the fresh water, and everything started to move again. Some of the locals satiated their wanderlust by traveling to Salisbury in Maryland or down over the bay, but when the temperatures finally rose, we took a walk along—where else?—one of our favorite places, the Bivalve Trail.

At sixty-one degrees, we enjoyed the most comfortable weather for January, but the marsh looked lifeless. The grasses were still a dull brown—many areas lay flattened, their stalks sheared off at the bases from the enormous ice blocks. A few optimistic young turtles sunned themselves on one of the far banks, the first ones of the New Year.

That white plastic bag, an eyesore since last summer, still remained caught on a bush in one of the guts. It served as a constant, nagging reminder to me of the waste that visitors threw away and that lay around us in this pristine landscape. I remarked to Debbie that one day I was going to wade over to the far bank and remove it.

The green-winged teal hadn't arrived yet, but we hoped to see some spring migrants. As Debbie and I started our walk, we finally could breathe in the warm, fresh air, filling our lungs after living cocooned in the stale air of our house. The distinct, spicy, resinous smell of fresh pine wafted around us and lingered in our noses while we ambled along. The breeze drifting through the tall loblolly pines caused the trees to sway gently; the familiar sound blended with the background symphony of the distant ocean waves. We strolled past melting woodland ponds that looked as if milk lay on their surfaces.

Then we came upon the familiar notice to the Bivalve Trail that led out to the heavenly view of the watchman's shack. Revisiting this path reawakened satisfying memories of when I found it for the first time last year. Hardly anyone knew about it then. Now I noticed the smallest changes, a fallen tree or a snapped off branch close to the pathway. The walk worked its magic on me again, enchanting me, as it was my place to think, where my mind could unravel. The pine needle-strewn pathway provided mystique and a sense of spirituality. The Bivalve Trail had no notion of my presence. I had meandered along it in the sweltering temperatures of summer while the heat jellied the air as I emerged on the shore of Tom's Cove. Now, here I was again, in the frozen weeks of January, and yet it held the same appeal and a new sense of anticipation, as this time I looked forward to the path revealing its grand view of our old friend, the watchman's shack in the bay. Walking the trail provided me with an individual viewpoint, to consider my place on the planet and the island.

We looked forward to seeing our old friend, the watchman's shack. We walked on the lush, silent carpet of brown pine leaves, along the dark pathway framed by the woods. We beheld the light at the far end of the tunnel and awaited our favorite view just ahead.

As the bay came into view, we stopped dead, stunned by the scene in front of us. The watchman's shack lay collapsed on its end at a forty-five-degree angle, sunk into Tom's Cove. Its dark gnarled support posts had been snapped off at random. Jagged sharp spikes pierced the water's surface from below the dark structure. It was a somber moment—our special view gone forever.

The tide was out. The frozen mud allowed me to walk out toward it, closer than I had ever been. On a typical day, it wouldn't have been possible, as most people would be up to their waists in mud. When I reached the water's edge, I was close enough to take some pictures of it lying pitifully on its gable end. The shack's roof always held an osprey's nest. Every year the birds came back, made their repairs and bred, but that was now gone. Fortunately, it was early in the season, so there was no one home yet.

The owner of the shack lived in town and clearly didn't maintain the support pillars. The harsh temperatures we experienced for a few weeks undoubtedly played a part in its demise. My theory was that the ice probably held it up in place, and then, given the recent temperature rises, the supports finally weakened and gave way when the ice thawed. Now the shack joined a host of other structures that lay unkempt and discarded to rot in the bay. Maybe the broken window frames I found earlier on the shores of Tom's Cove when I created my beach collage were from the shack. Since the land was federal property, maybe it was hard to get permission to repair structures.

If only I could have preserved this beautiful scene in my mind, frozen it in time, like roses that kept their scent for a week. It does, however, live on in the watercolors I created.

When I searched online, I came across a Facebook post about the shack's original owner. Way back in the 1920s, none other than William C. Bunting, the man who built the very house we purchased, owned this shack. It was as if he called me to view another building he constructed; a kindred spirit that joined the past with the present.

31

THE SEAFOOD FESTIVAL

The Deluxe Seafood Festival Tray

In the spring, Debbie and I secured space at the annual Seafood Festival held at Tom's Cove Park to sell some of my art. The rain cleared after two days of constant downpours. It was a bright and sunny day in the low sixties. We set up my exhibit booth inside a giant craft tent and then parked our car behind the tent with the other vendors. This was an untried adventure for me, so I didn't know what type of visitors came to this all-the-seafood-you-can-eat event, or how many. At first, we noticed families started to gather, setting up their exhibit tents, chairs, and coolers in the grounds.

The center of the park contained a mixture of picnic tables with benches and open grassy spaces for vendors to pitch their tents. The food vendors, arranged around the perimeter of the festival, offered "Little Neck" steamed clams, single fried oysters, fried fish, a full salad bar, sweet potato fries, shrimp, clam fritters, boardwalk fries, clam strips, raw oysters and clams, grilled chicken, clam chowder, hush puppies, and non-alcoholic beverages. Crabs were not in season at the festival, but there was everything else. The public deliriously enjoyed the last of the season's oysters served deep fried, broiled, or baked. This was early May and a month without an "r" in it. The air was heavy with an enticing pungent, salty, greasy smell that wafted and then lingered around the craft tent, where I hung my art. It was an early teaser for what the carnival would smell like in a few weeks' time.

On first appearances, this looked more like a rustic crowd, similar to the people we saw in the campgrounds, but we waited to see if we would meet any serious art patrons. It wasn't long before our first potential buyers arrived in the craft tent. A group of middle-aged unshaven men with beer bellies wandered up to my booth, each bearing an open Budweiser can in hand. I immediately doubted whether I should have bothered to attend. They didn't show much interest in what I offered and moved on to peruse the other vendors in the tent. Many others wandered in, wearing various combinations of camo, baseball hats, and T-shirts sporting an assortment of hunting and fishing slogans. It became clear they were here for the food and social camaraderie, not to buy a painting of the island, but that was okay.

Close to my booth, a group of young lads sold truck decals, which they generated on their printer. The Budweiser can toting crew flocked to their product, so they did well. Two women also sold jewelry near us. Their price point was low. Buyers could afford a set of earrings for only ten dollars.

When someone purchased a set of my notecards, we placed them into one of our used paper gift bags. We had brought along a varied selection of Christmas-themed branded store bags from fancy stores like Victoria's Secret. After the buyers left my booth, we noticed they paraded around the festival with their Victoria's Secret bag. This created quite a stir, as other attendees wondered if there was a Victoria's Secret booth in one of the tents. The rumors that circulated created some heated conversations around the craft tent, which we found highly amusing.

Suddenly there was great anticipation in the air. The food lines were forming, and everyone began to move out of the craft tent toward the vendors. After all, this was really why they came. Many attendees brought their own trays to carry their food back to their picnic areas. When they visited each food station, they loaded them up with a smorgasbord of shellfish.

The variety of construction methods and types of material people used to make their trays amused us. Some trays had fancy edges to keep the food from sliding off. Some had perfectly cut holes in the bases to hold drinks. One person fashioned a wooden box that used to contain clementine fruits, and some had purchased aluminum baking trays from the grocery store and fashioned holes on the sides for straps. The pièce de résistance, however, was a well-constructed wooden mahogany tray with sturdy sides supported by two straps: a leather strap around the person's neck and another that wrapped around the waist. The hands-free customized set up also featured a built-in drinks holder and looked similar to the traditional iconic ice cream usherette trays that used to be commonplace in the movie theaters in the 1960s, when concessions servers sold snacks at the front of the auditorium during the intermission.

The lines in front of the food stations formed quickly, so the visitors to our craft tent dwindled. We waited to see what kind of traffic came in later after they ate, and hoped not to shake a lot of greasy hands, many of which might thumb through my notecards. While everyone else enjoyed an abundance of seafood, feeling somewhat incongruous, I retrieved my lunch-box and pulled out my healthy lunch of fresh fruit and yogurt. Since I am allergic to shellfish, there wasn't much I could eat at the festival. Maybe I can enjoy it in my next life.

The people visiting my booth later in the day were similar to the folks who came into the tent earlier. I sold some prints and a few notecard packs, which covered my show fee. One person expressed interest in attending one of my art classes. Debbie reminded me that not everyone buys art, and I discovered that a substantial part of the island fell into this category.

Thankfully, not many cruised by with open Budweiser cans, but plenty sported previous Seafood, Oyster, or Blueberry Festivals on their T-shirts. In Chincoteague, people wear their T-shirts with pride, celebrating the various festivals they have attended during the year. Festival attendees preferred to spend twenty-five bucks on an event T-shirt rather than pay for a local piece of art from the island for the same price. People socialized and ate at this festival. It wasn't a place to expect a significant sale. I enjoyed myself regardless, and watching people proved a treat.

32

THE MAGIC WINDOWS

Hungars Episcopal Church

Two weeks after the Seafood Festival, we attended the final classical concert of the season given by the Orchestra of the Eastern Shore. We found this orchestra by accident, not realizing that such a wonderful orchestra existed on the Eastern Shore. So far away from any major cities, the island is essentially a cultural void when it comes to classical music. What transpired was an unforgettable experience provided in a beautiful historical setting. What's more, the concert was free and featured music I listened to while I painted in my studio. This special treat for me was an opportunity to hear the instruments live.

We drove more than an hour south on Route 13 to Hungars Episcopal Church near Machipongo. The town's name came from a Native American Indian tribe known as the Matchipungoes. The name means "bad dust," or "much dust," or "fine dust and flies."

We turned off Route 13 and took route 617 along a straight country road flanked on either side by dried, unharvested cotton fields. I wondered why no one harvested the cotton. Some cotton clumps even adorned the roadside trees as added decoration. Then we passed a small makeshift airfield where an orange windsock fluttered above the single hanger. We made a left, past a graveyard of rusted up old farm vehicles parked in rows. The landscape was as flat as a pane of glass with open fields bordered by patches of mixed woodland. We passed a group of dilapidated trailers and then, a half-mile later, a beautiful southern plantation home with a wraparound porch. The contrast was marked. We couldn't see the church at first for the mature trees surrounding it. Towering oaks and chestnut trees with huge girths grew in the churchyard amongst a mixture of old headstones, proving the age of the church—established in 1632. Some headstones had ornate stone carvings with balls on top and scary angels peering down at us.

The concert proved to be popular, as many cars parked on the grounds. We quickly found a parking spot on the grass and sauntered around the sizeable rectangular brick structure to find the entrance.

In the middle of nowhere, the church is one giant imposing brick building with huge, tall clear windows on two sides. Two old coaching lamps adorn the brick wall by the entrance. The air was redolent with the fragrant white blooms from a fringe tree outside the main door.

The striking interior was a vast, clean white space with high ceilings. It was jarringly sparse, but despite its stark appearance, there was a restful ambiance to it, the perfect place to hear a classical orchestra. There was no air conditioning, and people already waved their programs as fans.

The uncharacteristically clear tall church windows had spacious rectangular panes that reached up to the roofline, topped with rounded arches. I expected some stained glass or depictions of the saints or Bible stories, but there were none. Instead, the clear glass invited the outside world in, along with a tremendous abundance of light.

The church was pristine. The lack of color, which I hadn't expected for a church, made the mahogany furniture and railings stand out. Simple, elegant, upturned twin candelabra lights hung on the inside walls. In the center of the church, four giant white columns rose from floor to ceiling. The organ pipes were cast in silver steel. Simple black numerals announced the hymns, arranged on white lattice boards on the walls at the front. Such was the absence of distraction that it made it easy to concentrate on the orchestra in front of us and to appreciate the view of God's world out of the windows.

The pews were uncomfortable, made of solid hardwood, and in closed boxes like those that proliferated in churches of the day. In the past, a family might have their own box pew. It didn't matter to us, as the music was our focus.

Where the orchestra sat perfectly in chairs atop a luscious, soft, light green carpet, was the nave adorned with mahogany wood hand railings. Below the altar and hand railings were custom-made cream cushions that depicted wildlife and plants from the Eastern Shore—hibiscus, turtles, ducks, crabs, and wood thrush.

It was noticeably an older white audience—certainly not a jeans-and-T-shirt crowd. Some women wore colorful silk scarves around their necks. Debbie and I were the youngest ones there in the fully occupied sanctuary. At the very last minute, we noticed that no one had taken the front pew on the right side, and we moved up. I didn't know it at the time, of course, but our move to the front would allow us to experience something extraordinary.

The orchestra performed a brief tune-up, after which Paul Kim, the music director, walked up the center aisle to polite audience applause. He introduced himself and the orchestra and gave a short statement sharing his opinion of the value of music.

"I hope everyone can understand the role of music in our lives and the emotions it creates, whether this is sadness or joy. It interweaves beauty into the fabric of our lives. I hope today that our music does this for you, as these are beautiful pieces. I hope you enjoy them."

The first piece was Mozart's Symphony No. 29 in A major. What an experience. Right up close, I noticed the concentration written on the orchestra members' faces.

Dr. Kim dipped and wove away on his violin while conducting, giving an occasional glance to others to signal the start of the next passage. The musicians swayed in their seats, weaving the air with such energy around them and creating beautiful music that drifted and floated high up to the ceiling of the church.

If we hadn't moved seats, we would never have experienced the powerful sounds of the instruments up close. I couldn't help think how much a front row seat in a famous concert hall in New York would cost. Here we were, experiencing it free. As I daydreamed, I experienced a surreal moment.

As the last movement, the Allegro con spirito, played, I looked to the right of the altar, beyond the orchestra, and through the clear glass of the giant window. The tops of the tall loblolly pines in the distance appeared to sway in synch to the violins. The sun joined in too, peeking through the clouds off and on with its light passing over the trees in quick flashes. The theme of the music was both fast-paced and graceful, characterized by some fiery, impulsive horn passages that matched the appearance and shading caused by the sun. The combination of swaying treetops and passing light mesmerized me as if everything was in complete harmony. The outside concert followed the inside symphony precisely. Was I dreaming? Or was this a special show for me?

Once the piece finished, I turned to Debbie and asked her to look through the same window to see the sunlight dancing off the trees. The moment she did, the ephemeral show stopped—over as quickly as the music. The loblollies stood still in complete shade. I wondered if the show was mine alone.

I looked forward to the second piece, J. S. Bach's Brandenburg Concerto No. 4. As the orchestra began, I felt compelled for some reason to look to my left and through the window behind the orchestra. This view was very different from the one I just witnessed. Two flutes began a mellow wafting duet to open the Allegro. Further into the first movement, as if on cue, the sun suddenly burst out again and this time lit up a tall old beech tree with dead ivy clinging all the way up its trunk. As the orchestra played, some of the dried-up brown ivy leaves caught the breeze and began to fall, dancing and gently floating down to the music. The leaves fell at just the right moment, as each movement built up and then cascaded down. I watched the amazing control of the musicians as they slowly drew their violin bows across their strings to the very end, extracting every note they could. The sound quivered—piercing, flowing. The double bass player drew his bow at different angles to evoke deep, rounded, full rich tones, oaky with a thick, velvet complexity. Maybe I imagined it, but I swear that each ivy leaf fell in complete synchronization. Quite abruptly, the sun switched off my show again, just as it had before through the other window, then turned it on as if it was flicking a light switch. Dark storm clouds passed in front of the sun, hastening the approach for an imminent downpour. The clouds raced across the sky, providing a dramatic showstopper outside. The final Presto piece combined the sound of each instrument built upon each other in an overlapping sequence of heavenly music.

Once again, the show transformed me into a dreamy state, or maybe it cast me under the same hypnotic influence as the swaying treetops. I entered into a peaceful world where I floated in complete relaxation, oblivious to my hard seat and the others around me. On reflection, I think I was just tired, and the minute the orchestra began, I gazed outside and relaxed. The action through both windows appeared to coincide perfectly though as if they were performances for me personally. They added some absolute magic to my day. One never knows when nature might conjure up her own show for us to see, just like the sunsets that appear out of nowhere at the end of our day on the island.

We left the church totally calmed, the sweet music still ringing in our ears. We truly experienced an oasis of sophistication in a landscape that didn't offer much. We listened to instruments that sounded amazing up close and personal, perhaps the only string instruments for a hundred miles, which made it even more special in the intimate setting of a beautiful old church. The dedicated players practiced for hours to hone their music. Since we hadn't paid for such a treat, we dropped a generous donation into the basket at the end of the performance.

After the concert, I briefly spoke with Paul Kim, the conductor, and expressed my appreciation of the wonderful music I so enjoyed. I told him that on many occasions I painted along to this music in my studio. I could say from our conversation that he, too, was passionate about it as he discussed the various stanzas and complexities of various composers, his favorite being Mendelssohn.

Making the relatively long trip from Chincoteague down the strip to hear this wonderful concert was a highlight of our event calendar. We briefly lost ourselves in a bubble, a cultural oasis in the middle of vast open farmland. One would pay more than seventy-five dollars in New York for such a front-row seat like that, and yet we enjoyed it free. What's more, I experienced personally my own outdoor show, which made it even more special for me.

When we returned home later that afternoon, we ended the day similar to the way we began it, by sitting on our front porch, looking out over the bay. The music resonated in my ears.

As the sun set, we listened to a harbinger of spring, the shrill piping of the tiny chorus frogs or peepers, as they are known. As night came, they provided us with another orchestral concert, this time from the marsh, with their high-pitched flute-like vibrant voices. Some term their vibrating rhythm as "the night music of spring."

33

THE HARBINGERS OF SPRING

Our Mailbox

"Harbinger" means something that precedes or indicates the approach of something. Living on an island brings many harbingers to signal that spring is coming.

Thoreau once remarked,

One by one the long-absent feathered, furred, and scaled creatures of the marsh make their appearance on land and in the water and skies.

We waited to see the first flickers of life in the landscape and asked ourselves when the marsh would green up again.

The Chincoteague Wildlife Refuge announced a harbinger of spring with the appearance of the fleshy succulent plant sea rocket on the dunes. When would the noisy laughing gulls return, and when would the first campers and RVs thunder past our house again? Already flocks of grackles, starlings and red-winged blackbirds gorged themselves, stripping my large feeder in two hours. The grackles came back in spring to nest in the large clumps of bamboo across the road.

The first splashes of spring color already occurred on the mainland, where it was slightly warmer. As I drove to school one morning, the bare grassy fields bloomed with patches of purple lamium, indicating that spring was coming. The lamium formed a rich but sporadic carpet, dotted here and there across the flat, wide-open landscape.

Meadowlarks once again perched on the wire fence that surrounded the Wallops Flight Facility; their bright puffed-up yellow breasts shone in the early morning sun.

The birds reacted to the temperature changes and were the first to notice when the ponds melted. The common mergansers and belted kingfishers made a beeline for these unfrozen ponds. The stoic overwintering grey blue herons suddenly perked up and fed again, having endured an ice-locked landscape for weeks. In flight, their backs glinted blue to proclaim the new season.

In mid-March, while I was unlocking the back door to our house, there came a familiar, unmistakable call from some masked raiders. I looked out toward the bay, and sure enough, my buddies were back, squawking and jostling on the dock opposite. A great flock of exhausted laughing gulls flew in from the south that day and rested.

They're Back!

They looked immaculately dressed in summer plumage with bold dark brown hoods that gave them the appearance of masked bandits. I knew that once reenergized, they would fly off to the marsh opposite to form their colony once again and secure their spots for breeding. They would use the grasses sheared off by the winters ice blocks to build their nests.

The year's cycle was about to start over again when the curtain of green emerged from the mud. "Marsh Mud" is a popular ice cream flavor sold by the Island Creamery on the island, and it epitomizes the season that was about to come. The mud in the marsh is a rich, dark brown color like raw umber, and it began to show signs of life as the temperatures rose. The remaining ochre grassroots rose straight and firm, set like teeth into their impenetrable brown gums below. At first sight, the wet oozing mud could easily creep one out. Its surface glistened, the lifeless translucent jellyfish lying on top, and the smell of sulfurous rotten eggs. The marsh awakened from its short sleep that stretched from horizon to horizon by the familiar "tew" call of the tattler that carried far across the vast flat surface.

In early April, we noticed the first two black-necked stilts feeding on the mudflats out by the causeway. They looked resplendent in their striking black and white plumage as they picked daintily over the slabs of mud, strutting about delicately on their slender, bright pink legs. Forster's terns perched in a line back on the bridge over to Assateague.

A fox surprised us out on the Wildlife Loop. He was out in the open but keeping low, trying to stay hidden in the grasses as he hunted. He looked like a large dog, with lustered fur and a bushy tail flowing behind him like the wake from a boat. He looked cunning and pensive, pausing to sniff the air every few feet as he inched closer towards a great egret on the edge of the marsh. The egret, which had already fixed him from his raised view, in an instant took to the air. The fox turned, and with a last flash of his copper tail, disappeared into the swaying grasses.

It was a welcome surprise one morning to see the fishing boats back at the town dock, not that there were many these days. Surf fishermen were also back, catching on the beach, so it made sense the boats were back. The usual fishing boats— Lady Carolyn, Sharon Nicole, The Eagle, Papa's Girl, Capt. Ralph, and The Kirsten Lee—all were neatly tied up in a row. How amazing it would have been to see the waterfront full of boats way back. A new green boat, the Mary Elizabeth, was in town, docked beside Robert Reed Park. I always notice the newcomers to the island.

Just before the spring pony roundup, I took an early evening walk on the Woodland Trail. It was a calming experience, like last year's walk to the watchman's shack. The silence overwhelmed me. The woods were in between seasons, a time when the winter birds like sparrows and juncos had left, and the songbirds hadn't yet returned. The woods waited in expectancy for the rush that would come from every angle—the human tide, the passerines, and the ponies. Except for the loud drumming of woodpeckers on dead trees, I walked in peace. I didn't have to scan the sides of the path for the odd resting black snake or watch one slither across. It was too early for them. Before the undergrowth burst into green, I gazed into secret clearings visible inside the woods where old gnarled trees grew in peace. The spring growth would hide them again.

We also experienced some spring tides, a factor of the alignment of the earth, sun, and moon, whereby the gravitational forces of both the moon and the sun contributed to extremely high tides. On some days, the tide was so high that it was impossible to distinguish the channels from the marsh, and driving across the causeway made me sense I was adrift, unanchored in a changed landscape that was less distinct and not familiar anymore. Often, driving the causeway was an effective therapy for us. I can imagine a doctor saying to a patient, "Drive the causeway five times a week, and you'll be more relaxed."

In late April, a bolt of emerald green flashed by our kitchen window. He was back, examining the feeder, which I had hesitated to put out so early. He needed the nectar badly, considering he recently flew the entire way from South America. The ruby-throated hummingbird's return was heart-warming, reassuring in that, despite the many problems we face on the planet, and against many odds, this minuscule bird returned from his incredible journey and the world still worked.

Time and place was everything when it came to watching wildlife on the island. When I ambled along the beach, I couldn't help notice the impeccable timing among the shorebirds. I asked myself how individual sanderlings know when to turn in flight at the same time in their flocks. They flip and turn together in an instant, alternating their dark backs and then their white bellies that catch the sun. The sanderlings fly as one, and yet there is no apparent leader. When they feed in the surf, they sense the speed of every wave and know precisely when to move, as it forces them to run up the sand on their fast twinkling feet a few inches ahead of it. They are a marvel of nature. The birds are known as "hunakai" in Hawaiian, which means "sea foam." What an apt description, for that is exactly where we see them here. I grew accustomed to recognizing from a distance the differences between the sandpipers and plovers, as I did with the diving ducks and dabblers. The pipers probe and then strut, whereas the plovers peck and scurry.

Oystercatchers know when the incoming tide is at just the correct height for oysters to open their shells on the oyster beds at Queens Sound. They pry their beaks into a shell and force it open. The bittern has made his appearance in the same spot at the same time for two years in a row. He didn't look like he wanted to be here, but he was on time. In May, the red-headed woodpeckers appear on the refuge, the terns lined up to fish from the bridge, and the laughing gulls begin their colony in the same spot every year.

Getting to know the marsh landscape over our first year meant these observations became familiar and a treasured part of our everyday experience. We were part of the gentle rhythm of living on the island, where seasonal changes occurred, in the same way, every year. The birds, insects, and plants depended on each other as the cycle of the marsh repeated.

It was only April, but the temperatures jumped quickly from the sixties to the eighties in a matter of two weeks. The mainland was eighty-seven degrees when we drove over, but the island was only eighty degrees, thanks to the cooling effect of the waters around it. In the spring, the temperatures on the mainland rise quicker at first than on the island. The waters around the island warm slowly, and so the island takes a while to warm up. In the fall, the reverse is the case.

It was time to uncover our front porch chairs and enjoy dinner outside for the first time since last fall. It felt strange to sit outside, having been inside for months. I didn't bother to think about the mosquitos that I knew would arrive soon. Instead, I hung up the birdhouses around the yard, including a fun one Debbie gave me, a bright red British postbox.

In late April we watched the courting displays of red-breasted mergansers in Swan Cove Pool and noticed a few red knots feeding furiously, no doubt hungry and recovering from the prolonged flight from their faraway wintering grounds on the southern tip of South America. The East Coast is one huge flyway for birds on the move. Airplanes flying high above follow similar routes that birds take. Instead of linking city to city via an airport though, the bird migration routes link one wild place to another in some of the most remote parts of the planet.

The Forster's terns returned and perched on the bridge over at the refuge. This was a convenient spot for them to watch for fish below, without having to expend much energy hovering. The tree and barn swallows patrolled the air once again on the Wildlife Loop, especially around the Shoveler Pool, which they frequented in early spring.

The health of the human spirit is intrinsically linked to having birds around us. In fact, our health depends upon them, and yet many take birds for granted and hardly notice them. They offer many benefits other than drawing tourists. They help farmers stay in business, spread seeds, and prevent the spread of disease. They even help with dead bodies by devouring roadkill. In this landscape, birds surround us every day, and we welcome them back in spring, for it wouldn't be the same if they didn't come back every year.

May arrived quickly and was the richest time in the marsh as the yellow thistles bloomed along the wildlife trails, and interspersed clumps of vibrant red clover blossomed along Beach Road. Everything that was growing insinuated that it only had so much time to reproduce. Soothing variegated greens burst out everywhere, woven together in a chlorophyllous patchwork without boundaries. Distant blue-greens appeared with greyish sages, lime, mint, olive greens, emeralds, shamrocks, the dark greens of conifers. Hibiscus grew six inches a day, reaching for the sky, along with the new green spears of phragmites. Blue grosbeaks and indigo buntings fed along the green borders of the Wildlife Loop. Snapper turtles appeared like small rocks jutting out of the water. They arched over, their armored backs occasionally breaking the surface. Sometimes they hauled themselves up on the grass verges, their enormous bodies black with mud. A crumpled face emerged from the dark recesses of the shell and peeked forward to sniff the warm air.

The damaged hunter's blinds and debris dislodged from winter's wrath lay well buried amongst the tall grasses, thankfully out of sight. The marsh was in full voice, from the sounds of toads calling to each other, the laughing gulls screeching in their colonies, and the spring migrants calling from the canopy on the refuge. There was limited time to see the upper canopy birds, specifically the warblers, before full foliage came in. It was possible to walk the Woodland Trail looking for warblers in comfort before the mosquitos arrived, but by the second week in May, the leaves grew as colossal as rabbits' ears and limited any opportunities for spotting them. One bird that wasn't hard to spot, nonetheless, was the jewel-like cobalt blue indigo buntings that fed conspicuously beside the road along the Wildlife Loop. Since our house is known as the Hattie Bunting House and we saw a few indigo buntings on the refuge, I hand-painted these beautiful birds onto our mailbox.

An excerpt from Mary B. Moore's award-winning poem, *Indigo Bunting's Blue*, compares the colors of the bird:

> *It doesn't match the royal blue flame tips wreathing the stove's brass rings while bordelais thickens.*
>
> *It's bluer than the oxidized turquoise of Chartres' copper roof plates, than the eyelets of sky mirrored in the indentations where rainwater settles on the flat-topped stones in the seawall.*

A hive of activity occurred any day we ventured out in May, and it reminded me of the controversy surrounding whether kids got enough time outside these days. Some people say that if parents don't encourage this at an early age, kids are not well rounded. It is a well-known fact that many kids today grow up with an inside lifestyle, attached to their technology and not knowing the world outside, a sort of child divorce with nature. I was thankful that years ago in my teens I could roam the countryside for hours at a time, and my parents were rarely concerned. In fact, they didn't want to see me until dinnertime. Research studies show that if one goes outside with one's parents at an early age, it creates a more significant connection with them. There are many articles about this, but one thing does stand out, and that is that a life led in touch with nature does have a therapeutic effect on most people. I believe people need to experience nature, for it serves to define our place in the world and how we fit in. Chincoteague offers this in abundance.

The Friday evening of Memorial Day weekend presented an interesting opportunity to watch incoming visitor traffic from our front porch. Coming from the direction of the bridge was a distinct group of vehicles that made us laugh, many driving way over the island's twenty-five mile per hour speed limit. A procession of RVs contained pale-skinned drivers with their windows rolled down. The model names of their RVs were hilarious to read as they passed our house and made for the campgrounds. From our perspective, they were names feeding off images of the wild west, or big powerful animals. A few of the brands we observed were Montana, Coachmen, Puma, Chaparral, Eagle, Cherokee, Laredo, Jay Feather, Cascade, Sierra, Jayco, Wildwood, Tioga, Zinger, Kodiak, Windjammer Rockland, and Fleetwood Discovery. One RV even towed a truck with a golf cart in the back bed. As the endless procession passed our house shaking the ground, we wondered who needed so much stuff for a short weekend stay.

There was a mixture of BMWs and Lexuses, some containing affluent, well-dressed visitors on their first visit, others with kids peering out of the back windows at the scenery around them. Then came the Yukon XLs and Suburbans crammed with people, and hatchbacks with canoes protruding out of the rear windows.

At one point, a massive rumbling noise came from our right. Debbie turned to me and said, "Don't look now but the Raptor is back."

Once again, the Star Wars-looking box of tricks on wheels passed the house, the mother of all RVs, this time pulled by an even more ominous looking giant black tractor trailer. Last year we didn't recall such a large truck towing it. Two hours passed, and then a state-of-the-art giant RV rolled by that we added to our RV spotter's list. I laughed—this one boasted an impressive name, The Seismic Wave, scrolled across its header as it passed the house and shook the tarmac. I considered that someone sitting in an office somewhere came up with these crazy names.

The drivers coming from the left looked rougher, often with a tattooed arm hanging from the driver side window. One man, apparently proud of his well-kept vintage red Chevrolet truck, rounded the corner for the second time in the day, chugging off down the street like a Panzer tank. Other trucks followed with splattering wet-fart mufflers.

While we enjoyed dinner on our front porch, we were continually amazed at the condition of vehicles that drove past our house: beaten up trucks that sounded like they could fail any second, many with a gazillion fishing rods hanging out the back, or their back beds crammed with a mishmash of used furniture. The vehicles that continued straight down Main Street toward the southern end of the island appeared to have more junk in them, spare wood hanging out the back, bedraggled plants, or various nondescript metal objects that we couldn't make out.

The massive RVs, on the other hand, tended to turn left and headed towards Tom's Cove campground. The occasional line of student scooter renters passed on their puny annoying engines sounding like strangled weasels, thinking they looked so cool.

I didn't care for the unnecessary vehicle noises that invaded our world again and made the porch rumble. There were too many of them everywhere these days, and the island was no exception. After the roving dinner crowd died down, the quieter vehicles, like the electric rental carts, passed by so we could enjoy our summer view with less interruption.

Only when we reluctantly turned on the air conditioning on hot, humid days did we realize we could isolate ourselves from the noise. We prefer the windows open though, so we simply build the vehicle noises into our summer routine. No wonder we yearn for the less busy months.

As the crisscross traffic chaos unfolded, swallows careened around in the sky above the street, oblivious to the human craziness happening beneath them. The party house catty-corner to us once again erupted back into life, with the arrival of a varied assortment of Land Rovers, Audis, and BMWs. There wasn't enough room for all eleven cars, so they parked some in front of our house. The visitors then partied most of the night, whooping and hollering on the back porch and disturbing the neighborhood. It was such a relief when they departed a few days later. The day they left, they dragged a large black bag full of their empty beer cans and bottles out to the curb. Once again, they didn't turn off their air conditioning or their back porch lights.

We decided to take a short trip to the beach. We always visited early in the day, so we could sit out for a while when it wasn't busy, and then come home for lunch before the crowds built up. We drove on the back roads to avoid the traffic on Maddox Blvd., the main thoroughfare to the beach.

We set our beach chairs up and settled in for a tranquil morning. At first, we enjoyed some wonderful peace with very few people—just couples ambling along in the surf and shell collectors staring down, looking for that unique shell—the sun still low in the sky, not blazing hot yet, with a gentle breeze that caressed our skin. It was a slow start to the day, as most visiting families ate their breakfast and weren't out yet. The angle of the sun made the ocean waves sparkle as they rolled over lazily to greet the day. A sense of space, calmness, and civility prevailed before the onslaught. The ocean issued a familiar mantra of white noise, as the waves gently kissed the shore.

Abruptly and all at once, the human noises arrived, along with boogie boards, coolers, dads digging in umbrellas, families carrying buckets and spades, and screaming kids. I opened my eyes from my relaxed state and turned around to see a blaze of colorful parasols filling every space along the beach. Unfortunately that day, we experienced beach comers with no accounting for taste or respect for others. A colossal family set up too close to us with a huge tent canopy and an army of plastic lawn chairs. The only thing they forgot was their sixty-inch television. They constantly shouted and whistled at their children who played down by the water's edge.

I was dismayed to see directly in front of the family a few surf fishermen casting heavy leads with their bait. Bathers were oblivious to a surf angler hurling a six-ounce lead over their heads at great speed. This could have seriously injured someone. Mercifully, the fishermen, realizing the potential danger, eventually gave up as the bathing numbers grew.

The shell hunters now strolled through mostly picked-over shells. Had they been early, they might have found a special one. A group of noisy teens arrived with their boom box playing some offensive music. They had no regard for others or any awareness that perhaps people didn't want to listen to their invasive rap tunes. Some of us actually enjoyed peace at the beach.

It astonished me some days just how entitled visitors to the island behaved. Some even believed it was okay to kayak over to where the ponies grazed, get out of their kayaks, and stand next to the ponies, taking selfies. The ponies are wild animals, and you never know when they might feel threatened and react. I tried to relax, despite the noise around me, when I overheard some college girls close to us saying they couldn't wait to go clubbing later on the island. Little did they know the nearest club was in Salisbury or Ocean City, fifty miles away. The final straw came in the form of a newlywed couple with a newborn. They set up their beach chairs practically on top of us, despite plenty of other spaces to sit. As they dug their umbrella in the sand, they uncovered garbage left by others who didn't have the decency to take their litter home. When they proceeded to change their baby's diaper, the smell was the final nail.

It was time to go home and return another day when the public was not so overbearing., When we packed up, the wind changed direction as if on cue from a gentle sea breeze to a hot breath coming off the land. It brought the biting flies onto the beach, just what was needed to punish the invaders of my peace and seclusion. We pulled out of our parking space, and immediately another car pulled in; the lot was full. For those who visit the beach, there is an overload of senses, and for some, they have had no exposure or familiarity with nature. They merely see it as just another theme park, where they must stand in line to use the porta potty.

We returned home and sat on our porch, where we experienced instant therapy, noticing the return of brown pelicans in the bay, flying in their family groups with their familiar flap and glide technique.

Monday came, and we viewed the same RVs returning home in a mass exodus. I could see the lines of RVs a few minutes later on the causeway out in the bay pulling their homes behind them like sluggish snails.

The warm season returned, and we looked forward to seeing what it yielded. When would I get my first mosquito bite? Who might come to visit? Did the same events occur again this year? Three things hadn't changed. The tourists returned, so did the laughing gulls, and the wildlife provided endless enjoyment throughout our year.

34

THE ELUSIVE STRIPER

Some fishermen might laugh when I say that the striper has been hard for me to catch. I haven't put in the hours many people have, but I have been in the surf when numerous fish were present and still wasn't lucky.

My poor luck goes back ten years, and over that time, the striper migrations up the Eastern Shore have been patchy some years. I could have ventured out on a charter boat, but instead, I wanted to experience catching one for myself off the surf. So began my quest since I moved to Chincoteague.

Striped bass provide some of the best sport fishing on the Eastern Shore. I recalled my hike to the Coast Guard Station back in August when a Teaguer told me that May and November were the best months. In mid-May, my chance came when a run of fish occurred off the beaches. The local tackle shop, Steve's, posted numerous pictures of surf fishermen proudly displaying their striper catches on their Facebook pages. I was ready for some action.

It was a Sunday, and anglers crowded the beach, so I trudged further along the shoreline to find a quiet spot. I noticed one fisherman using six rods, which seemed a bit overkill. I thought to myself, *What happens if he hooks multiple fish at the same time?* It was sixty-nine degrees and overcast, but the sun peeked through in between the occasional shower. I fished on a falling tide, which the striper sages stated was not ideal, but the fish might bite for the first two hours.

I chose a spot randomly, not knowing if it held fish since I wasn't that great at reading the beach. Other fishermen told me to look for cuts and holes in the sandbars, but I wasn't that experienced to know what they looked like. I was a novice, like the great writer Mark Twain was when he learned from the veteran steamboat captain Horace Bixby how to steer his paddle steamer through the shifting sandbanks of the Mississippi.

In John Macfarlane's book, *The Old Ways*, he writes,

Horace Bixby taught Mark Twain to read the surface for depth: how small perturbations might infer large submerged truths, a long slanting line that might suggest a reef.

I saw examples of how waves looked when they approached sandbars, cuts, and holes online, but no one actually taught me how to read beach structure. After baiting my hooks with cut bunker, I set my two rods in their sand spikes and sat for what felt like ages, blankly staring out to sea in a trance. I glanced up every so often at the rod tips to watch for any sudden tugs, not knowing what a tug might look like with a striper on the line.

After a while, a group of fishermen set up not that far from me. They appeared very organized and immediately proceeded to dig in the sand for something. I was curious about what it was, and casually wandered over to introduce myself and have a chat. So began my delightful encounter and adventure with the three Franks. There was Frank Senior, Frank the father, and Frank the father's son. Frankly speaking, (ha ha) I could not resist that, it was rather hilarious. I began by inquiring about the fishing.

"It's been great," Frank Senior replied. "We are on a run. In the middle of the week, we caught thirty shorts (smaller stripers), and today hope we'll get a larger one. We can take only one fish over twenty-eight inches this year, and not two as before since the rules have changed."

This was news to me, as I didn't know the limit changed.

I asked what bait they used and quickly realized that I had the wrong bait. On seeing me pull out my bunker, Frank Senior remarked, "Don't use bunker, the fish are feeding on mole crabs in the surf. I'll show you what a mole crab looks like. Come over here and take a look."

I hadn't seen a mole crab or sand flea, as they referred to it, so Frank Senior picked one out of his bucket. It reminded me of a miniature armadillo with an oval-shaped hard shell, about an inch and a half long with a bundle of legs under its shell. It looked more like a shrimp to me on the underside with two antennae that it used for filter feeding in the surf.

Frank the father dug for fresh crabs with his light, short-handled spade.

"Once you find a large one, dig closer to that as more will be there," he said, "Because the swash zone changes with the tide, so do the location of the crabs. You have to move quickly, throwing and spreading the sand sideways, so the crabs are visible before they burrow back into the sand. Also, look in the hole when removing the spade as the crabs often fall down into the bottom again. After catching a few, fill a bucket with sand and water and put them in. That way they'll stay fresh while you are fishing. You will need a lot due to the losses. I put at least two on a hook."

Frank the father showed me how he located them.

"Look for a spot near the water where there are Vs that appear hardly visible as the wave rolls out. The V is the set of antennae that belong to a mole crab."

He then loaned me his shovel, which was very generous of him, so that I could gather some for myself. It wasn't easy, as I dug around in a random manner trying to locate them. Then I found one. I quickly picked him up and plopped him into my bucket. After that, I was on a roll and found plenty nearby. When I returned the shovel to Frank the father, he pulled a crab out of his bucket.

"Now I'll show you how I hook them," he said. "Thread your hook up through the body, toward the head, and out through the outer shell. You will have to rebait every fifteen minutes due to the losses. Put two crabs on at a time and use an eight/zero circle hook. Are you using a high-low rig?"

"Yes," I answered. A high-low rig has a lead sinker at the end of the line, and two dropper loops come off the main line further up with a hook on each end. This presents chunk baits at various heights in the surf and parallel to the beach.

For the first time, I was able to locate my own mole crabs quite successfully and made some mental notes on how to catch them another time. I also got some lessons on reading the water as Frank the father showed me where there was an immense suck out, where the waves collided and the water forced into a confused mess. Outside this area was where the fish congregated.

I continued to fish alongside the Franks for another two hours. During that time, they caught a short striper and a twenty-six-inch black drum keeper. They then packed up and wished me luck as they left. I thanked them for their advice and quickly moved into their spot, hoping that their luck rubbed off on me. Unfortunately, like many of my previous adventures, I blanked that day but learned a lot from the Franks.

I stopped at Captain Steve's Tackle shop on the way home to get some larger hooks and more high-low rigs for another outing, as I was determined more than ever to catch a striper.

Free mole crabs make sense compared to the more expensive store-bought bait, and you get a workout digging for them. When I got home, I rummaged around in the garage to find a rough, worn spade that my father used to shovel coal back in Wales. I brought it back from the UK as a memory of him and didn't consider it useful again. As it was shorter than most spades, it might have a purpose yet to locate mole crabs, but unfortunately, I felt the weight from the heavy, sturdy metal plate firmly set into the thick wooden handle. It weighed too much for me to lug along the beach with my gear; a lighter, collapsible spade worked better. Then an amusing thought came into my head. What if my father could see me now digging for mole crabs on an Atlantic beach, using the spade he previously used to shovel coal in the kitchen of a Welsh homestead?

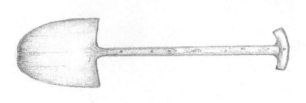

The Welsh Coal Shovel

My third and final attempt to catch a striper was on a Wednesday before the holiday weekend. After that date, the forecast predicted heavy rain, and the crazy Memorial Day tourists came back so that the beaches would be crowded. For this trip, Debbie joined me, as she was curious about surf fishing.

It was warm and sunny, in the low seventies. No one was fishing on the beach, so I wondered if the fish slept in that day and the memo hadn't reached me. Despite the lack of fishermen, nonetheless, I decided to head to the very spot where the three Franks fished the previous Sunday, hoping that the hole, or "suck out," as they referred to it, might still be there. It was quite a hike, but I was hoping for third time lucky. Debbie helped me set up the chairs and equipment, and then I dug for mole crabs for the first half hour, collecting a bucketful to last the late afternoon and into the evening. On my previous sessions, I nearly ran short of them because the tide advanced so quickly up the beach that they got harder to find nearer the top of the tidemark.

After I set my rods up, I proceeded to bait up the two hooks on each rod every fifteen minutes with two mole crabs on each hook. I repositioned the rods every so often, moving them further up the beach as the tide came in quite quickly. It added to our fishing pleasure to see dolphin offshore, and two pelicans came by. My white plastic rod holders often gave away and fell over frequently, as the incoming tide washed around them. I had made these at home from cutting PVC tubing and then shaping the ends.

As each rod and its holder started to fall over onto the sand, I darted over and grabbed it. It became an annoying routine until one time I looked down at one rod, and the line was flying off the spool, turning wildly and spewing sand in every direction. I picked the rod up and engaged the bale arm. I immediately felt a heavy, dead weight on the other end. I quickly loosened the drag slightly to allow the line to give. The reel still churned, with line flying off at a heck of a speed, so I was careful not to tighten the drag up too quickly in case I snapped off whatever it was. I played it safely by loosening the tension on the drag, a yard at a time. Other fishermen might have advised me not to do this, as it gave the fish more line when I should have checked and muscled it in. I had only seventeen pounds of line on my spool, so whatever I had caught was taking a ton of it, and the end of the line was imminent. I thought fast and took a chance when I felt less resistance and reeled in more line. I was lucky, as the incoming waves helped me play the fish in.

Every time the fish paused, I used the natural onshore current to gain more line back, slowly gaining a few feet at a time, cranking and waiting, then cranking and waiting again, as my muscles and that of the fish wore out. My heart pounded in my chest as the dead weight drew ever closer to the beach.

The anticipation was nerve-racking but also exhilarating as I waited to see what my prize was.

Debbie grabbed my camera and came down to the shoreline to stand alongside me, ready to take a few photos.

"Do you think it's a Striper?" she asked.

"I have no idea, but whatever it is, it's putting up one hell of a fight. I have to be careful as it comes closer, in case I break him off."

Eventually, my unknown prize tired, as there was no more tugging on the line, simply a solid mass somewhere out there languishing in the murky rolling waves. Suddenly three breakers out, my reward broke on the crest of a wave, ever so briefly in the shape of a bulky silver bullet. At first, it looked like it had three fins, but I wasn't sure as it rolled beneath the surface. It was enormous and sent an exciting shiver through me, as I hadn't ever caught such an impressive fish as this before.

"Yeeks!" I shouted, and then it appeared briefly again, much closer. A flash of sunlight bounced off its gleaming silver scales that glistened and flashed pure white for a second or two before disappearing beneath the waves. It was my first striper, at last, a fish I sought for ten years. Previous outings ended with either no fish or my timing was terrible. Mind you, the hours put in by me are no match for those who spent weeks targeting this species. I took my time getting him safely to the shoreline and then waded in to lift him out. I didn't know how to bring him up onto the beach, so I let the wave action roll him onto the sand. He lay there panting like a massive dog on its side with its mouth open.

"Wow!" I yelled to Debbie. "Look at the size of him!"

What a gorgeous beast he was—and a wonder to look at on the beach, illuminated by the golden rays of the evening sun.

I felt the strength of my fish the entire way into the swash zone and marveled at finally seeing a giant striper up close in person. I was awestruck. It felt like it weighed a ton as I heaved him up onto the dry sand to make some decisions. His head and girth were substantial, and his build spoke of his notorious power.

Robert Liguori spoke of the fish's power in his poem titled, *The Striper's Soul.*

My rod just bent in half!
My heart is pounding fast!
My line is spooling out,
What a sudden blast!

He's on, I set my hook!
And then I set again!
I give him time to run,
My rod just bends and bends!

While I had played the fish, Debbie frantically tried to unravel the line on the other rod, which I had crossed over when I hooked the fish. I asked her to reel the second rod in should another fish strike, but I hadn't given her any instructions in the ensuing chaos. She hadn't known what to do, so she was in an awful pickle, which I apologized for. The other white sand spike (used to hold the rods in place) had careened off into the surf and was lost, but that didn't matter now. Ultimately, I truly landed a wonderful fish after trying for so many years.

As the fish lay there gasping for air, I was suddenly overcome with doubt about whether to keep it. He measured close to forty inches from tail to mouth, so it was a magnificent specimen. Part of me wanted to let him go, but I had waited so many years for this that I was inclined to keep him and enjoy the fillets he would give us. Debbie chimed in and reminded me of the wait.

So we carried my fish, wrapped tightly in my large beach towel, a thousand yards back to the car. It was an arduous and burdensome walk, so I promised myself I would invest in a hand-pulled beach buggy for subsequent trips.

While driving to Captain Steve's Bait and Tackle shop to have him weighed, it was somewhat disconcerting to hear my fish occasionally thrashing around in the towel on the back seat of the car. I was the only fisherman that day to check in a fish for weighing, as everyone else had taken the day off. He weighed in at thirty pounds and later Captain Steve's posted the photo on their Facebook page. Persistence finally paid off and the endless digging, baiting, and rebaiting with mole crabs constantly for the week was worth it.

I asked the staff at Captain Steve's about how to fillet the fish, as I didn't know. A quick video on YouTube assisted me, making the process much easier. We got about sixteen fillets off the fish, but there was quite a bit of waste in the over-proportioned head, lungs, and rib cage. Since most of the fish comprised its extensive rib cage and head, there wasn't much meat on it. I took the remains to the back of our property and lobbed them into the gut. Keeping some bones for fish stock was ideal, but they weren't easy to cut into smaller pieces, so maybe a shorter striper was better for that.

Later on, after doing some research, I discovered that wild striped bass (a whole fish) yields only a third to skin-on fillet, whereas a salmon (head-on gutted) yielded three quarters to skin-on fillet. One evidently got a lot more off a salmon than a striped bass.

The surf-fishing quest was an awesome experience, but I don't know if I would take another grand fish like that again. This may sound ridiculous to regular fishermen, but while it was fun to do it once, the conservationist in me couldn't get used to taking large fish regularly out of an already impoverished ocean.

35

HIDDEN GEMS

Pastel of Pitts Creek Landing

R oute 13 is the main highway down the Eastern Shore and the only one lit. Many years back, people referred to it as the stone road, but I am not sure if it was ever actually stone. All I know is it would qualify for a great Roman road. Everyone drives down Route 13 to the Chesapeake Bay Bridge, passing through undifferentiated towns with few distinctive features, stopping only for gas or a quick snack at Royal Farms. On either side of the highway are vein-like, unlit, country roads that lead back to the bayside or seaside. Strung along these deserted roads are spaced-out single-family homes or groups of trailers, separated communities where often a white clapboard church or barn is the largest building around.

We have made numerous trips down the Eastern Shore and over the Bay Bridge to Norfolk. Every time we make the one-and-a-half hour journey south, we comment on how scarcely any development has occurred, other than the numerous chicken houses hastily built across the landscape. It seems that no other major industry wants to come here.

Some of the houses along the highway are in disrepair, often in a worse state when we make our next trip down. Some of these homes are historical, but no one has the money or time to restore them to their former glory. We note how a business may have closed, or a house collapsed. Despite the gloom, however, the burgundy blooms of the mature crepe myrtle bushes line the highway and add color to our drive.

The real beauty of the Eastern Shore lies hidden off the highway, in the views from private homes that face the bay or sea, within concealed historical buildings that hold a host of treasures and stories, and in the gorgeous private gardens behind these historical homes.

Similar to the discovery of enchanting homes during the Homes for the Holidays tour on Chincoteague, on the mainland, there are also hidden gems.

We enjoyed seeing some of these magnificent homes on the House and Garden Tour that has occurred every year at the end of April for over seventy years. This tour offers a view that very few people know when they drive along Route 13. The properties provide a welcome change of scenery and an opportunity to step back in time into some gorgeously restored period homes hidden down secluded roads. It opened up our eyes to places we could never have known existed.

This tour took us out of our usual lives into another world. Some homes were steeped in history, including trading and slavery. Some were full of furniture the owners collected on travels all over the world—one even displayed an original Picasso. We drove on far-reaching, straight private roads flanked by dense woodland to both historical and modern homes hidden away from Route 13. The historical homes were intentionally located close to the water because the owners relied on the delivery of supplies along the Chesapeake or from the sea. The modern homes now, of course, have the roads in place to deliver their supplies.

The home sites, only revealed on special occasions, are in secluded spots amongst acres of land for added security, and they often overlook beautiful scenic creeks that sprawl out below them. Unless one participates in the house tour, you wouldn't know of their existence. This rarefied world represents a massive difference between the haves and the have not's who live along Route 13.

Upon arrival at the first property, called Walston Place, we noticed two things: The parking lot wasn't full of the usual pickup trucks we had become accustomed to seeing, but rather BMWs and sleek SUVs; and the audience was predominantly white, older, and appeared more upscale. They mirrored the same audience we saw at the classical concert in Machipongo.

At every location, the tour guides were attractive, well-heeled, middle-aged women dressed up fashionably for the day. They had the Lilly Pulitzer look, wearing colors to match the exquisite, cleverly positioned flower arrangements, which matched the décor of the rooms. The guides provided as much entertainment as the properties themselves. The women greeted viewers at each property, relating its history or pointing out facts about various artifacts in each room.

The attention to detail in each property was impeccable. Each period home was restored to a high order with the best furnishings, and there was an academic, educated atmosphere in each place. Despite the fact that we didn't meet many owners, I tried to figure out their interests by looking at what books were on their shelves, or in one case, observing a large collection of old vinyl records.

I also noticed that some properties contained neglected graveyards, sometimes close to the property itself. I was curious as to why people were buried on the land, so I did some research. I found a fascinating article on Delmarvanow.com written by Jennifer Cording. This is what I learned:

According to Miles Barnes, librarian at the Eastern Shore Public Library and a well-known Shore historian, "Planned cemeteries were not fashionable, or practical, until around the turn of the 20th century."

Prior to this, John T. Williams Jr., a third-generation funeral director at Williams Funeral Homes in Parksley, Virginia, said, "Whoever owned the land picked a spot and started burials there. It was usually a high spot on the farm. The remains faced east, as Christian tradition dictated. This was so the dead were ready to rise in their graves to meet Christ who appeared in the east. Sometimes, farmhands or slaves were buried in the plots, along with family. Farmers tend to respect (the family graveyards) as much as possible and literally plow around them. When they sell the land and the deeds transfer, the descendants have the right to visit the plot indefinitely.

"State laws do govern where a cemetery may or may not be located," John Williams continued, "basically not within 250 yards of a residence, unless one has the homeowner's permission. Less distance is allowed in some circumstances."

In some of the plots I viewed, some of the graves looked sunken and rotten. I learned that in Virginia and in Accomack County, there are no laws to govern the condition of a rotted, sunken grave—even those exposing human bones. Public health officials admit there is nothing to enforce.

According to Miles Barnes, "It was the coming of the railroad that changed the way people buried people on the Eastern Shore. We have no native stone, so any stone had to be brought in. Until the arrival of the railroad in 1884, only the wealthy could afford to bring stone in."

The railroad linked to the wealthy, as it transported the huge volumes of their produce off the Eastern Shore. According to Barnes, "There's no dating of the great majority of English and African graves on the Shore," Barnes said. "We walk on the dead on the Shore every day."

One of the modern homes we visited was located on a spit of land named Cove's End. The owner designed the house in the shape of a flying bird. As we toured, we made our way along its wings and ended up at the head, which was a marvelous dining room with large windows overlooking the creek below.

Each year the homes on the tour change, so we look forward to discovering more hidden places tucked away from Route 13.

At Chatham Vineyards, we decided to do some wine tasting in their modern facility located in a separate building away from the main house. Once again, well-dressed, attractive women wearing stylish puffer vests welcomed us in the refined atmosphere of the tasting room, surrounded by oak barrels. We sampled six varieties of wine and then purchased a glass of our favorite for each of us, retiring to a perfectly positioned outside fire pit to sit and savor the experience on a beautiful sunny day. Our server brought out a delicious cheese platter served on a slate slab. The vast flat fields of the estate stretched out before us, with vines strung out in neat rows. The smell of wood smoke, combined with the sharp, gamey aroma of cheese, hung in the air as we sipped our crisp, fruitful wines. Everything was rather bucolic; nevertheless, something bothered me. I couldn't help notice and wonder about an abandoned home standing by itself near the incoming driveway. What family once lived there? The juxtaposition of these dwellings, those with plenty in the old Chatham home, and those who had been less fortunate in the smaller homestead were noticeable on many of our visits that day.

Suitable work is hard to find on the Eastern Shore, so the owners of these magnificent properties tend to be retired or derive their income from other places. Here we glimpsed the Eastern Shore's landed gentry in their beautiful homes, but I couldn't help sense a mammoth disconnect. A similar difference existed between the stately homes on the north end of Chincoteague Island and the trailers in other parts of the island. Here is a region where there are such drastic differences seen within three miles of each other.

When I drove out of the driveway from the historically restored Metomkin Farm, I only traveled half a mile when I looked to my left and spied a damp, unkempt trailer buried in thick woodland. A brand-new Nissan SUV was parked outside it.

The Virginia Eastern Shore Land Trust asked eight well-known artists to create paintings of these magnificent homes on the shore to sell to benefit the Land Trust. I was invited to participate. I visited a home known as Pitts Neck, not far from Chincoteague. With its grand brick façade, it looked imposing in the photos that the VES Land Trust emailed me. The owner, Wayne Williams, attended our church and invited us over for a tour. I planned to take some reference photos for the painting I would create.

It wasn't an easy place to find. We drove north along Route 13 to the other side of the bay and then made a sharp left onto a straight country road, which then twisted and turned through a flat landscape.

Vast fields opened up, some ripening with wheat, others full of fast-growing corn bordered by thick stands of woodland. Single-family homes spaced out randomly, a few tucked into the shaded woods. The periodic abandoned farmhouse didn't surprise me. A newish looking car tucked behind an unkempt barn gathered weeds. I had to be careful not to take Routes 708 or 704, as they split off in different directions. *How did someone find this place at night?* I thought. I had almost reached the bay. My enthusiasm waned as I began to wonder if the great home I was seeking existed.

As the road bordered by high hedges curved, suddenly a fantastic red-bricked building with tall chimneys set back from the road appeared. Just for a moment, I thought I was back in England and about to drive up to a duke's country house. It looked as if it had been picked up from the English countryside and plopped down in America. What an impressive find! It had beautifully manicured lawns, and crepe myrtles and hollies lined the straight shell driveway, evenly dispersed leading up to the old brick building.

I drove slowly up the drive and parked in the back. Immediately, I noticed a very old addition with a partial roof under restoration. I would learn from Wayne that this was the oldest part of the house, built in 1692. The main house was built in 1734. I didn't have to knock, as Wayne Williams, clutching his small poodle named Bailey, had already opened the back door. Wayne is a quietly spoken man in his seventies with a distinguished look about him. Very methodical in his mannerisms, he has a calming effect—he's the sort of guy you would want flying the plane if there was a problem.

We wandered through the modern part of the house and sat in his sumptuous sitting room with its stately brick fireplace. Light flooded in from every window. The views were beautiful. Wayne proceeded to tell me the history of this residential gem.

"Robert Pitt was the original owner back in 1663. I believe there is a connection to William Pitt, but that hasn't been proved. Robert came from wealth as his father owned a fleet of ships."

Wayne recounted the evidence he discovered on the property about the previous existence of Native Americans. When Wayne drilled wells to put in a geothermal system, the contractors uncovered numerous Native American artifacts. About seventy-five feet from the house, they struck a trench seven or eight feet long by two feet deep full of human bones.

When Wayne's wife requested a survey be conducted to move their driveway, the surveyors stated that they didn't uncover enough domestic artifacts for it to be a homestead. It transpired that this was an ossuary or ceremonial group burial site for Native Americans.

A short distance from Pitts Neck is the hairpin turn of the Pocomoke River. When John Smith arrived in 1608, a year after his landing, he mapped the Chesapeake Bay. In doing so, he sailed up the Pocomoke River searching for fresh water, as they were running low. He stopped at Pitts Neck, where the natural bend in the river made for a perfect landing. Wayne has consulted numerous well-known historians and historical documents. He learned that John Smith spent the night with the Native Americans close to his property.

I was mesmerized as Wayne told his story in his calm, relaxing way. I felt surrounded by the ghosts of the past and their untold stories—in, of all places, the Eastern Shore. The fact that this history took place just twenty miles from Chincoteague Island was also quite remarkable. Up until this time, the only other home of historical significance I knew of was the Timothy Hill House on the island.

Wayne explained that the density for large colonial homes is much greater further south on the Eastern Shore. "There are not many further up north," he said. "The development on the shore started further down and progressed up. The irony now is Northampton County is the poorest on the shore."

When I thanked Wayne for the fascinating tour of his house, he made a poignant last comment. After I congratulated him on all his restoration accomplishments, his parting words to me were, "I am doing very well here, but I have no backup. Sort of like flying without a safety net." I assumed he was referring to having no one who would take the place on and care for it.

The upkeep on these lovely homes is enormous, just as it is with those I had seen on the Garden Tour.

A few weeks later I created a pastel painting of Pitts Neck. I chose an unusual angle from which to paint. Way back behind the house, a track led back through the ripening corn to the creek. Halfway along, a small ridge rose up across the track. I stopped and climbed out of my car and stood on the roof from where I had a unique view of the magnificent house. I took a few photo references. I learned there was even more history from where I painted.

Wayne told me that the slight ridge was made up of oyster shells.

"Why in the middle of a cornfield?" I asked.

"It was the site of two slave cabins located away from the house," Wayne replied. "The slaves discarded their oyster shells onto the ground outside, which over time built up into quite a pile."

It made me appreciate just what history lies beneath our feet on the Eastern Shore. It made me think about all the stories I had heard on the Tump. In only one year, I had learned so much about my new home—all about what the Irish referred to as just an insignificant chunk of land.

Chincoteague is so much more than just a chunk of land. It's a special place deeply steeped in history.

EPILOGUE

Debbie and I are lucky because we have been able to slow our lives down from the hectic pace of New Jersey. We no longer endure a commute and pay high taxes. Any stress that arises we instantly forget at the sight of an amazing sunset or a flock of egrets gliding effortlessly past our house at the end of the day. Many people come to Chincoteague when they want to retire. We are younger than the average retiree, and we still have our physical abilities and the energy to enjoy the island.

We have met genuine, honest people who don't need to impress us with their cars or jobs; who often don't look at their watches. The local mentality of attending to tasks somewhat more slowly—and not always on time—can sometimes be frustrating, but for the most part, the benefits far outweigh any aggravation. The beach and Wildlife Loop are a mere ten minutes from our home, so any stress from the day can instantly be relieved by visiting either place or by sailing out in the bay in front of our house.

Some people are surprised when we tell them we survived the year without a TV. We are not people who depend on technology to enrich our lives. So much is available through our computers that we haven't the need.

Debbie reorganized our garden with beautiful dahlias that we had no idea grew well here, and we successfully transplanted plants from our mature gardens in New Jersey. The start of my island art career has been successful with numerous original art sales at our makeshift gallery in the house. It is a pleasure to talk to interesting people from every part of the U.S., many of whom had Chincoteague on their bucket list.

We dislike those who visit the island with a party mentality, as they add nothing to the island except their noise. Fortunately, most visitors are not like this. The wake the revelers cause on the island is noticeable during the busy months. On Labor Day when they leave, it is always a relief, so our neighborhood can get back to its quiet self again.

We also experienced a year of construction from the building of Loraine's house. The constant sound of nail guns, forklift trucks, and table saws was exasperating.

We have learned to live with the screeches from the laughing gulls in the early morning and tourists blasting the horns on their scooters all day long. When I drive to school on the mainland, I listen to the radio and sometimes catch news of the traffic delays for those stuck in their cars in Washington or Norfolk. We have none of that here, except for the short delay caused by ducks crossing the road in the early morning.

They say that blood runs thicker than water, so when it rains, my mind wanders back to North Wales, and I suffer what Welsh people call a bit of *hiraeth*, which means longing. Chincoteague is another shore away from Rhos-on-Sea back in Wales, yet both are similar in many ways. They host the regular rhythm of life played out by the daily tides and setting sun, supported by the magnificent backdrop of nature and the changing seasons.

Around the Christmas holidays, I miss my family in the UK, the rugby, Welsh rain, and a great tasting cup of tea. I miss the British sense of humor and how we connect with each other on another level instantly when we meet. We Brits grew up with the *Carry On Movies*, *Only Fools and Horses*, and *Benny Hill*, so maybe that is why we share the same sense of humor. Could it be our therapy for enduring such lousy weather and imperfect healthcare? I know that for me, a hearty laugh during the day can ultimately make a huge difference. Fortunately, I have found a handful of Brits, Teaguers and Come'eres to add that sense of humor that I miss.

I often find the opportunity to laugh on the island. One very hot day while driving home from the gym, I spotted JJ Jamaican John riding his bright yellow and green bicycle, smoking a cigar, and wearing his distinctive woolen bobble hat in

Jamaican colors. I rolled down my car window and yelled, Hi, JJ! to which he replied, Hello there, Mon. I chuckled to myself and thought, *Who would have thought I'd be on an island in the U.S. waving to a Jamaican I hardly know, who wears a bobble hat in eighty-degree weather?!* It is this crazy quirkiness I love about the island. Spending one evening sitting on our front porch can yield a plethora of similar characters.

Debbie and I can always travel back to our much-loved cities in Europe. During my years of travel, my heart has embraced many landscapes that now lie within it. On occasion, we take a drive off the island to Norfolk or Washington, DC, to experience greater sophistication in a more cosmopolitan atmosphere. Some days we admittedly crave integration, culture, and civility in the stylish places we have known in Europe. When we leave the island, it reminds us there is a massive world out there with a lot more to explore, but then we look forward to coming back. We only hope that we never reach a point where we take this beautiful island for granted. There is always peace and tranquility here, and an interesting chat with an eclectic mix of people—Come'eres, Teaguers, and, of course, the tourists.

I am sometimes inclined to pinch myself that I really live here and not merely exist as I did before. It doesn't offer a living in the sense of realistic wages, but it certainly offers a fulfilling life.

One gets a sense, when one crosses the causeway, of coming home to something honest and genuine. These qualities endure warmly in memory. There is so much that nurtures the soul here: the silence and solitude in winter, the wonder of nature, and the clean, expansive beach.

Debbie and I use our talents as teachers to serve God's purpose and to help His children. Our lives have taken on a kind of ministerial service. When you are teaching kids who haven't had much education, anything you can spill into their brains is good. Many of our students cannot see a future for themselves on the Eastern Shore, so we try to inspire as many as possible.

I have much to learn about Chincoteague, but during our first year here, I enjoyed seeing the island in every one of its moods, its many kinds of weather, and its community with all its strengths and weaknesses. If I am to stay, grow, and weather the years, a place must welcome me, nourish me, and allow me to flourish. This certainly seems possible in the short time I have lived here.

For those who might consider doing what we have done, I encourage you to take the risk. Opting out of a stressful life takes courage and a belief in oneself. Don't wait until it's too late. Our many walks in the marsh impressed upon us that the meaning of life is not about a fat bank balance or a fancy job. It is hard to compare these stressful accomplishments with the euphoria of seeing a snowy owl on the beach.

We laughed at a recent obituary in the paper, which read, John died from complications from a life well lived. It sums up everything important about living.

As Hunter S. Thompson once wrote,

Life should not be a journey to the grave with the intention of arriving safely in a pretty and well-preserved body, but rather to skid in sideways in a cloud of smoke, thoroughly used up, totally worn out, and loudly proclaiming Wow!

The natural world is with us every day, a closeness that is hard to ignore. One becomes conscious of every sound in an undisturbed landscape. For me, the Chincoteague Wildlife Refuge is a place to enjoy nature, to relax and lose myself, whether this is walking the trails, driving the loop, or strolling the beach. I can describe little of the refuge as wild or untouched in the true sense of the world. Yet given its unique location and the no-pets-allowed policy, it offers a more remote experience than many places. These days everywhere is transformed, amended, and corrected to suit the needs of those who manage it. Public opinion and money affect the decisions made on how a piece of land is used, hence the current debate on moving the existing beach north.

We share similar frailties with those creatures that live out in the open where the wind rages and the tides constantly batter; those exposures curtail their lives even more. We are therefore bound to everything around us.

While I eat my breakfast, a casual glance out of our large kitchen window can often reveal a beautiful and graceful bald eagle cruising effortlessly over the backyard with its sharp white head caught in the early morning sun. We cannot help but be intimate with this kind of wildness around us. Perhaps the words from the great environmentalist John Muir sums it all up.

Nature's peace will flow into you as sunshine flows into trees. The winds will blow their own freshness into you, and the storms their energy, while cares will drop off like autumn leaves.

WORDS OF GRATITUDE

First, I would like to thank my editor, Donna Mosher, for once again working with me to create another book.

My deepest thanks to those individuals mentioned in this book. Each one of you has added to my enriched understanding of the island, its history, and the many challenges it faces today. In particular, I would like to thank the following Teaguers who took the time to talk with me: Judy and Terry Howard, Denise Bowden, Roe Terry, Helen Merritt, Dino Johnson, Bonnie Stump, Barbara Walker, Amy Lewis, Cork McGee, Terri Cherrix Rose, and Stephanie Downing.

I am grateful to those people who added the Come'eres' perspective and with their own contributions add much to the fabric of the island. In particular, Captain Barry, Captain Spider, Captain Doug, Lin & Sam Mazza, Jon and Jane Richstein, Lynne Ballerini, Cindy Faith, Tom Cardaci, Joe Adams, JJ, Julia Strain, John Beam, Alex Hubb, Bill and Dottie Troxler, Scott and Susy Norris, Barbara and David Wiedenheft, and Caroline and Howard Lubert.

Many others advised, enlightened, and guided me with incredible generosity of their time.

I thank the staff and biologists at the Chincoteague Wildlife Refuge: Aubrey Mills, Shase Sands, and Matt Young for their invaluable advice on the fauna and wildlife of the refuge. In addition, I thank Wayne Williams, the owner of Pitts Creek, and Dr. B. Miles Barnes for his invaluable economic history of the Eastern Shore. I thank Evelyn Shotwell and the Chincoteague Chamber of Commerce for their information on visitors to the island.

Last but not least, I want to acknowledge our friends and family who visited us: Amanda Thomas, Robert Thomas, Charlotte Thomas, Charlotte McCoy, Hilary Thomas Dorer and Ward Dorer, Jacki and Chuck Klaniecki, Ellen and Gary O'Neill, Gwyn Nielsen, and Dave Hennel. You let us experience the island through your eyes, enabling me to add the visitor's perspective.

BIBLIOGRAPHY AND NOTES

CHAPTER 2

Cocker, Mark. *Crow Country.* Jonathan Cape Ltd; First Edition, 2007
Louv, Richard. *Last Child in the Woods.* Atlantic Books, 2010

CHAPTER 4

Fisher, K. Arthur. *The Eastern Shore Wordbook.* Self-published. ASIN: B00CNI8A68, 1996

CHAPTER 8

Wohlleben, Peter. *The Hidden Life of Trees.* Greystone Books, 2016
Macfarlane, Robert. *The Old Ways: A journey on foot.* Penguin, 2013
John Clare 1793-1864
Jackson, John Brinckerhoff. *A Sense of Place, A Sense of Time.* New Haven, CT: Yale University Press, 1994
Poem by Stacy Smith. From an Eagle's View

CHAPTER 9

Louv, Richard. *What the Robin Knows.* Mariner Books, 2013

CHAPTER 10

Poem by R. A. Marschall. Ibis

CHAPTER 12

Decline of the Front Porch. Retrieved on November 8th, 2018 from http://xroads.virginia.edu/~class/am483_97/projects/cook/decline.htm
Poem by Patricia Neely-Dorsey Front Porch
Muir, John. *The Wilderness World of John Muir.* Mariner Books, 2001
Ruskin, John. Feb 4, 1884 *The Storm Cloud of the Nineteenth Century* Lecture delivered at the London Institution. Also in *The Works*

of John Ruskin, Vol XXXIV, Ed. E.T. Cook and Alexander Wedderburn. London, 1908

Davidson, Peter. *The Last of the Light*, Page 32. Reaktion Books, 2017

CHAPTER 14

Dickinson, Emily. A Route of Evanescense 1879

Ettlinger, Steve. *Twinkie, Deconstructed: My Journey to Discover How the Ingredients Found in Processed Foods are Grown, Mined yes, Mined, and Manipulated into What America Eats.* Plume; Reprint edition, 2008

Gerber N.N and Lechevalier H.A 1965 *Geosmin, an earthly-smelling substance isolated from actinomycetes.* Applied Biology, 136: 935 -938. *Retrieved on Nov 14th, 2018 from https://prairiepiece.word-press.com/tag/petrichor/*

CHAPTER 17

Yeadon, David. *Seasons on Harris.* Harper Perennial, 2007

Visitor Stats provided by Virginian Tourism Corporation.

CHAPTER 19

Ghost Crabs. Retrieved on August 20th, 2018 from https://www. outerbanks.com/ghost-crabs.html

CHAPTER 20

Maxwell, Gavin. *Ring of Bright Water.* Little Toller Books, 2009

Thoreau, Henry David. *Walden; or life in the woods.* Dover Publications, 1995

Emerson, Ralph Waldo. *The Complete Works, ed. 12 vols.* Boston, MA: Houghton Mifflin, 1903-4

CHAPTER 21

Ruskin, John. *Of the Open Sky.* Modern Painters I, Part II, Section III 1819-1900

Griffiths, Jay. *Country Life Magazine* page 124, June 27, 2017

Andrews, W. Linda. "Benefits of Sunset Gazing" *Psychology Today*, July 16, 2014

Macfarlane, Robert. *The Old Ways: A Journey on Foot*, Penguin, 2013

Oyster Castles Retrieved on Nov 6th, 2018 from http://www.allied-concrete.com/materials/oyster-castles

Davidson, Peter. *The Last of the Light.* Page 203 Reaktion Books, 2017

CHAPTER 22

Photo of Shelf Cloud storm by Oxana Bukreeva, 2018

CHAPTER 23

Johnson, P. Emily. *She Wields a Pen: American Women Poets of the Nineteenth Century* University of Iowa Press 1997

Emerson, Ralph Waldo. *The Complete Works, ed. 12 vols.* Boston, MA: Houghton Mifflin. 1903-4

CHAPTER 24

The term *Ass about Face* is a British phrase meaning to fall backward the wrong way around.

The Triffid is a fictitious tall, mobile, prolific, and highly venomous plant species, the titular antagonist in John Wyndam's 1951 novel, *The Day of the Triffids,* and Simon Clark's sequel, *The Night of the Triffids.*

Ruelland, Kenny. *The Mysterious Autumn Calls of the Spring Peeper,* Retrieved on Nov 5th, 2018 from www.amphibians.org August 2017

Murray, W.H. *Mountaineering in Scotland.* J. M. Dent & Sons Ltd 1947

Information on saw-whet owls https://www.nps.gov/asis/learn/nature/birds.htm

CHAPTER 27

Liberthson, Dan. *The American Bittern. A Poetry of Birds: Poems about birds and the photographs that inspired them.* Gatekeeper Press, 2017

Information about Snow Geese V flying formations taken from the Federal Junior Duck stamp curriculum- Youth Guide, Page 152

Lewis-Stempel John. *The Wood. The Life and Times of Cockshutt Wood.* Penguin Random House, 2018

Pfeiffer, Bryan. *Yellow-rumped Warbler- the Winter Warbler.* Retrieved on Feb 16th, 2018 from https://www.birdnote.org/show/yellow-rumped-warbler-winter-warbler Jan 29, 2018

How do birds keep warm in the winter? Dec 18, 2017 Page 179. Retrieved on November 8th, 2018 https://www.fws.gov/midwest/news/WinterWarmth.html

Species List for Chincoteague and Wallops NWR's Retrieved on November 4th, 2018 from https://www.fws.gov/uploadedfiles/appendix%20L_CHN%20Draft%20CCPEIS.pdf

CHAPTER 32

Source for place name Machipongo, *Eastern Shore News* article *Funny Local Names and how they got that way*, Held at Saxis Island Museum. http://www.saxisislandmuseum.org/files/Download/Eastern%20Shore%20Names.pdf

Also from Ryan Webb at: https://blog.esvatourism.org/2018/08/07/eastern-shore-town-names/amp

Kim, S. Paul Nov, 2018. *Orchestra of the Eastern Shore* Retrieved on Nov 8th, 2018 from www.orchestraes.org

CHAPTER 33

Moore, B. Mary. Mar 3, 2017. *Indigo Bunting's Blue.* Written by Dennis Forney and retrieved on Nov 10th, 2018 from https://www.capegazette.com/article/artistry-and-poetry-indigo-buntings-old-trucks/126714

"What do birds do for us" retrieved on March 28th, 2019 from https://www.audubon.org/news/what-do-birds-do-us

CHAPTER 34

Macfarlane, Robert. *The Old Ways- A Journey on Foot.* Penguin, 2013

Twain, Mark. *Life on the Mississippi 1883.* Penguin Books, 1986

Poem by Robert Ligouri "The Stripers Soul"

Hovey, Matt. May 18, 2010. *Fish Yields-Or how much does this really cost me?* Retrieved on Oct 15, 2018 from *http://seafoodshop.blogspot.com/2010/05/fish-yields-or-how-much-does-this.html*

CHAPTER 35

Cording, Jennifer. *Sunken graves and exposed bones, but law doesn't act.* Retrieved on July 17, 2017 from https://www.delmarvanow.com/story/news/local/virginia/2015/03/05/sunken-graves-exposed-bones-va-law-act/24428569/ 2015

NOTES

I have witnessed the destruction of two beautiful views on the island. In January 2014, I was one of the first to see that the watchman's shack fell into Tom's Cove. Since it sat on federally owned property, the owner no longer could repair it. Years of neglect made it weak and prone to the weather. In January 2017, I was then witness to the destruction of the Bivalve Trail, a sacred place for me that led out to the beautiful view of the watchman's shack. The reason given was a needed clearance of the trail and the immediate area due to Pine Bark Beetle infestation.

A year after meeting Gustav, I was relaxing on our front porch watching the incoming RVs for Memorial Day weekend when another incomer visited me. This one was familiar. A lone laughing gull made its way across the grass in front of our porch. At first, I didn't pay much attention to it, as it looked like all the other laughing gulls, but then I noticed the way he walked and how he kept looking at me, his head tilting to one side every so often. It reminded me of Gustav—but that would be ludicrous. The bird flew off, and I thought nothing of it.

Five minutes later, he was back, but this time he landed on the pathway leading up to the house. The gull slowly walked towards the steps, giving me a full-on stare. I swore he called, *Hi it's me, don't you recognize me? How have you been?*

Given the way the bird acted, I was sure he was Gustav, but then again, maybe I was hoping it was. The gull turned and walked out toward the street. As he took flight, I saw an unmistakable white mark above his eye and quietly said to myself: *Yup.*

I expected the tourists to come back—but not Gustav.

ABOUT THE AUTHOR

Daniel, proud Welshman, teacher, artist, and author, became interested in birds at the age of eleven after spending time with the famous British Ornithologist, Sir Peter Scott and it was birds which were the subject of his first artworks. Dan is a self-taught watercolor and pastel artist, and was drawn to Chincoteague Island because of its art community, birdlife and life by the sea. He is the author of *The Come'ere, From Wales to Chincoteague Island* and his art is displayed at Tryfan Gallery, named after his favorite Welsh mountain.

f Tryfan Gallery
danielpturnerthomas.com